Learning about Education

Innovations in Education

Series Editor: Colin Fletcher (Reader in the School of Policy Studies, Cranfield Institute of Technology).

There have been periods of major innovation in public education. What do the achievements amount to and what are the prospects for progress now? There are issues in each slice of the education sector. How have the issues come about?

Each author analyses their own sphere, argues from experience and communicates clearly. Here are books that speak both with and for the teaching profession; books that can be shared with all those involved in the future of education.

Three quotations have helped to shape the series:

The whole process – false starts, frustrations, adaptations, the successive recasting of intentions, the detours and conflicts – needs to be comprehended. Only then can we understand what has been achieved and learn from experience.

Marris and Rein

In this time of considerable educational change and challenge the need for teachers to write has never been greater.

Hargreaves

A wise innovator should prepare packages of programmes and procedures which . . . could be put into effect quickly in periods of recovery and reorganisation following a disaster.

Hirsh

Current titles in the series

Learning about Education

An Unfinished Curriculum

David Hamilton, 1943-

Open University Press
Milton Keynes · Philadelphia

Open University Press
Celtic Court
22 Ballmoor
Buckingham
MK18 1XW

and
1900 Frost Road, Suite 101
Bristol, PA 19007, USA

First Published 1990

British Library Cataloguing in Publication Data

Hamilton, David, *1943*—
    Learning about education: an unfinished curriculum.
    (Innovations in education)
    I. Title.   II. Series
    370′.1

    ISBN 0 335 09586 0
          0 335 09585 2 (paper)

Library of Congress Cataloging-in-Publication Data

Hamilton, David, 1943—
    Learning about education: an unfinished curriculum / David
Hamilton.
        p.   cm. – (Innovations in education)
    Includes bibliographical references (p.   )
    ISBN 0 335 09586 0 – ISBN 0 335 09585 2
    1. Education. 2. Literacy. 3. Teaching. 4. Learning.
I. Title.   II. Series.
LB14.6.H36   1990
370–dc20   89–48157 CIP

Typeset by Inforum Typesetting, Portsmouth
Printed in Great Britain by St Edmundsbury Press Ltd
Bury St Edmunds, Suffolk

Education, like most meetings between two people,
is a chancy business.

(R.S. Peters, philosopher, 1967)

Contents

Acknowledgements

For their assistance in the preparation of this book, I would like to thank Gaby Weiner, Stephen Kemmis and Colin Fletcher, who felt its ideas deserved a wider audience; undergraduate students at Glasgow and Deakin Universities, who were supportive yet critical of earlier drafts; Susan Bain and Mebrouk Khireddine, who furnished pivotal ideas; and, not least, Andy Sanders and Douglas Bain, who rendered vital support at an early stage in its preparation.

David Hamilton

Series editor's introduction

The pace of modern life, the need to understand almost instantly, can seriously damage our chances of understanding anything properly. If I were asked quickly what education means, I would probably say 'teaching' or 'schools'. Yet I would sense that it means more than that and hope that the questioner would not probe too deeply.

But it is each person's right to know what education means. Teachers, and trainee teachers particularly, need to know where the word comes from as well as the activities and attitudes which it describes. If they do not know, with confidence, their part in the whole and their place in a history, they can become touchy technicians, frustrated by what they have to do and the changes they are ceaselessly expected to make. This is an eternal danger as well as an immediate issue for teachers. They can so easily become 'deprofessionalized' and 'deskilled' and depressed. If they know what education means clearly, economically and accurately for themselves, their self-esteem and self-determination would be much more sure.

David Hamilton realized this timeless truth years ago and set about developing a course which would respect teachers' rights to know about education. There would be psychological knowledge, political history, and so on: not as subjects but as sources of insights. Since the earliest relationships, human beings have been learning about growing up, about thinking and about ways of guiding learners. There were schools two thousand years ago but at the same time what we now call schools are relatively modern inventions. David Hamilton invites his readers to take an idea at a time, see where it came from, how its forms altered and what it means for education today and tomorrow. He writes as a warm person who has thought and researched so that he can explain without pomposity or waffle. This book was a long time in the making and that gives it a rare quality.

I learned and learned from each chapter. I turned from being reluctant to admit how little I knew, to gaining for myself some useful certainties. I now feel that behind the gentleness of Hamilton's invitation to learn with him he has a great gift. In business-type phrasing I feel I can 'own' being a teacher, I do not feel 'owned' by education. Better, much better than that, I can see the common ownership of education and that it could never be otherwise. I have been helped to accept my place in something bigger and to assert my purpose in something better than most. I knew I needed to know 'things', David Hamilton knew too. The difference is that he set about working out how to give what he knew to me. This book makes me glad to be a teacher.

Colin Fletcher

Prologue

The principal giver of instruction is our own past history.

(Jerome Bruner, psychologist, 1974)

It was my first morning as a temporary teacher. Nearly thirty adolescents had settled themselves into orderly rows of desks. Suddenly, a bell rang in the corridor. It came earlier than I had expected. Two children rose from their seats and, uninvited, made their way towards the classroom door. I had not foreseen this hyperactivity in my lesson plan. What was happening? 'Dinner tickets, sir', came the unsolicited explanation from a seated child. The fast disappearing pupils had, it seems, set off to collect their tokens for free meals. I resumed the lesson plan, albeit uneasily. I had no wish to underscore the ticketed pupils' embarrassment and humiliation. More than a week passed before I realized my error. I had misread the situation completely. The minor exodus comprised the children who paid for their tickets: free meals were the day-to-day experience of the majority of the class. Ultimately, therefore, the social embarrassment and humiliation were mine.

Since that gentle yet memorable incident – which occurred nearly twenty years ago – I have experienced many comparable interruptions and deflections in my work as a student and as a teacher. Such incidents have ranged from the amusing to the highly emotional. In turn, all have given me food for thought. Together, they have left me with a heightened awareness of the complexities of teaching and learning. The life of a school, like the life of a human being, does not take place in a social vacuum. It is part of a much larger universe that is, itself, in a constant state of flux. To understand the small world of schooling, much can be gained from investigations of its wider context. In my own case, I feel that such reflection has increased my sensitivity as a student and as a teacher. As my vision has been enlarged, I believe that my grasp has been strengthened.

This book, then, explores the breadth and depth of education and schooling. It builds upon a course which, between 1978 and 1989, I gave annually to a group of undergraduates at the University of Glasgow. Week by week, small-group discussions accompanied my presentations. On many occasions, students reported their own equally memorable classroom experiences. Some students expressed anger about their schooling. Others recalled the positive support of individual schoolteachers. But many of them – even the most vocal – found difficulty in drawing wider lessons from their anecdotal experiences. They could speak volumes about isolated incidents. But, like me, they did not always find it easy to translate anger or gratitude into insight or understanding.

My predecessor on the Glasgow undergraduate programme had offered a 12-lecture history course. I was expected to organize my own teaching along similar lines. Unfortunately, however, my knowledge of the kings and queens – or Acts and facts – of education was, and still is, relatively limited. How could I validly fill the lecture time placed at my disposal? I was sympathetic to the view that an awareness of the past might be relevant to an understanding of the present. But how could I give substance to this notion? More specifically, how would it *illuminate* the present? It would be easy to write an antiquarian text about the passage of past events. But what would be gained from an endless catalogue of unconnected and eminently forgettable incidents? Eventually, I recognized the root cause of my difficulties. An aspiration to innovate is not the same as the capacity to innovate. In short, I was a teacher without a text.

In my uncertainty, I turned to a slim volume that had already voiced some of my broader educational interests. Despite its title, Joan Simon's *The Social Origins of English Education* (1970) is not a chronological account of early English education. Rather, the author introduces her book by begging a series of open-ended questions about the basis, organization and purposes of education and schooling. She queries the status of the human animal (is society anything more than a human zoo?). She asks about the ecological adaptation of *Homo sapiens* (are humans merely a direct product of their environment or 'the system'?). And she focuses attention upon distinctive human attributes (how has the evolution of the human species been affected by language and speech?). By such means – and drawing upon notions from anthropology, biology and elsewhere – Joan Simon adopts an important perspective. She identifies education as an essentially human process, one that has played a major part in shaping the course of human evolution and the uniqueness of human society.

I was keen to build upon Joan Simon's book in my teaching. But a major disruption occurred a few days before my first presentation. I learned from the university bookshop that *The Social Origins of English Education* was out of print. Inevitably, the students who had signed up for the course were short changed. They had to fall back upon my hurriedly prepared notes and hurriedly organized lectures.

As the years passed, I gradually expanded the course notes. But they still remained unfinished and unpolished. My thinking always seemed to run ahead of my capacity to express my ideas clearly in a written form. In their feedback on the course, students reported reactions that ranged from severe indigestion to mild intoxication. They pointed to inadequacies, contradictions and confusions in my formulations; and, equally important, they reported degrees of difficulty in entering and understanding my arguments.

Year by year, I was able to amend my presentations in the light of these criticisms; but, after 1982, my text remained untouched. Eventually, however, the supply of copies ran out. Worse still, the original set of duplicating stencils went missing. Worried by the prospect of becoming textless again, and encouraged by outsiders and by the publishers, I set about preparing this version for a wider audience. What, then, are the themes and viewpoints that have shaped the organization of this book?

First, I am unwilling to claim that schooling is necessarily a 'good thing'. I do not, therefore, regard its present form as the unfolding of a glorious idea disseminated by Christian missionaries more than a thousand years ago. Instead, I try to acknowledge that schooling is a two-edged social instrument. It is as much a tool of oppression as it is a lever of liberation. The history of schooling, therefore, is best seen as a history of changing circumstances, not a history of inevitable progress. Accordingly, the political, power-based dimensions of schooling – past and present – receive due attention in this book, as in J. Karabel and A.H. Halsey's *Power and Ideology in Education* (1977) and C. Karier, P. Violas and J. Spring's *Roots of Crisis: American Education in the Twentieth Century* (1973). Equally, I am very aware that many accounts of schooling are written by, and for, winning participants in the educational race. They recount a world that is cosily familiar to their readers. But is it also familiar to the unplaced runners and outright losers of the educational race? Can a book about education, therefore, do justice to the inner-city Boston circumstances of Jonathon Kozol's *Death at an Early Age* (1968) and to the rural Italian circumstances of the School of Barbiana's *Letter to a Teacher* (1970)? And how should books about education and schooling respond to the vivid accounts of Scottish teenagers gathered in Leslie Gow and Andrew McPherson's *Tell Them From Me* (1980), and the telling reminiscences, collected in Bristol, Manchester and elsewhere, that are analysed in Stephen Humphries's *Hooligans or Rebels?: An Oral History of Working-Class Childhood and Youth 1889–1939* (1983)? Indeed, at one stage in its preparation, this book had the working title *A Loser's Guide to Education and Schooling*.

A second thread that runs through this book has already been touched upon. It is the distinction between education and schooling. As a social process, education is much older than schooling, as old as the human species itself. Moreover, throughout its history, education has been an untamed, undisciplined, unorganized, unpolished, everyday activity. It was, and is, an integral part of everyday life – initiated as and when it was required. Schooling, on the other hand, is a relatively recent human invention. Historically, it is the domesticated offspring of earlier educational practices. Its domestication and refinement have largely been the responsibility of socially developed civilizations. As a result, the practices of schooling are fenced in and nourished by a complex network of rules and regulations. These, in turn, give a characteristic shape to the material artefacts of schooling – its textbooks, desks, registers, blackboards, etc. Indeed, most histories of education focus preferentially upon these cultivated artefacts. As a result, they might be more vividly understood as histories of schooling. Certainly, few of them treat the distinction between education and schooling as worthy of serious attention.

A third influence on the organization and content of this book has been my interest – shared with Joan Simon – in the role that education has played in the transformation of the human species. The human species has accumulated a vast storehouse of experience during its existence. And it is often assumed that education revolves around the transmission of this stored up experience from generation to generation. But is this stockpile analogy adequate to the educational record? Year by year, does the stockpile merely grow in size? Or does later experience lead to the modification of earlier experience? In short, is the accumulation of human experience a transformative as well as a cumulative process? And what are the social consequences of such transformation? How important, for instance, was the change over from oral to written literacy, as discussed in Michael Clanchy's *From Memory to Written Record* (1979) and in Ivan Illich and Barry Sanders's *The Alphabetization of the Popular Mind* (1989)? What educational and social significance should be attributed to the invention of moveable type printing, as documented in Elizabeth Eisenstein's *The Printing Press as an Agent of Change* (1979)? And what are the consequences of a shift from print-based to electronic media, as examined in the futurology of Stewart Brand's *The Media Lab: Inventing the Future at MIT* (1988)?

A fourth strand in this volume is the attention given to changes in the terminology and semantics of education and schooling. The Latin and Greek words for 'school' (*ludus* and *schola* respectively) denote the pursuit of leisure activities. What does this tell us about ancient schooling? Likewise, what inferences might be drawn from the fact that the words doctor and docile come from the same root – the Latin word *docere* (to teach)? Such questions not only open up windows upon the past, they also point to important differences between the past and the present. The study of terminology fosters an appreciation of changes in the organization of social life. More generally, too, the study of language also provides access to the condensed wisdom that guided the practices of the past. The educational record is littered with prescriptions like 'spare the rod and spoil the child' or 'as the twig is bent, so the tree groweth'. In turn, such formulations become the truths which shape and legitimate future practice. They are both a summation of past experience and a springboard for new practices. What, for instance, might be made of the exhortation, included in a British government policy document (*Education: A Framework for Expansion*, 1972), that a minority of students should be allowed to study specialized subjects 'to the top of their bent'?

Another consideration shaping the organization of this book has been a concern to acknowledge the seamless quality of educational practice. In the twentieth century, the study of education and schooling has become fragmented. It has been divided up among groups of specialists – psychologists, sociologists, administrators and managers. Wittingly or unwittingly, it is assumed that only persons in possession of such specialist knowledge can reach an informed understanding of education and schooling. A social consequence of this assumption is that the world of twentieth-century education and schooling is populated by two tribes: a small cadre of *experts* and a much larger community of *operatives*. Members of the latter group – notably teachers and learners – are expected to be doers, not thinkers. Most of them have relatively little time, opportunity or encouragement to reflect upon the short- or long-term merits of the prescriptions of experts. And they have even less time to explore the wider implications of education and schooling. But should education and schooling be left solely to the guardianship of politically interested experts?

Another guiding assumption – one that follows from the previous argument – is that to experience education and schooling is not the same as to understand education and schooling. Understanding and appreciating a task is not the same as doing a task: it draws upon a wider frame of reference. Understanding may be triggered by experience: Isaac Newton's encounter with a falling apple is a classic, if apocryphal, instance. Ultimately, however, understanding arises from intellectual activity. It is acquired through discussion, reading and reflection – the reworking and recasting of experience. And the crucial difference between experience and understanding is neatly captured in the aphorism 'once you know what you are doing, you are no longer doing it'.

Many people, including students in higher education, are denied opportunities to evaluate and rethink their experiences. Books, for instance, are often expensive, if not unreadable; libraries are overcrowded, if not unwelcoming; teaching rooms are cold, draughty and uncomfortable; and many teachers declaim statements and avoid questions rather than give their attention to promoting discussion and accepting dialogue. This book, therefore, seeks to overcome such shortcomings. It is not a series of golden tablets inscribed with *all you ever need to know about education and schooling*. It is a series of prompts and provocations, not a catalogue of truths and prescriptions.

Finally – and for related reasons – this book questions the assumption that there can be a predictive science of education and schooling. Instead, it seeks to acknowledge that education and schooling are necessarily unstable and unpredictable. Much that passes for prediction is in fact, more accurately described as projection. At root, education and schooling are social encounters whose participants (teachers, learners, etc.) are highly reactive. Indeed, if humans lost their reactivity (or wilfulness), they would cease to be human. In these terms, therefore, the education and schooling of human beings can never take place under fully controlled conditions. Education and schooling have an in-built instability, which acts like a grain of sand. It may cause the process to grind to a halt; or it may engender unimagined pearls of innovation.

Summary

Dissatisfied with conventional treatments, I have written this book as an examination of the positive and negative roles that education and schooling have played (and can play) in the creation, maintenance and transformation of the human species. In so far as I have used examples from the past, the following chapters draw upon the history of education. But in so far as I have highlighted a set of pivotal concepts (e.g. schooling, education), these chapters are also an essay in educational theory. In attending to history, I have tried to make the past more accessible; and, in attending to theory, I have tried to make the present more comprehensible. Either way, this book is dedicated to extending the educational grasp of its readers.

CHAPTER 1

In the beginning

Every individual lives from one generation to the next; and contributes, however minutely, to the shaping of society and the course of its history.

(C. Wright Mills, sociologist, 1959)

In the late 1850s, Charles Darwin and the American naturalist Alfred Wallace confronted the Victorian intelligentsia with the claim that human beings were directly related to other members of the animal kingdom. Before Darwin, it was conventionally assumed that humans differed from other animals, to the extent that they had a soul. Further, souls were deemed to be the special gift of God who, many years previously, had created mankind independently of other living creatures.

In the century before Darwin, the animal kingdom was envisaged as a great chain of being. Humankind took its place at the top of the chain; and the lowliest organisms congregated at the bottom. This natural order of things was assumed to be immutable and fixed for eternity. Inevitably, then, the basic premise of evolutionary theory – that each species is an ever changing entity – was nothing short of revolutionary. Darwin had arrived at his theory in the 1830s but, recognizing its controversial tenets, waited until 1842 before committing it to paper, as a 35-page pencil sketch. Only the circulation of equivalent ideas by Wallace prompted their joint presentation to the Linnaean Society of London in 1858 and, in the following year, to the publication of Darwin's *Origin of Species*.

Although Darwin was cautious in his claims – the title he offered his publisher was *Abstract of an Essay on the Origins of Species* – and although Darwin had taken great care to win the support of major British scientists, *The Origin of Species* was still accused of being an atheistic and blasphemous anti-Bible. It was commonly assumed that Darwin had rejected the power and primacy of God's design and, in its place, had substituted blind chance as the ultimate source of the order of things.

In biological terms, the Darwin–Wallace theory was important because, supported by vast amounts of data, it proposed that differences between humans and other animals should be regarded as matters of degree, not as a matter of kind. Whatever else they were, human beings were also animals. Nevertheless, Darwin's and Wallace's ideas did little to dismantle the great chain of being. Certainly, leading scientists no longer held that each species had a preordained and static position in the great chain of being. But the chain metaphor was retained in their belief that evolution was a race in which some species had made more progress than others. Given the European origins of the great chain of being, it is hardly surprising that white European males were accorded a place at the top of the ladder, with white women and non-white humans occupying successively lower ranks on the scale of being. Stephen Jay Gould has engagingly explored the political and pseudo-scientific basis of this differentiation in *The Mismeasure of Man* (1981), a volume whose sexist title deliberately underlines the gender bias of much nineteenth- and twentieth-century social theory.

Re-examination and reconceptualization of the great chain of being has continued throughout the twentieth century. Much of the research and debate, however, has been framed by post-Darwinian questions such as 'What are the human species' most evolutionarily significant features?' and 'What part did these features play in the human species's rise to prominence?' Answers to these questions have been sought in a variety of ways. One approach has been to focus upon settings occupied by animals (e.g. chimpanzees) assumed to be subordinate, yet closely related, members of the great chain of being. Over the years, too, anthropologists have examined the life styles of materially limited communities; palaeontologists have excavated fossil beds believed to contain traces of early humans; and, more recently, biochemists, endocrinologists and geneticists have sought to evaluate evidence drawn from the organs, cells and chromosomes of humans and their near relatives.

Another approach has been to extrapolate from twentieth-century human beings to their early ancestors. In a sense, this approach tries to strip down the human species and, thereby, find its true essence. Such a study – the examination of early humans – has a long history. It provided the stimulus for Daniel Defoe's *Robinson Crusoe* (1719), Jonathan Swift's *Gulliver's Travels* (1726), and, more recently, William Golding's *Lord of the Flies* (1954).

Other recent scholarly examinations of the human condition have often focused upon human speech and human use of tools. They have repeatedly asked whether such activities hold the key to human uniqueness. In fact, systematic observation of apes has cast doubt upon such claims. It now seems accepted that chimpanzees, like many other animals, use primitive implements in their natural habitat (e.g. to poke insects out of holes). And it has also been claimed that chimpanzees can manipulate abstract symbols in a manner approaching the linguistic competence of human beings. But, critics ask, are these observations valid? Is the tool-using capacity of apes merely copied from their human observers and keepers? And can the linguistic behaviour of chimpanzees be satisfactorily distinguished from sophisticated mimicry?

Finally, archaeologists, palaeontologists and others have given much attention to the social consequences of changes in the human body. They have reflected, for instance, upon early changes in the life style of the human species. How important, they have asked, is the upright gait of human beings, and the resultant release of arms and hands for other tasks? And what evolutionary significance should be ascribed to the skeletal structure of the human hand (which allows objects to be readily manipulated between fingers and thumb)?

Unfortunately, however, few of these questions appear to have generated consensus among the scientific community. Indeed, one of the most readable reviews is deliberately – and significantly – entitled *Bones of Contention: Controversies in the Search for Human Origins* (Lewin 1989). Is it possible, then, to summarize the insights gained over the decades since Darwin? Overall, research seems to indicate that, in their internal make up and external life style, humans, apes, and their common ancestors are very similar. Equally, there is widespread agreement about the significance of certain evolutionary events (e.g. the acquisition of upright mobility). Nevertheless, scientists interested in human evolution still seem to be a long way from agreeing upon which events came first in the evolutionary sequence. And a further reason for the lack of consensus is that since such research is conducted by human beings about human beings, it is neither disinterested nor dispassionate. Like abortion-prompted discussions about the sanctity of human life, debates about the origins and make up of the human species always invite the same kind of theological fervour that originally surrounded (and, to a degree, still surrounds) the Darwin–Wallace propositions.

Nevertheless, most commentators seem to accept that apes do not build computers, write sonnets or fly to the moon. Perhaps the simplest explanation of these differences is as follows. In the prehistory of humankind, small biological changes (perhaps not yet identified and dated) gave certain individuals a much greater purchase upon both themselves and their environment. *Homo sapiens* emerged as a group of social animals who sought to shape themselves and their world to their own constructive (and sometimes destructive) designs. As a consequence, the human species gained an immense social advantage within the animal kingdom. It ceased to be a product or prisoner of its environment. It broke out and created a new world – a social environment that stood between its biological self and its material surroundings. And it is in this new, non-animal world that the human species has created its own homeland and its own life styles.

Mental and manual tools

At some point in the break out sequence, members of the human species must have developed the capacity to think and to reflect upon their circumstances. Early humans did not simply react to their environment; they were able to take stock of their surroundings. Earlier experiences, stored as memory traces, could be revisited, re-evaluated and recast. These mental manipulations (i.e. thinking rather than remembering) enabled early humans to reimagine the past and, in the process, to rethink their place in the world. The concept of social change became thinkable and the practice of social change became doable. The *status quo* lost its aura of permanence. It was never the same again.

The emergence of human awareness also had other consequences. Thinking became more than the manipulation of memories. It became a productive activity, a means of apprehending (literally, grasping) the world and rebuilding it in the form of new mental constructions. Indeed, thinking is one of the most important forms of human tool-use. And through extending their appreciation of the natural and social worlds, human beings have enlarged their capacity to make the future more than just a rerun of the past.

The development of abstract reasoning, like the development of tool making, enabled the human species to break further away from its animal contemporaries. Gradually, too, the mental toolbox of the human species changed in character. Over thousands of years, number systems (one, two, three, etc.) were joined by more complex concepts such as 'zero', 'infinity' and 'decimal point'; and the organization of social life became suffused with notions such as 'government', 'democracy' and the 'welfare state'. Humans built their homes around increasingly complex structures. But, in the process, they also devised a set of mental structures that raised an equivalent shelter – a comparable sense of organization – over their social existence. Ultimately, humans were able to find a place in the world that was both materially comfortable and intellectually comforting.

Production and reproduction

The creation of inside-the-head solutions to practical difficulties enabled humans to overcome survival problems that might, otherwise, have led to their extinction. *Homo sapiens* has never succumbed to environmental change. Sufficient numbers have always survived. Whereas other species have survived by finding a supportive ecological niche, humans have been able to custom-build their own niches. For humans, therefore, survival is not simply a matter of finding an evolutionary lifeboat; it can also be based upon a strategy of lifeboat building. Necessarily, then, survival of the human species has been based as much upon intellectual activity as upon physical struggle. It has rested not merely upon procuring enough food for tomorrow, it has also been accomplished through the allocation and preservation of enough seed for next year.

In reality, humans possess two survival mechanisms. First, human beings are able to survive by instinctive behaviour – a mechanism that is probably more important to other animals. The relevant feature of instinctual behaviour (e.g. the suckling strategies of new-born infants) is that it is transmitted genetically. The second survival mechanism – social learning – is a non-genetic process. Later generations survive and flourish with the assistance of lessons learned socially (i.e. non-genetically) from earlier generations. Furthermore, social learning is one of the most important features of the evolution of the human species. That is, the humanity of the human species is based on intergenerational learning, not upon the vagaries (or 'blind chance') of genetic transmission.

Yet, as suggested in the prologue, social communication from generation to generation is inherently unstable. As messages are passed from person to person and from generation to generation they are exposed, consciously and unconsciously, to interference and distortion. The received message may bear little relationship to the original signal. In a apocryphal example from the First World War, frontline troops signalled: 'Send reinforcements, we are going to advance' – a request that was logged at headquarters as 'Send three and fourpence, we are going to a dance'.

The instability of social transmission among human beings – a recurrent feature of teaching and learning – stands in marked contrast to the relatively faithful communication of information through genetic channels. Further, these differences in the fidelity of transmission suggest a conceptual distinction – between production and reproduction – that helps to clarify important differences in educational practice. The clearest case of faithful transmission occurs in single-parent, or asexual, reproduction. Typically, the parent sloughs off part of its body which then develops into a new member of the species. Genetic information is transmitted unchanged to the offspring, and the entire process is usually known as cloning. Necessarily, differences between the parent and its offspring are slight. In short, cloning is associated with high levels of intergenerational stability. By contrast, two-parent or sexual reproduction is more complicated. Offspring receive genetic information from two sources and, as a result, differ visibly from either of their parents. Accordingly, slow intergenerational change takes place, the kind of biological evolution identified by Darwin and Wallace.

But how do these sexual behaviours illuminate educational practice? When social communication entails distortion free transmission and intergenerational stability, it fosters cultural reproduction. The practices learned and adopted by the offspring are very close to those communicated by the parent. Each child is a living facsimile of its parent. On the other hand, when social communication promotes new forms of behaviour and understanding, each new generation differs visibly from its parents. Cultural production is the outcome.

In practice, of course, social transmission and social learning are always a combination of reproduction and production. Nevertheless, educational practices differ in terms of the emphasis they give to production and reproduction. When social practices are directed towards conserving a way of life (e.g. maintaining the *status quo*), they tend to be concerned with reproduction. When social practices are directed towards the transformation of a way of life, they tend to be concerned with the production of new cultural forms. Education and schooling are key agencies of social transmission. And they, too, can be examined for the role they play in intergenerational reproduction and production.

Economy and culture

As noted earlier, early humans did not merely adapt responsively to the exigencies of nature, they also began to act positively and develop new survival solutions. For instance, life support systems emerged (e.g. forms of shelter and fire) which enabled human beings to domesticate hostile elements of their surroundings. Further, this domestication process – the taming of the environment – enabled human beings to transport their houses and hearths to all parts of the globe.

Early humans probably shared a scavenger–hunter existence. But, as they migrated across the globe, the focus of their hunting and scavenging varied from climatic zone to climatic zone. Some human groups built their lives around the vagaries of sea fishing, others relied upon the seasonal rewards of fruit gathering and others still, took advantage of the infrequent entrapment of large animals. Not surprisingly, the life styles of these different consumers began to be linked with the life styles and life cycles of their staple foods (plants and animals). Moreover, these links took a variety of forms. For instance, humans probably spent as much time dreaming about their food and fuel as they did gathering and consuming it.

Foodstuffs, therefore, figured prominently in the mental worlds of early human beings, as they still do. Like the sacred cow of the Hindu, discussed in Marvin Harris's *Cow, Pigs, Wars and Witches: The Riddles of Culture* (1978), foodstuffs not only began to be regarded as day-to-day sources of sustenance, they also became powerful symbols of survival. Within each human group, therefore, essential artefacts took on more than a survival significance. They began to be seen, inscribed on standing stones and cave walls, in a spiritual or magical light. In turn, humans acquired an enlarged and supernatural (or non-worldly) sense of their life style – a state of affairs reflected in the title and contents of David Attenborough's *The First Eden: The Mediterranean World and Man* (1987). Together, these material resources and mental assumptions constituted, and still constitute, the way of life of human groups. Foodstuffs and fuel provide the resources for living, while mental assumptions, an outlook on life, furnish the reasons for living.

But what is the relationship between material resources and mental assumptions, between economy and culture? Is a culture merely the mirrored reflection of its accompanying economy? Is the relationship, simply circular and self-confirming? If so, the culture would merely reflect (or reproduce) the economy and vice versa. Social change, therefore, would be impossible. As already noted, however, a culture is an enlarged conception or reflection of an economy. Just as human thought processes extend beyond a person's immediate environment, so a society's culture – its collective assumptions – necessarily transcends the limits of its economy.

Nevertheless, there may be a direct relationship between a culture and its host economy. Many societies, throughout recorded history, have consciously cultivated substances that elevate their members on to new mental planes. Fermented barley (and its derivatives) play this role in Scotland; and grapes, mushrooms, marijuana and poppy derivatives serve equivalent purposes elsewhere. As important, humans have learned that altered mental states can also be induced without the aid of externally derived material stimulants. Music, meditation, dance and other forms of exercise provide such opportunities. It may be no accident that, throughout the world, there is a close association between music, dance and narcotics.

Through such practices and substances, people are 'taken out of themselves' (a loose translation of the Greek word for ecstasy). They gain entry to a mental world that is only partially encompassed by their material world, a disjunction central to the neurological case studies reported in Oliver Sacks's *The Man Who Mistook his Wife for a Hat* (1986). A gap is opened up between the material world that people inhabit and the mental world that they dream about. Where they are, and where they would like to be, are not the same place. Their 'consciousness' (culture) is not the same as their 'being' (economy). And it is in the attempts made by humans to close that gap – to bring heaven down to earth – that the mainspring of social evolution is to be found.

Summary

Small changes in biology seem to be associated with the peculiarly human attributes of *Homo sapiens*. The human mind – working in conjunction with the human body – developed the enduring capacity to be rather more than a storehouse of memories. It began to act as a buffer zone. Information from the senses was not simply accumulated; it was recast and reused in many different forms. In turn, the capacity to manipulate manual and mental tools enabled human beings to rehearse the future with their minds, share the future with their neighbours, and to create the future with their hands, as discussed, for instance, in Tom Ingold's *The Appropriation of Nature: Essays on Human Ecology and Social Relations* (1986). Such visionary activities were disseminated through social rather than through biological channels. Empowered by the lessons of social experience, and aided by social dissemination, the break out of the human species took place. Early humans began to occupy hitherto unwelcome environments. They migrated with their material possessions on their backs and the remainder of their culture in their heads. But however far their bodies travelled, their minds travelled even further. The march of human history had not only begun, it began to seem unstoppable.

CHAPTER 2

From survival to subordination

We had the experience but missed the meaning.

(T.S. Eliot, poet, 1943)

As already suggested, the early history of the human species is a chronicle of biological and social survival. Yet, as humans survived, so they also changed their life styles. They became increasingly conscious of their place in the world and of their capacity to change – or domesticate – their immediate surroundings. Gradually, the human species hijacked its own biological evolution. It became less concerned with biological evolution and more concerned with social improvement.

Planning for the future of the human species took many forms. At one level, it must have entailed the development of future-oriented linguistic forms (e.g. the future tense). At another level, it must have encompassed the invention of organizational forms that would outlive their creators. And, not least, planning for the future must have embraced a social re-evaluation of child-rearing practices.

Human socialization and acculturation

The survival of individuals to sexual maturity takes place largely through the processes of nurturing or upbringing. In the nurturing process, children become humans: for instance, they develop a capacity to use abstract thought and language, to a degree unknown among other animals. But these skills do not arise fortuitously. Rather, they are fostered in a particular cultural context. Our thoughts and our language are no less part of our life style than the foods we eat and the games we play. Upbringing, therefore, is a combination of two processes: socialization – which makes us all human – and acculturation, which enables us to become students in higher education, French models, Italian waiters, American footballers, Soviet gymnasts and so on.

Socialization, therefore, is not the same as acculturation, despite the fact that they occur simultaneously. Human beings become socialized through their communication with other members of the human species; and they become acculturated because the content and form of the communication varies from one social context to another. To talk of socialization is to refer, preferentially, to the attributes that all humans share; whereas to talk of acculturation is to focus on differences of life style.

Typically, cultures differentiate themselves linguistically in their languages, dialects and accents. But cultural identity is also stored and transmitted through many other channels, including the ways that people design their habitations, wear their clothes, eat their food, give each other flowers and hold each other's bodies. In these terms, joining a culture – or acculturation – is rather more than becoming a human being. It is an intensely social experience comprising induction into a complex array of conventions and practices. Collectively, these practices form the fabric of a culture. They provide the reasons and resources for living and, in the process, provide reassurance to the members of a culture. To be acculturated is not merely to become human, it is also to acquire a life style and, just as important, to acquire an associated outlook on life.

But full membership of a culture is rarely acquired instantly. Typically, it requires an extended period of induction. The transition from candidate member to full member, or from outsider to insider occurs only when the novitiate has learned how to behave with full cultural propriety. Somehow, the newcomer has assimilated the conventions – the inner logic – that sustain the fabric of the culture. A culture, therefore, is not merely a way of living or a set of practices, it is also a repository of deeper meanings which must be decoded before a newcomer can really feel at home in the receiving culture. It is one thing to mimic a life style; but it is something else to understand and appreciate it. People can be shown *how* to dress and how to eat. But these practices only become fully accepted when people understand *why*, in terms of the logic of the culture, they should eat and dress in such ways.

Acculturation is therefore based on the transmission and reception of cultural messages. Moreover, the idiosyncracies of the logic (or 'riddles') of the culture means that many cultural messages are incomprehensible to outsiders. In such terms, acculturation becomes a process whereby noviciates gradually crack a cultural code (e.g. the queuing conventions of different cultures). But there is an in-built problem with this model of cultural communication (and, hence, with all forms of education and schooling). How can coded messages be successfully communicated to someone who does not already have access to the codebook? To overcome this difficulty, newcomers need to receive a compound message, one that also includes extracts from the codebook of the culture. Human acculturation is as much a process of explanation as it is a process of demonstration.

Upbringing, education and schooling

As a major activity of acculturation, child rearing is also a process of transmitting and decoding cultural messages. Among early humans, child rearing presumably took place alongside adult activities. Youngsters were not given a life style. Instead, they picked one up as they engaged, like other animals, in their own survival activities. Subsequently, however, child rearing became a more culturally focused activity. Individuals and groups began to recognize the survival potential of an improved upbringing. They took steps to transform its form and content. In short, they began to reorganize the encoding and decoding procedures of their culture.

Viewed from the twentieth century, the net result of this reorganization was the consolidation of a distinctively human activity – education. As humans adopted routines and rituals to cultivate the environment, so they also invented routines and rituals to cultivate themselves and their successors. These routines and rituals became the object of repeated, if not continuous, renewal. Gradually, education was transformed from a human activity into a human institution. It became a highly visible feature of the cultural landscape. Significant areas of educational practice became separated from everyday life. For example, they were deemed to be the responsibility of specialist personnel (tutors, child minders, teachers); they were conducted through specialist activities (e.g. games, exercises, homework); they were linked to specialist materials (e.g. toys, textbooks, teaching machines); they were associated with specific periods in young people's lives (e.g. before the onset of puberty); and, finally, educational activities were identified with specialized locations (e.g. nurseries, kindergarten, playing fields).

In the transition from a process to an institution, education also underwent a further change. It became less of an undisciplined, *natural* process and more of a regulated, cultural institution. In turn, these qualitative changes in education meant that it also acquired a new designation – schooling. The rise of schooling, therefore, was rather more than the rise of schools, teachers and textbooks. It also entailed a major reconceptualization of social learning. Experience which, previously, had been passed on in a non-formalized fashion became the subject of sophisticated human reflection. In an important sense, the history of schooling is the history of attempts to overcome the acculturation (i.e. coding and decoding) difficulties described earlier in this chapter. Questions like 'What should be taught?', 'Who should be taught?', 'Where should they be taught?' and 'How should teaching be conducted?' were moved up the cultural agenda, in order that acculturation might be rendered more effective. Nevertheless, this was not a process that occurred overnight. It was not until the sixteenth century that schooling began to be opened to

all children, regardless of their sex and social status. And it was not until
the nineteenth century that all British children were officially required to
attend school.

Thus, schooling was more than just a technical innovation, a set of
tools designed and constructed to extend the intellectual reach of the
human species. Rather, schooling rose to prominence as a political institution. In the process, it was charged with meeting political goals. It left
behind issues of survival and focused attention on more abstract entities
such as spiritual salvation, social progress and citizenship. Schooling is as
much a political institution as an educational institution. And, given its
political remit, schooling has acquired a distinctive culture. It is an island
of established order within a much wider – and much less colonized –
educational archipelago.

Such, then, was the historical fate of education. It began, long ago, as
an embedded social activity; it emerged as a visible set of practices; and it
matured as a partitioned and formalized social institution. Today, education operates in parallel and in concert with schooling. Necessarily,
though, schooling receives more political attention than education. In the
twentieth century, for instance, schooling has been repeatedly called upon
to compensate for older educational agencies (e.g. employers, the church
and the family). It is claimed that the latter have relaxed or abandoned
their former educational and cultural responsibilities. Yet, can schooling
fill the educational space relinquished by other institutions? Does schooling compensate for education? Or does it, rather, replace education with
something else – resulting in the consequences discussed in Paul Corrigan's *Schooling the Smash Street Kids* (1979), Lynn Davies's *Pupil Power:
Deviance and Gender in School* (1984), Paul Willis's *Learning to Labour*
(1977) and Madeleine Arnot and Gaby Weiner's *Gender and the Politics of
Schooling* (1987)?

Education and the division of labour

The long-term history of education and schooling can be examined from
many perspectives. One valuable approach is to reflect upon schooling in
terms of the division of labour. An important element in the organization
of schooling has been the subdivision of human experience into separate
categories and activities. In the twentieth century, for instance, adolescent
children rarely learn about the complexities of modern life. Rather, they
learn the mysteries of physics, mathematics, geography (etc.) – elements
of a cosmology that is only obliquely related to the cultural and material
world that they inhabit outside school. Schooling, therefore, conventionally addresses the complexity of human experience by passing it
through a prism marked 'the technical division of labour'. Just as the

complexities of house construction can be broken down into roof building, plumbing and electrical installation, so schooling has also been conceptualized as a comparable set of discrete activities.

Educational Jack-of-all-trades survive, conspicuously in nursery and primary schools. But modern education (including primary schooling) is increasingly organized like modern house building. Separate tasks are allocated to separate specialisms (e.g. physics, mathematics, geography). More important, these discrete activities become associated with specialist personnel. The technical division of labour, therefore, merges with the social division of labour. Schooling is not merely reduced to a series of tasks, it also assumes that each task should be the responsibility of a different person.

These social divisions produce their own subcultures. As the common pool of stored experience is fragmented, new territories of knowledge and expertise are created. Furthermore, these territories became marked out with property rights of access and exclusion. Schooling becomes a world of multiple territories, not all of which are rendered accessible to outsiders. As society divides up experience, so experience divides up society.

Power and the division of labour

The division of experience also has implications for the distribution of power in society. Experience is a form of cultural property (e.g. craft-specific knowledge) that is consigned from generation to generation. Yet, whatever its form, culturally relevant experience also provides learners with cultural leverage. But if such resources are differentially distributed, they can easily become linked to differences in cultural power. Eventually, powerful sections of a culture or community begin to exert their influence over other human beings. And, as they consolidate their power and authority, such groups not only enhance the upbringing of their own young, they also seek to intervene in the educational activities of the less powerful – their subordinates.

Calls for universal schooling in the sixteenth century illustrate these developments. Typically, they were related to the Reformation, a political project whose adherents – as its name suggests – sought to re-form (i.e. re-build) society around a new social agenda. The Catholic Church, which had exerted its own forms of authority for several centuries, was undermined by vigorous social, political and theological dissent, portrayed in Richard Tawney's *Religion and the Rise of Capitalism* (1942). Town-based merchants and wealthy artisans accrued sufficient economic and political advantage to threaten the economic and ideological power of the land-dependent aristocracy and the established church. Small merchants and artisans were the social upstarts of the Reformation drama; the established Church and its rent- and tax-farming allies were the defenders of the faith; and the rural peasants were the innocent, if somewhat jostled, bystanders in this spectacle.

Reformers like Martin Luther (1483–1546), John Calvin (1509–1564) and John Knox (1505–1572) projected a new view of society, one that, so they claimed, included all social groups, not merely the ruling or aspiring elites. For instance, the key Scottish text of the day – the significantly titled *Book of Discipline* (1560) – argued that all children, irrespective of rank and gender, should be brought up in 'learning and virtue'.

These arguments are sometimes hailed as the seedbed of common or comprehensive schooling. Certainly, all children were expected to receive formalized instruction under the aegis of the state and/or its allied church. But it is incorrect to assume that the call for everyone to go to school was the same as a call that everyone should go to the same school. It seems, in fact, that the schools of the sixteenth century differed considerably. Indeed, they consciously differentiated themselves according to whether they offered instruction through the medium of Latin – a distinction that served to separate the upper and lower ranks of society. Some post-Reformation schools, therefore, confirmed the social ascendancy of young members of political elites, while others merely served to secure the economic and cultural acquiescence of the remaining members of society – contrasting states of affairs illustrated in Gerald Strauss's *Luther's House of Learning: The Indoctrination of the Young in the German Reformation* (1978) and George Huppert's *Public Schools in Renaissance France* (1984).

Power and social engineering

Central to the reformers' vision, however, was the assumption that schooling could, in fact, serve as a social engineering device. Schooling was seen as a lever of massive social reform, a means of redirecting the whole of society. In an important sense, the educational initiatives of the Reformation, both Catholic and Protestant, were designed to interfere with the intergenerational transmission of experience. Parents were to be constrained from passing on their own experience, and universal schooling was the mechanism proposed to effect this social interruption.

A variety of political initiatives flowed from this view of social reform. For instance, the reformers recognized that the dissemination of their ideas required the recruitment of faithful teachers and preachers. Accordingly, universities were founded (e.g. Leiden, 1572) or reformed (e.g. Glasgow, 1577) to become staff colleges of Protestantism, just as new guilds of teachers were created to become missionaries for the Catholic

Reformation – the Jesuits and the Ursuline Sisters received papal recognition in 1544 and 1540 respectively.

Together, these developments in the provision of, and the provision for, schooling have led the sixteenth and seventeenth centuries to be remembered as the founding epoch of 'modern' (as opposed to 'classical' or 'medieval') schooling. Certainly, events of those centuries – not merely the Reformation – dramatically increased the profile of schooling. In many North European countries, schooling became a nationwide phenomenon, even if schools were not yet strongly networked or formalized into national systems of schooling (a later development).

The emergence of differentiation in schooling also had an important impact upon the literature of education. Previously, most educational writers had concerned themselves with the upbringing practices of the powerful sections of society. But, from the sixteenth century, a new genre of educational literature appeared: documents prepared by one section of society about the schooling (or disciplining) of their subordinates. Necessarily, this literature embraced a 'top down' view of schooling. The horizontal division of educational labour was visibly recast as a hierarchical or power-based division of labour.

Summary

In the early history of the human species, survival activities were probably accompanied by both social reciprocation and social differentiation. Nevertheless, gradual reallocation of cultural tasks in the interests of social efficiency seems to have foreshadowed important changes in social structure. A technical division of labour emerged which, in turn, laid the basis for the emergence of a social division of labour. Child rearing underwent a similar transition. As human beings began to take a self-conscious interest in enhancing the economic and cultural potential of young people, they not only turned socialization into education, they also began to reallocate the tasks of child rearing so that horizontal parity was exchanged for hierarchical control.

CHAPTER 3

Educational communication and cultural literacy

In the agricultural society the old man is the wise one; in the industrial society he is a has-been.

(Carlo Cipolla, historian, 1973)

The activities of socialization and acculturation are accomplished through the medium of human communication, a social process extensively documented in Raymond Williams's *Contact: Human Communication and its History* (1981). Through communication – a word which derives from a Latin root meaning to share – stored up human experience is distributed across the cultural networks that unite different groups of human beings. But how does this communication, sharing or transmission operate? And in what ways, if any, can human communication also be regarded as an educational activity?

In evolutionary terms, much of the information that passes among animals has little educational significance. Communication, therefore, is not the same as education. For instance, when animals transmit alarm or courtship signals to each other, their behaviour is driven more by biological instinct than by social learning. Typically, the arousal of the recipient is triggered by the arrival of a predator or a potential mate. The resultant reaction (e.g. blushing) is spontaneous. It is rarely motivated by a carefully pondered decision. Communication between transmitter and receiver arises simply because of their mutual presence. The in-coming animal might be deemed the source of the message. And the aroused animal might be deemed the receiver of the message. But have teaching and learning also occurred?

Teaching and learning are special forms of communication. They operate when communication is accompanied by heightened levels of consciousness among teachers and learners. They are shaped, that is, by the wishes, intentions and values of teachers and learners. Further, teaching and learning are also shaped (or constrained) by social rather than biological circumstances – the cultural assumptions, conventions and codes that surround, yet also separate, the teacher and the learner. Together, these aspirations and circumstances mean that teaching and learning occur across a cultural medium. Moreover, many teachers and learners find this medium to be foggy or cloudy. It hinders satisfactory communication. Teaching and learning, therefore, are never easy. They always include an element of demystification.

Showing how, playing how and telling how

When animals communicate socially, they do so without the obvious assistance of speech. Human learning also arises from non-verbal communication. In such circumstances, adults serve as models; and learners gradually, if sometimes selectively, 'pick up' the appropriate behaviour through watching the demonstrator. Sometimes, such learning is neither intended nor expected by the model; sometimes, on the other hand, modelling is deliberately organized to assist the learner. Either way, learning derives from the process of showing how. Further, a notable feature of such teaching and learning is that it often takes place on the job: it is typical, for example, of the acculturation of craft and trade apprentices. Typically, too, teaching (or modelling) through showing how is a repetitive process. It continues – usually self-consciously on the part of the teacher – until the designated learners can faithfully copy the teacher's actions.

Homo sapiens seems to be unusual among members of the animal kingdom, in that it can also teach and learn in other ways. One of the most important forms of human teaching and learning is accomplished in off the job settings. Separated from life in this way, education begins to become a specialized and socially visible activity. Learners acquire the necessary experience off stage, under surrogate conditions. Central to this form of teaching and learning are the notions of 'rehearsal' and 'play'. Learning through play, therefore, is regarded as a rehearsal for later life. Learners, adults as well as children, gain confidence and competence in social and other activities without being exposed to unnecessary risks. Indeed, renaming play as 'simulation' has made it possible for adults to acquire, safely and inexpensively, the competences of airline pilots and space astronauts.

But, culturally and educationally, play is also important in two other respects. First, organized play can be used to cultivate life styles as well as specific skills. Through play (e.g. 'doctors and nurses'), children not only learn how to do things, they also begin to learn the cultural value and social meaning of such activities. In Britain, for instance, the nineteenth-century schooling of middle- and upper-class boys placed considerable stress on competitive games as a means of inculcating values such as 'fair play', 'manliness' and 'gentlemanly conduct'. Sporting competence – the acquisition of specific skills – was secondary to the inculcation of the social and political values discussed in J.A. Mangan's *Athleticism in the Victorian and Edwardian Public School* (1981) and *The Games Ethic and Imperialism* (1985). Meanwhile, the female counterparts of such schoolboys enjoyed (or struggled against) a different kind of secondary learning – inculcation of the domestic values and social attributes discussed in Sara Delamont and Lorna Duffin's *The Nineteenth Century Woman: Her Cultural and Physical World* (1978). Indeed, such forms of secondary learning may be the most important aspect of learning through play.

The second feature of play is that an element of indeterminancy surrounds the transferability of off-the-job learning to on-the-job practice. If the off-stage context of play differs from the context of real life, the resultant learning may not be smoothly transferred to the real world. In the extreme case, the learner remains intellectually and socially in the play area, and at a cultural and emotional distance from everyday life. Hence, calls for schooling to move closer to the real world – and become *relevant* – are a call for schooling to abandon its historic role as a socially separate set of rehearsal rooms. The enhancement of relevance is not easily accomplished in the context of schooling.

Play is therefore a two-edged educational instrument. It may be culturally valuable as an agency of socialization and acculturation. But a price may have to be paid for the discrepancies that result from the learner's off-stage and on-stage performances. There is always a gap between teaching through play and teaching through life. Learning to climb on an indoor climbing wall is not the same as learning to climb on a dark, windswept, ice-covered mountain side. The institutionalized contexts of teaching and learning are rarely the same as the disorganized, and sometimes unfathomable, contexts that make up real life. Historically, then, the formalization of schooling introduced an element of slippage between school and life.

Such slippage can be regarded in two ways. On the one hand, it can be identified, disapprovingly, as an undesirable inefficiency in intergenerational transmission. Play is deemed to be merely a pale substitute for life. Yet, on the other hand, slippage can also be regarded approvingly – as when scientists and artists 'play around' with old ideas and come up with new and socially valuable notions, procedures and solutions. In such circumstances slippage turns the intention of cultural reproduction into a source of cultural production.

As well as the educational possibilities of play, the human species has also developed another source of off-the-job learning. Showing how is joined by telling how. Learners gain access to new forms of behaviour by being transported even further away from life – to a rehearsal room inside their heads. For instance, to teach an unfamiliar route, the teacher might conjure up a map inside the learners' heads and transport them verbally along the desired pathway. The telling–how process is initiated and sustained by such linguistic openings as 'Imagine . . .' or 'Picture in your mind . . .' Such teaching and learning revolve around the manipulation of mental images. Historically, the development of telling how was crucial to the accelerated social evolution of the human species. Teaching and learning ceased to be hands-on (i.e. showing how) activities. They began to be conducted, in effect, through a sharing of minds.

By shifting teaching on to a cognitive plan, the scope for telling how became much greater than that for showing how. Experiences could be brought to mind more readily than they could be brought to hand. Over the centuries, however, the boundaries of human communication have constantly been redrawn. The emergence of telling how increased the potency of cultural transmission, deepening the forms of experience – abstract as well as concrete – that could be communicated through educational channels. Above all, it opened up forms of cultural transmission, from epic poetry to historical narrative. Indeed, as this line of argument indicates, the processes of telling how have many cultural and historical affinities with story telling.

The separation of telling how from showing how also had a structural consequence for education and schooling. Teachers emerged not only from those who were competent at showing how but also from those who were skilled in telling how. Teachers surfaced as a separate social category, via a distinction that survives in the aphorism 'those who can, do; those who can't, teach'.

Language and thought

The emergence of telling how was linked, inevitably, to the emergence of more abstract forms of language. The language of early humans was probably closely linked to the manipulation of the environment. It was a language of representation. It consciously mimicked and manipulated, through sounds and bodily gestures, socially significant objects and activities. Then as now, language activities were essential to collaborative aspects of human life (e.g. the collective hunting of large animals). And echoes of this early collaborative and communicative language survive in team games, like football and hockey, where participants pursue a wild or runaway ball until it is killed and put in the net through their efforts.

In general, language served as a tool, a means of increasing the reach, power and effectiveness of individuals and social groups. Gradually, however, the communication that accompanied everyday survival, like the sounds used to accomplish the kill in hunting, was generalized to other spheres of life. Language became decoupled from its originating contexts. It took on a life of its own. In turn, social interaction took advantage of opportunities offered by this decoupling (or slippage): communication became connotative as well as denotative. A word could denote (i.e. stand for) something; and/or it could connote (i.e. carry additional meanings). Language, therefore, became a multi-message system, a medium suffused with uncertainty and imprecision. In the extreme, the literal (or denotative) meaning of a word or phrase can become completely masked by its accompanying connotations. Life can become a 'bowl of cherries' (or, conversely, a 'bed of nails'). Indeed, the development of human language and communication has advanced to such a degree that speech can also be ironic; that is, a statement can mean exactly the opposite of its literal meaning. It should be no surprise, therefore, that teaching and learning are complex communication activities.

Signs, symbols and cultural literacy

From this perspective, the most important feature of human communication is that it builds upon many layers of meaning. It is a subtle, finely woven medium whose meanings have to be extracted rather than received. Necessarily, transmitters of meaning (e.g. teachers) cannot guarantee the faithful or hi-fidelity dissemination of their messages – circumstances well documented in Terence Moore and Chris Carling's *The Limitations of Language* (1988). Language can be as much a source of social division as a tool of social unification. Symbol-laden communication may foster solidarity among insiders who grasp its meaning. But the complexities of communication may also intensify the barriers that exist between the insiders and outsiders of a culture. To those on the inside, culture-bound communication operates in an aura of sharing. Yet, to those on the outside, that same culture-bound communication evokes feelings of discomfort: outsiders may feel that the complexities of language will be used against them. Like the catalogue system of a large library, a cultural code can be a forbidding threshold to some and a welcoming gateway to others.

To enjoy the fruits of the cultural heritage of a social group, noviciates and outsiders must learn to read the signs and symbols of the hitherto alien culture. And full membership of a social group is achieved when newcomers begin to acquire two skills: the ability to receive (i.e. read) and the ability to transmit (i.e. write) the messages of a given cultural code. Necessarily, then, participating membership of a cultural group is closely tied up with culture-specific knowledge and with the acquisition of varying degrees of cultural literacy.

Cultural literacy may also be tied up with economic proficiency. To be able to read weather signs is economically important within a fishing community, just as the ability to read market reports may be economically important in the stockbroker belt. In turn, economic intelligence serves as a cultural power base. Further, cultural literacy and economic power are also linked, in different ways, to the practices of socialization, acculturation, education and schooling. To those within a group, power is given through socialization and acculturation; to those who join the group, power is acquired (or shared) through education; and to those outside the group, power is (or can be) denied through schooling. In cultural terms, therefore, schooling may act against the empowerment of learners.

Cultural storage

Experiences happen only once. Yet, if they are to remain part of an individual's personal heritage they must be retained. But experience is rarely stored as itself. More often than not, it is retained in a codified form. For instance, human memory is based on the storage of chemical and electrical traces in the brain and nervous system. But humans also have an unrivalled capacity to store experience outside their bodies. Objects such as totem poles and stone circles are clear examples of culturally coded and socially stored information. They represent, in a shorthand yet memorable form, experiences that are revered, treasured and deemed worthy of recall. At best, they consolidate the past of a social group. Individuals also retain comparable objects (e.g. locks of hair, birthday books, concert programmes and school photographs). In one sense, such cultural and personal artefacts are part of life. Yet, they are also larger than life. As valued memorabilia, they are important personal and cultural markers. They testify to life's continuity, past, present and future.

Cultural storage, therefore, is a highly selective process. Yet, through time, the human species has greatly extended its storage capacity. Indeed, these two activities have converged. Much cultural storage in the twentieth century is little more than archival. Experiences are stored in the modern equivalent of charterhouses, to be recovered only under exceptional circumstances. Today, the human memory has become less of a storehouse of raw experience (i.e. memories) and more of a repository of instruments that can unlock experiences stored elsewhere (e.g. in the Yellow Pages). Powers of detailed recall, therefore, have declined in importance as symbols of cultural status and authority. Displaced from the sphere of economic production and political power, the display of detailed recall has survived on the margins of society, in the after-work world of cultural sideshows (e.g. pub games, music hall acts and television quiz shows).

Summary

Many accounts of schooling indicate its importance as a transmitter of culture. This chapter has suggested that cultural transmission is not an automatic, knock-on process but rather one that incorporates intellectual processes of encoding and decoding. These processes are fostered through acculturation. But they are also cultivated through education and schooling. Equally, they have also been dramatically affected by changes – also described as improvements – in the devices used for the storage and communication of experience. Nevertheless, there is another side to these historical transformations. The elaboration of human communication has also served to accentuate the gulf between doers and tellers, between insiders and outsiders and, in the realm of cultural power, between the haves and the have nots. People can be deprived of the nourishment of cultural literacy just as easily as they can be deprived of the sustenance of wild berries, fresh salmon and sun-dried grapes. At times, however, cultural literacy – access to cultural codebooks – has been extended to people outside the host culture. At other times, cultural literacy has been deliberately manipulated (e.g. via language policies) to reaffirm, if not reinforce, the gap that separates insiders from outsiders. Education and schooling, therefore, can be agencies of cultural manipulation just as much as they can be agencies of cultural transmission.

CHAPTER 4

Education and literacy

Here's freedom to him that would read,
Here's freedom to him that would write.

(Robert Burns, poet, 1792)

The concept of literacy was defined very broadly in the previous chapter. It referred to a person's ability to read and sometimes write down the cultural symbols of a society or social group. Essential to this argument was the difference between appearance and meaning or, to put it another way, between signs and symbols. Signs and symbols are both representational: they stand for something else. But a sign has a visual resemblance to the notion that it signifies, whereas a symbol, on the other hand, is always a codified message. This difference is demonstrated by the British road sign for a school. Today, schools are announced by means of a sign – a pictorial representation of a schoolgirl and schoolboy. Before the 1960s, however, schools were announced by means of a flaming Olympic torch, a symbol looking like a soft ice-cream that actually stood for the torch of learning.

The modern school sign was introduced, presumably, to conform with cross-national standards. But it is an open question whether any legislation can make signs valid across cultural boundaries. Like the washing instructions on international clothes labels, international road signs are inevitably a source of cross-cultural confusion and within-culture humour. Their meanings are rarely unambiguous. No sign is purely representational or culture free. The gap between the sign itself and what it stands for, and between the writer and the reader of the sign, always offers scope for slippage of meaning.

Written language, like sign language, is also a message system that utilizes signs and symbols. Certain forms of writing (e.g. pictographic writing) are built as representation systems. Their meaning can be uncovered by appreciating the physical similarities between the written signs and the objects and notions that they stand for. Alphabetic writing – as used in this book – is based on a much more elaborate system of coding. It is a non-representational system of communication. There is no physical connection between a text and what it signifies (or stands for). And, for this reason, alphabetic or alphanumeric literacy is comparable with cultural literacy. Likewise, alphanumeric literacy is not simply a set of decoding skills, it is also a political resource – an item of cultural property and an instrument of cultural power. Equally, the history of alphanumeric literacy is not simply about the spread of cultural power, it is also a history of the carefully managed distribution of cultural power. Literacy does not flow from person to person. Rather, it is consciously channelled to further social and political aspirations. In short, the history and politics of alphanumeric literacy cannot be separated.

Many writings on alphanumeric literacy fail to recognize the importance of this political dimension. As Harvey Graff has suggested in *The Labyrinths of Literacy* (1987), such writings subscribe to a 'literacy myth'. They take the view that literacy, like schooling, has only socially positive dimensions. They claim that its introduction and dissemination have been an unequivocal source of human improvement and human progress. Yet, the notion that literacy is all things to all people should be treated with caution. Certainly, the acquisition of alphanumeric literacy seems to have been associated with the rise of specific social groups. But it may also be true that the literacy myth is most enthusiastically celebrated – in literate media, of course – by those who have benefited from its powers.

The history of colonialism offers an illustration of the politics of literacy. As European armies conquered overseas territories, alphanumeric literacy, and the cultural messages that it carried, was deliberately substituted for indigenous form of communication. The conquered peoples were left stranded in a cultural vacuum. Their own languages and cultural codes ceased to have official currency and were replaced by cultural artefacts assiduously distributed and closely regulated by the colonial masters (e.g. through control of schooling and print-based mass media). The uneven distribution of alphanumeric literacy was, therefore, integral to the achievement and survival of political domination.

Nevertheless, the creation of a cultural vacuum, and its replacement with stunted forms of the dominant culture ran into the problem of human reactivity. Typically, subordinate groups reacted to the spread of alphanumeric literacy in two ways. Their political programmes called for the restoration and preservation of old cultural codes (e.g. traditional spoken and written languages). And their programmes also demanded institutional resources (e.g. schools and adult literacy programmes) which would give them full, rather than stunted, access to the codes and codebooks of the politically dominant culture. Indeed, such calls for access to the 'really useful knowledge' of the dominant culture commonly arise in all kinds of divided societies. They are reported, for instance, in Frantz Fanon's analysis of colonialism, *The Wretched of the Earth* (1965). But they also occur in social contexts divided by class and gender, as discussed in Brian Simon's *The Two Nations and the Educational Structure 1780–1870* (1960), and Nonita Glenday and Mary Price's *Reluctant Revolutionaries: A Century of Head Mistresses 1874–1974* (1974).

Overall, then, alphanumeric literacy can usefully be regarded as a cultural tool. It supplies power to its possessors and, like other tools, provides them with a means of escaping their immediate environment. Yet, as noted, literacy is not universally distributed. Indeed, to appreciate its historical significance, it is probably more important to consider the uneven cultural distribution of literacy than it is to understand the new powers made available to those who decoded its mysteries.

The mystery of alphanumeric literacy

As suggested, the mystery of alphanumeric literacy derives from the fact that it is a form of symbolic rather than representational communication. To learn to read and write is, therefore, to translate mystery into mastery. The power of alphabetic literacy, cogently outlined in Eric Havelock's *The Origins of Western Literacy* (1976), is associated with the fact that only 20–30 symbols are needed to represent the entire range of sounds and meanings used in different cultures. The handful of symbols used to create these high levels of generalizability stands in marked contrast to the thousands of characters necessary in Mandarin Chinese. The alphabet is a highly abstract codebook.

Early written scripts – like hieroglyphics – were based on the codification of ideas (e.g. 'horse', 'love', 'mother') and comprised a series of pictures. Alphabetic scripts have a completely different derivation. They are the codification of sounds, not ideas. The range of sounds used in spoken communication is built up from a small set of fundamental sounds (vowels) which are open to modification by the remaining letters of the alphabet (consonants). Thus, if a language is standardized phonetically, it can be read aloud as soon as the sounds of the letters and syllables have been learned. Russian and Swedish are two languages which come near to meeting this criterion. They can be competently read aloud with only a few hours' practice. But to read the sounds of a language is not the same as being able to read the meanings of a language.

How, then, does the alphabet convey meaning – its ultimate purpose? As the example of Swedish and Russian suggests, there are two processes entailed in extracting the meaning from an alphanumeric script. First, a pattern of sounds has to be derived from the letters; and, second, the resultant patterns of sound must be translated into units of meaning. This double-decoding is the basis of the so-called phonetic method of teaching reading. Children are trained to build up the sounds of words as a prelude to extracting the meanings of words. Likewise, children and adults who have reading difficulties are often encouraged to 'read it aloud', so that they extract the meaning of sentences from sounds rather than from print. And one of the signs of skilful reading is that people can read silently without moving their lips. As readers gain in competence, therefore, the double-decoding processes merge. In effect, individuals 'read it aloud' inside their heads, simultaneously and effortlessly extracting the meanings coded in the sounds. As a result, the dual decoding tasks cease to be visible in the behaviour of a competent reader. Reading appears to be little more than a process of seeing, despite the maxim that 'there's more to seeing than meets the eye'.

How, then, is alphabetic writing related to alphabetic reading? Are the processes of writing merely the reverse of the processes of reading? Is writing merely the translation of thoughts into sounds which are then reduced to inscriptions on paper and other media? If so, did reading and writing gain simultaneous cultural currency? And were they disseminated in tandem? In fact, the historical record suggests otherwise. Within alphanumeric cultures, the skill of writing seems to have diffused much more slowly than the skill of reading. No doubt this delay had something to do with the fact that writing requires sophisticated manual skills and specialist, if not costly, writing materials. But writing also differs from reading in another important respect. Reading is a means of revisiting the accumulation of past experiences; whereas writing is also a means of organizing and distributing visions of the future. In short, writing – the power of the pen – goes beyond the power of reading, and is not its mirror image.

For these reasons the history of literacy is really two separate histories whose divergence and convergence can be illustrated by reference to four historically significant processes: (1) the rise of personal property; (2) the growth of trade with distant parts; (3) the emergence of the town as a manufacturing centre; and (4) the development of large-scale factory production.

Literacy and property

From the earliest times, inscribed signs, whether on tally sticks, parchment, vellum or paper, have been used to record or display the extent of the 'earthly possessions' of human beings. But possession is not the same as ownership. During the early Middle Ages, for instance, it was assumed that everything belonged to God and that, accordingly, humans merely possessed their material goods (which included their children). Land, for instance, was merely held by stewards or occupied by tenants. Likewise, rights of occupation, or tenancy, were based on oral testimony (i.e. word of mouth).

Over time, however, patterns of land transfer changed. Although transfer was usually based on intergenerational inheritance, land often passed to relative outsiders, especially in times of famine and epidemic. As Michael Clanchy has elegantly demonstrated in *From Memory to Written Record* (1979), medieval transfers of this kind were increasingly recorded in a written form. Moreover, matters became even more complicated after the twelfth century. Stewardship (or possession) of God's land gave way to more powerful forms of tenure based on outright (i.e. freehold) ownership.

Tenure documents, however, often enjoyed only limited circulation among the senior owners and stewards. Tenants' rights of inheritance were, therefore, rarely acknowledged or recorded. In times of dispute (e.g. the enclosure movement in England and the Highland clearances in Scotland), small-scale tenants could appeal only to oral tradition for their land rights, whereas owners had recourse to written documents to enforce their entitlements.

As God's most senior steward, the Church not only enjoyed the fruits of large land holdings, it also retained the services of skilled copyists. Groups of men and women – many of them housed in convents and monasteries – became, quite literally, the keepers of God's word. And, to this end, they made copies of theological documents that might otherwise have been lost in the turmoils that accompanied the fall of the Roman Empire (*c.* AD 500). Well-versed in a variety of transcribing techniques (e.g. the preparation of parchment), these copyists – *clerks* as well as *clerics* – also turned their hands to non-religious texts. These included not only *pagan* texts (e.g. writings by Aristotle), but also more earthly documents such as details of harvest yields and land stewardship.

The development of record keeping – an early account of harvest yields was prepared for the Bishop of Winchester in 1208 – also marked the emergence of a literate administrative strata in society (e.g. notaries, scriveners, accountants and calligraphers). Above all, it fostered the expansion of the supply of readers and writers who serviced the documentary requirements of the powerful, and often non-literate, sections of society. For chivalrous medieval knights, possession of literacy was a cultural frill: their word was still their bond. Yet, for propertyless peasants, literacy was equally a social hindrance: their word had, in effect, become their bondage.

To this degree, writing in the Middle Ages was primarily a matter of record keeping, not communication. Documents were drawn up, endorsed with a signature or a signet, and lodged in places of safe storage (i.e. charterhouses) to be resurrected only in disputatious times. Cultural communication remained predominantly an oral activity. People did not send documents, they sent messengers, a practice which has survived into the twentieth century. Important communications from the Catholic Church to its members are still carried from Rome by a papal *nuncio*, the Latin word for an announcer or messenger.

Literacy and trade

Towards the end of the Middle Ages, the character of European cultural literacy was affected by a cluster of new factors. A major stimulus was the discovery of classical texts which had been lost, displaced or misplaced in the social upheavals (e.g. colonization by the Huns, Vandals and the Ostrogoths) that accompanied the decline of the Roman Empire. Together with commentaries, these texts, which passed from Greek into Latin via Hebrew, Persian and Syrian, comprised a new and unexamined storehouse of human experience, a corpus, among other things, of biological, physical, medical, astronomical and mathematical knowledge.

Gradually, this new learning – sometimes known as Aristotelianism – spread out across Europe and, in all kinds of different ways, stimulated intellectual inquiry by memorable philosophers such as Albertus Magnus (?1195–1280), Thomas Aquinas (1225–1274) and William of Occam (1285–1349). The intellectual voyages undertaken by late medieval philosophers also stimulated the comparable intellectual journeying of Renaissance figures such as Leonardo da Vinci (1452–1519). Indeed, many of these Renaissance voyages were also tied up with an international search for raw materials (e.g. silver, gold and spices) financed by merchants from communities in the Low Countries and the Mediterranean (e.g. Rotterdam, Lisbon, Genoa, Venice). Columbus's journey across the Atlantic in 1492 was, therefore, as much a commercial voyage in search of new sources of colonial wealth as it was an intellectual exercise to clarify the geography of the world. Indeed, it was the wealth acquired by the merchants that supported the scientific explorers of the Renaissance. Necessarily, then, intellectual innovators of that period were more closely allied to the merchant classes than to the Church. Gradually, early scientists put aside the teachings of the Bible and appealed, instead, directly to the book of nature, a transition which led them to become known as natural philosophers. Not surprisingly, this shift of attention away from theological texts and their associated doctrines did not always meet the approval of the established Church – a state of affairs, like the trial of Galileo (1564–1642), extensively examined in Arthur Koestler's *The Sleepwalkers* (1964).

Around 1450, a further technical development, that of printing with movable type, heightened the transmission potential of writing. Most early printed books were devoted to traditional texts (e.g. the Bible) rather than to the more speculative – and secular – new knowledge. Eventually, however, the new literature of the Renaissance was readily disseminated by means of the printing press, as chronicled in Lucien Febvre and Henri-Jean Martin's *The Coming of the Book* (1976). In turn, the primacy of oral knowledge and the dominance of the Catholic Church began to be undermined. Above all, printing made possible a revolution in self-instruction and, in the process, fostered the growth of personal libraries. Learners acquired greater access to texts and commentaries previously guarded by their teachers. Equally importantly, they also acquired access to an alternative literature, to pamphlets composed by religious and political heretics.

Besides recognizing the commercial utility of the printing press and the new learning, the merchants also distanced themselves from medieval forms of scholarship by placing less emphasis upon Latin. The language of the marketplace ceased to be the same as the longstanding language of the Church. It became, then as now, the vernacular of the most powerful merchants. In these and other respects, the merchants were an upstart social group. They did not fit easily into the hereditary aristocracy of the land or the ecclesiastical aristocracy of the Church. Powerful merchants, of course, could buy direct entry into polite society. But many others used a more indirect method. They deployed their economic power to acquire cultural power. And it was through these efforts that upstart social groups acquired (or cracked) the cultural codes of the dominant culture. Further, new social groups also began to transcend the dominant culture by constructing their own distinctive life styles or manners. Indeed, the importance of manners to the cultivation of life styles is acknowledged not only in the motto of Winchester School (founded 1382), *Manners Maketh Man*, but also in a vernacular acknowledgement heard in twentieth-century Glasgow, *Manners is a braw thing*.

In Britain schools have always played an important role in the establishment and refurbishment of life styles. During the Renaissance, for instance, St Paul's School was established in 1510 by the Mercers' (i.e. clothmakers) Company of London. Such an initiative – discussed in Joan Simon's *Education and Society in Tudor England* (1966) – was intended to create a new kind of adult, the Christian gentleman. St Paul's, which served as a model for the foundation of many later schools, was designed to provide a general (i.e. broad) education for privileged members of the laity. The products of such schools, equipped with accounting, law, and modern languages, were expected to make their way in civil as well as ecclesiastical society.

In creating their own schools and in developing a modern approach to the teaching of classics and other subjects, the merchants created a distinctive life style for themselves. Some of them made use of schools for this purpose. But many others also took advantage of an important educational boot-strapping device – the self-instructional improving text. These texts were manuals of etiquette or manners that recounted the forms of social conduct sought by aspiring social groups. One of the earliest and most influential improving texts was written by Desiderius Erasmus (1466–1536), a merchant-sponsored scholar who hailed from the important trading centre of Rotterdam. Erasmus's manual – which gave the word civility to the English language – was called *On Civility in Children* and was first published in Latin in 1530. Aided by the new technology of printing, it achieved enormous circulation. It appeared in more than thirty editions in Erasmus's lifetime, and more than 130 multi-language editions by 1800. As reported in Norbert Elias's *The Civilising Process* (1978), it offered advice on propriety ('don't wipe your nose on your sleeve'); table etiquette ('it is not very decorous to offer something half-eaten to another person') and deportment ('do not expose without necessity the parts of the body to which nature has attached modesty').

From an educational perspective, improving texts are historically significant because they contain life style information that is not accessible through the normal channels of intergenerational acculturation. In short, improving texts are an important means whereby children acquired – and still acquire – life styles different from those of their parents. Improving texts achieve their social popularity, and shape their readers' life styles, to the extent that they contain information 'my parents/teachers never taught me'. Classic twentieth-century cookery books and child-care manuals, like Mrs Beeton's *Book of Household Management* (1859) and Benjamin Spock's *Baby and Child Care* (1946), achieved much of their popularity because new generations of middle-class parents were required to feed and rear their families without the support previously offered by trained cooks and nannies. Likewise, recent improving manuals have helped to shape the sexual manners of generations whose access to artificial contraception far surpasses that of their parents.

Improving texts, therefore, are social passports that enable outsiders to become insiders. Erasmus's *On Civility in Children* met the aspirations of a small but powerful social group anxious to become more literate in the cultures or moral codes of the dominant sections of society. At different times, too, these codes of manners became known by different keywords. If ascendant members of Renaissance society aspired to become *civilized*, their medieval knightly counterparts sought to appear *courteous*, and their nineteenth-century descendants hoped that they could pass as *cultured* citizens.

Literacy and urbanization

Manners are very close to morality. Hence the manners of the merchants – the way they ran their lives – were a crucial feature of their commercial ethic. Nevertheless, the entrepreneurial code of 'buying cheap and selling dear', meant that merchants regularly ran into difficulties with the producers (from whom they bought) and with the consumers (to whom they sold). Indeed, it was heightened instances of this tension that, among other things, fuelled the Reformation in Western Europe. Broadly speaking, the social upheavals of the Reformation were a reaction against exploitation by merchants. It was prompted by the rural producers (i.e. successful peasants with a surplus to sell) and carried through with the aid of skilled artisans in urban areas who, as both sellers (of their own produce) and buyers (of the produce of others), were open to double exploitation by the merchants.

The economic upheavals of the Reformation also occurred in the wake of a period of colonial expansion (again the work of the merchants and their supporters). Political disputes over the control of ports and trading routes were fought out in the sixteenth century, leaving Britain, France, Spain and Holland in a state of economic disarray. Increased taxation, a burden which ultimately fell upon the peasants, and the introduction of less labour-intensive forms of agriculture (e.g. sheep rearing), drove people off the land and into the towns.

The traditional rulers (whose wealth was derived largely from holdings in land) and the monopolistic merchant dynasties could not contain the opposition that came from the small merchants, the peasants and the early members of the urban proletariat. The traditional fabric of society was undermined and alternative worldviews came to prominence. The viewpoint of the primary producers (peasants and artisans) was voiced most cogently by Martin Luther. His writings and preachings called for a return to simple values and a life uncorrupted by self-indulgence, idleness and authoritarian (i.e. hierarchical) forms of social and ecclesiastical organization. For Luther, social reform would re-establish a life of personal piety untrammelled by the intervening apparatus, institutions, and officials of the Church. To this extent, early Lutheranism was a personal religion. Its adherents reformed themselves by looking inwards to their thoughts, feelings and conduct. Furthermore, the faithful were offered personal access to God's teachings: Lutherans believed that everyone should be taught to read Bibles translated into the vernacular languages of Europe.

John Calvin, on the other hand, adopted an outward going, interventionist view of social reform. His ideas were part of an urban movement that, economically, combined the interests of small traders with those of the skilled artisans. Unlike Luther, for instance, Calvin articulated the view – popular with traders – that the granting of credit and the charging of reasonable interest rates were acceptable forms of commercial practice. Calvinism became a much more organized, formalized and institutionalized religion. If inner faith was the key tenet of Lutheranism, outward discipline was its Calvinist counterpart. And if the family was the basic unit of Lutheranism, the organizational unit of Calvinism was the community or congregation.

Calvinist teachings, therefore, paid attention to two complementary issues. First, they focused on the individual, stressing the Christian importance of personal responsibility, personal discipline and personal asceticism. And second, they focused on the organization of society, emphasizing that it should be uniformly refashioned according to God's biblical prescriptions. Together, these political arguments – discussed in John Morgan's *Godly Learning: Puritan Attitudes Towards Reason, Learning and Education* (1986) and Richard Tawney's *Religion and the Rise of Capitalism* (1942) – shaped Calvinist theories of literacy and education as well as a Calvinist theory of politics and government. Indeed, these various theories fed off each other.

Together, Calvinism and Lutheranism profited greatly from Gutenberg's invention. The provision of multiple copies of God's word in a language that the faithful could understand – discussed, for instance, in Frank Davies's *Teaching Reading in Early England* (1973) – gave the Protestant communities in Britain, France, Holland, Switzerland and elsewhere an interest in schooling – and reading – that marked them out from Catholic communities. Nevertheless, their investment in schooling and reading also had a more complex social consequence. Reading is a generalizable skill. To be able to read the Bible is also to be able to read other writings about society, social conduct and social change. In promoting reading, therefore, Protestant authorities also gave the faithful access to heretical notions. Accordingly, the promotion of heresy was an inevitable consequence of the promotion of Protestantism. It is no accident, therefore, that the history of the Protestant Church is a turbulent chronicle of theological dissent and congregational secession.

Literacy and industrialization

The various movements in trade, industry and urbanization that came together in the sixteenth and seventeenth centuries took on a new character in the following century. Water-powered machines took over significant areas of manual and domestic production. Workshops that, previously, had formed part of domestic dwellings were transformed into much larger productive units or manufactories. By the nineteenth century, the development of steam-powered versions of earlier machines, and the creation of railway and steamship networks, brought distant parts of the world into closer communion and greater interdependency. Before the nineteenth century, the fortunes of nations had waxed and waned with the success or failure of their staple agricultural produce (e.g. wheat or wool). By the beginning of the nineteenth century, however, the economic fortunes of trading states began to be linked more closely to the booms and slumps of factory production than to the ups and downs of agricultural husbandry.

The economic innovations of the Industrial Revolution stimulated important changes in the circumstances of many people drawn to work in factories. For instance, the labour requirements of large-volume factory production took workers away from their domestic settings. Many children worked as diminutive and nimble adjuncts to manufacturing machinery. Housing ghettos were the result of large-scale migration towards centres of employment. And, not least, the release of workers in times of slump created factory communities sporadically full of young, able-bodied and, as important, disgruntled adults.

In turn, these demographic processes disrupted earlier patterns of domestic and community life. The employment of adults outside the home left many children unattended. Child employment meant that many children failed to enjoy the disciplines of schooling. Migration inserted people from agricultural backgrounds into the machine-driven rhythms of factory life. And unemployment imported poverty and social unrest into factory-based communities.

New kinds of schools – and other institutions – were established to compensate for these factory-related developments. Infant schools, for instance, were established to allow mothers of young children to work during periods of labour shortage. And Sunday and evening schools were organized for children who otherwise worked full-time during daylight hours. Despite their different names – factory schools, Sunday schools, evening schools, infant schools – all these educational institutions were designed to accommodate the consequences of industrialization. In short, they came between working-class children and their parents and, in the process, they interrupted (or replaced) earlier patterns of parent–child acculturation.

The new schools of the Industrial Revolution adopted a new social agenda. They sought not only to inculcate virtue – as had been the case since the Reformation – they also aimed to remould their pupils to fit in with the needs of the Industrial Revolution. Schools, for instance, began to place much greater emphasis on continuous and regular attendance. And, having secured or rescued their charges, school superintendents developed elaborate pedagogies to ensure that all children remained busy at their allotted tasks. Some reformers held that rote methods were no longer adequate to the new circumstances surrounding the Industrial Revolution. They believed that schoolchildren should understand as well as remember their lessons. In effect, they proposed that schooling should be organized around a new and more powerful discipline, one that would mean the same to schooling as the machine meant to factory production.

Two developments flowed from this reconceptualization of schooling. First, much greater attention began to be given to the education, training and competence of elementary school teachers. Rote methods (or catechesis) were given much less attention and, instead, teachers were expected to become accomplished in more intellectual methods of instruction. They were expected not merely to inspect the contents of pupils' minds (e.g. by hearing memorized lessons), but also to exercise the minds of their charges (e.g. by questioning them on their lessons). The second development, promoted alongside the spread of elementary instruction, was a major expansion of the school curriculum. Children began to be taught through secular (i.e. worldly) as well as religious topics (a fact well-documented in the facsimile pages appended to G.S. Chalmers's *Reading Easy 1800–50*, 1976). It was assumed that if children knew how the world worked, they would be more ready to accept their allotted, if unnatural, place in the scheme of things. But, as in the case of teaching Protestants to read, the secularization of the elementary school curriculum also broadened the intellectual horizons of learners in new and unplanned directions. Indeed, one of the outgrowths of nineteenth-century elementary schooling was a wide range of educational institutions (e.g. libraries, Sunday schools, evening classes) founded by, and for, members of the working class.

Another educational consequence of the Industrial Revolution was that writing began to enter the core curriculum of schooling. But this curriculum innovation did not meet with unqualified approval. Some people argued that writing – a business skill – should not be taught in Sunday schools (i.e. on the Lord's day). Others claimed that it would promote crime ('if you teach them to write, they will learn to forge'). And many more commentators tacitly assumed that the acquisition of writing skills would elevate children above their proper station in life. Nevertheless, there was a powerful educational lobby that recognized the importance of writing skills to the administration of the factory system. In a manner reminiscent of the Middle Ages, the factory system was also associated with a separation of ownership from possession (or occupation). When the manager of a factory was also the owner, management was by word of mouth. But as expansion began to be financed through partnerships and multiple shareholdings, owner–managers began to be replaced by hired managers who, by analogy, merely occupied their factories. In turn, management became a specialist occupation. As intermediaries between employers and employees, managers were expected to keep records and compile written records for their employers. Likewise, they were also required to act upon written documents emanating from their suppliers and clients. In such tasks, managers were assisted by male clerks who, by necessity, were expected to have achieved greater levels of written literacy than their parents. The army of clerks expanded with industrialization. And schools made an equivalent effort to supply such personnel.

Just as the dissemination of reading skills was assisted by the technology of printing, so the spread of writing in commercial institutions also received a comparable technological stimulus. The traditional barrier to the spread of handwriting was the cost of quills, penknives and paper. But the invention of the mass-produced and low-cost steel-nibbed pen in the 1830s ushered in a new era of writing, and new forms of writing (i.e. copybook handwriting).

As noted earlier, there is a close relationship between property ownership and the creation of written records, and between writing skills and forms of accounting. Indeed, many reports produced by factory managers included details of production, summaries of wage costs and details of factory maintenance. For this reason, writing and practical arithmetic were often taught in schools as a joint skill known, in Scotland if not elsewhere, as 'casting accounts'. The teaching of arithmetic, therefore, was directly linked to the production of bills and receipts, which is why problems of the kind 'If 54 men build a house in 90 days, how many men can do the same in 50 days?' (*The Compendium of Arithmetic*, 1824) figured so largely in the schoolbooks of the nineteenth and twentieth centuries. In earlier centuries, arithmetical knowhow was a craft skill, restricted to specialist occupations (e.g. surveying); and often taught as a separate school subject (e.g. 'mensuration') But the factory system and the associated spread of wage labour drew more and more people into the cash nexus and into the day-to-day use of arithmetical knowledge. To this extent, there is a closer historical association between writing and arithmetic (and their entry into the school curriculum) than there is between writing and reading.

Summary

Literacy is an extension of the species-wide powers of speech and thought. In effect, the refinement of literacy (e.g. the invention of alphanumeric symbols) has enabled human beings to 'speak' and 'think' in new ways. Nevertheless, the spread of literacy has been a two-edged process. For some human beings, it has been a source of social emancipation yet, for others, it has seemed more of an agency of social control. Thus, the history of literacy is not only the history of the spread of a set of technical skills but also the history of changing access to cultural resources. Those who aspired to retain the *status quo* sought to harness, if not control, literacy through censorship, licensing of approved printers, and the taxation of publications. But this was rarely sufficient. People who had been taught through authorized texts simultaneously acquired tools which gave them access to politically contentious works like Thomas Paine's *Rights of Man* (1791) and Mary Wollstonecraft's *Vindication of the Right of Woman* (1792). And many of those, like Robert Burns, who were inspired by such unauthorized texts extolled the benefits of self-instruction. Using an appropriate metaphor, E.P. Thompson points out in *The Making of the English Working Class* (1968) that despite the conformism of official schooling, 'the towns, and even the villages, hummed with the energy of the autodidact'. Again, education could not easily be accommodated within the framework of schooling.

CHAPTER 5

Teaching, curriculum and learning

Domestic education is the institution of nature; public education, the contrivance of man.

(Adam Smith, economist, 1759)

By comparison with other animals, human beings have a large measure of choice in the rearing of their young. And the exercise of such choice, coupled with the existence of alternatives, accounts for the cultural diversity of *Homo sapiens*. Human education, like human upbringing, also entails the exercise of cultural choice. To educate someone, therefore, is to reconsider and redirect their cultural and economic fortunes. In short, education turns them into someone else. And responsibility for such redirection largely rests with learners and their teachers.

Schooling is comparable to education and upbringing. It, too, is an option-laden intervention in the lives of human beings. But it differs from education and upbringing in so far as less responsibility and fewer choices are made available to teachers and learners. Instead, cultural power and responsibility remain with outside agencies, notably the Church and the State. To this degree, schooling is about the management, even the manipulation, of the choices of teachers and learners. And school curricula are one of the key political devices used to accomplish this management and manipulation.

Curriculum

Biological evolution occurs when a species repeatedly samples its changing gene pool. Equally, social evolution is built around successive samplings of the changing heritage of human experience. In neither case, however, does evolution occur randomly (or by 'blind chance'). Like the selection of a mating partner, the selection – or sampling – of past experience is influenced by many external factors. For these reasons, then, a curriculum is a social artefact. It is configured according to those elements of a cultural heritage that are deemed worthy of transmitting or communicating to a new generation of learners. To this extent, a curriculum draws upon the past but is shaped according to the future. Above all, it embodies a vision of the future, of the world that is to come.

But a curriculum is more than a vision; it is also a cultural tool. And, like all tools, a curriculum is shaped by its users, both those who wield it and those whose lives are managed – or steered – according to its pre-scriptions. Moreover, as a power tool, a curriculum is more likely to reflect the cultural selections, values and aspirations of powerful social groups than the cultural assumptions and aspirations of powerless groups.

From an historical perspective, school curricula, and the visions that they embody, are fragile and fluid. Curricula may embody visions or blueprints of the future. But their relationship with the future is always problematic. An ideal curriculum is both a blueprint for the future and, as important, a set of procedures for realizing such goals. But many curri-cula, however, are far from ideal. Destinations may be specified without including an indication of the routes to be followed. And routes may be presented as compass bearings that point across otherwise uncharted terrain.

To this extent, curriculum design, construction and implementation is a multifaceted production process. New curricula usually meet the light of day as rough-hewn outlines. Thereafter, they are repeatedly re-fashioned by curriculum committees, government inspectors, textbook publishers, etc. Indeed, the curriculum introduced into a school may bear little resemblance to the curriculum produced on the drawing board of its originators. The prolongation of curriculum construction can be regarded from two contrasting angles. One view is that the gradual distortion of a curriculum vision is a retrograde process: the eventual activities steered by the curriculum are merely a shadow of the intended curriculum. The contrary view, however, is that the prolongation of curriculum produc-tion should be regarded as a strengthening activity. The curriculum starts out as a shadow but is gradually transformed into a tried and tested artefact.

Whatever its value, the production process – from raw to fully fashioned curricula – has been on the agenda of schooling for several centuries. It has changed substantially over the same timespan. Today, most forms of schooling operate with fully fashioned curricula. But this was not always the case. In the Middle Ages, for instance, university teachers worked with relatively raw materials. Experience was selected without much thought being given to the form in which it should be organized or transmitted. In Glasgow, for instance, the university's teach-ers met on the opening day of the academic year to decide which source texts (e.g. works by Aristotle) they would use. Thereafter, they gave public readings and commentaries on their chosen works (the word lec-ture, like the word lesson, comes from the Latin verb 'to read'). As this suggests, there was no prescribed – or universally agreed – order in which texts were to be read by the teachers and studied by the learners. Above all, very little of the teaching presumed the existence of a set programme or course. Instead, student learning was a pick and mix affair. Students came and went according to their own circumstances. Many of them migrated from university to university (i.e. from teacher to teacher) to accommodate their intellectual, social and political interests.

Gradually, however, the raw material of university teaching was subjected to increasing formalization before it reached the hands and minds of teachers and learners. Indeed, the rise to prominence of the word 'curriculum' in the late sixteenth century is one indication of this reorganization. As suggested by its origins – the Latin word for a course or track used in athletic competitions – a curriculum embodies a route or journey undertaken to reach a destination. Its etymology suggests above all that a curriculum prescribes a sequence or *course* of learning. Precurriculum texts did not, it seems, refer to the sequential aspects of teaching and learning. Instead, they denoted the structuring of a student's studies by reference to terms like *reges* (rule), *leges* (law) and *disciplina* (discipline). Nevertheless, sequential terms like *ordo* (order) began to appear in the University of Paris in the early part of the sixteenth century. They formed part of a major revision of the University's practices that came to be known as the *Modus et Ordo Parisiensis*. And, in turn, these organizational innovations served as blueprints for the post-Renaissance reform of other universities.

The midwife of the educational term curriculum was probably the much older phrase *curriculum vitae*. If *curriculum vitae* is a course of life, a *curriculum scholae* became, by analogy, a course of school. Further, the educational annexation of the curriculum notion also seems to have been associated with two other suppositions. First, it began to be assumed that learning should follow a clearly defined sequence (i.e. a course); and second, that such courses should be rounded and coherent entities. In other words, curricula were to be well ordered, both in the sense of sequence (as in the phrase 'order of events') and in the sense of structure (as in the phrase 'an ordered society').

The connection between curriculum and ordered (or formalized) schooling can also be related to the fact that some of the earliest uses of the term curriculum appear in the records of two Calvinist institutions – Leiden and Glasgow universities. As already indicated, Calvinist theology placed great emphasis on social discipline, and upon the right of church officials to intervene in the lives of the faithful. As John Calvin preached in 1539, 'the body of the church, to cohere, must be bound together by discipline as by sinews'. Very probably, these notions extended to educational institutions run by Calvinists. Thus, the concept of curriculum may have held the same sense of order in Calvinist theories of schooling as the concept of discipline held in Calvinist theories of social administration.

The connection between curriculum and Calvinism deserves further examination. Curriculum may have made early appearances in Calvinist circles, but the latter half of the fifteenth century was an era when all educational institutions – Catholic as well as Protestant – were engaged in reorganization and reform. It is no accident, therefore, that a manual designed for Jesuit schools, the *Ratio Studiorum* (a title that can be translated as scheme, programme, order or logic of studies), was published in 1599, less than thirty years after the appearance of the term curriculum.

The meanings attached to *curriculum* and *ratio* also relate to another organizational innovation. The term 'system' came to prominence in the seventeenth century, at a time when much attention was paid to the movement and configuration of the sun and its adjacent planets. The appearance of the term 'curriculum' was, therefore, not only part of the ordering of schooling, it was also part of the systematization of schooling. To this extent, a curriculum is a unified system of interconnected elements. Just as a harmony was ascribed to the movement of the planetary spheres, so it is likely that a comparable harmony was sought in the interconnectedness of the elements (or subjects) of a curriculum.

Nevertheless, the subsequent history of the curriculum idea has paid only partial attention to the unity and coherence of curricula. There has been a permanent tension between the breaking down of curricula into smaller units (e.g. subjects, lessons) and the building up of curricula to preserve their overall integrity. Typically, curricula have been reorganized to make them more accessible to learners. Thus, the wholeness of human experience is broken down into a series of separate intellectual units (e.g. subjects), separate texts (or textbooks), and separate units of instruction (e.g. lessons). But the formalization or systematization of schooling may have served only to widen the gap between learners and the cumulated wisdom of their forebears.

It is not unreasonable to claim, therefore, that medieval students, who lived in the pre-curriculum age, were intellectually much closer to Aristotle than their twentieth-century counterparts who are expected to rely on selective, if not watered-down, versions of Aristotle's writings. The fashioning and fragmentation of a curriculum is, therefore, a double-edged process, a thesis forcefully propounded with reference to Renaissance and Reformation schooling in Anthony Grafton and Lisa Jardine's *From Humanism to the Humanities* (1986). Students who read original sources were exposed directly to the values of humanism; whereas students who were taught via separate subjects (viz. the humanist curriculum) may merely have been exposed to the latter-day values of the curriculum builders or the sixteenth century. Such systematization of a curriculum may increase the marketability of schooling (e.g. by producing attractive learning materials). But, as a consequence, it may also yield adults who have been schooled (or textbooked) rather than citizens who have been educated.

The recent history of school curricula in the United States and the United Kingdom further illustrates this tension. In the early days of the curriculum notion, teachers took their students through an entire course or programme of study. Gradually, however, single-subject teachers – who taught the same topic year after year – were introduced into schools and colleges. Single-subject teachers may, perhaps, have been instrumental in enhancing the quality of individual parts of the course, but their rise to prominence also had the complementary consequence of reducing the overall coherence of the course. Curricula became fragmented, dispersed aggregates of subjects rather than unified programmes of study.

The twentieth century has seen further curricular fragmentation. The introduction of curriculum options (or electives) has recast the notion of a curriculum, not as a course but as a branching tree. By selecting options, each student takes a different learning route. More recently, the curriculum tree has itself suffered major surgery. Today, many programmes offered in schools and colleges are little more than piles of pre-cut timber, relabelled as modular curricula. At best such educational offerings are courses in a culinary, not a curriculum, sense. But what would John Calvin have made of these curricula? What, and where, are the sinews – or over-arching concepts – that hold them together? Indeed, the inter-relationships between the units of a modular course are probably as much a mystery to the teachers of the separate units as they are to the students who seek a coherent path through the advertised programme.

If a curriculum is more than the sum of its parts, it comprises not only a range of individual units but also the interrelationships and interactions that hold the units together. A curriculum, therefore, is an ordered or structured entity. It is more than a cluster of educational topics, just as a house is more than a pile of bricks. If an educational programme can be reduced to a list of topics or subjects, there is good historical and etymological grounds for labelling it as a syllabus rather than as a curriculum. The word syllabus, related to the term syllable, is most readily translated as 'table of contents'.

In an important sense, a curriculum is a carefully selected and carefully structured storehouse of experience. The contents of the storehouse are chosen for their capacity to shape learners in particular ways. And the contents of the storehouse are arranged according to the sequencing that best achieves the reshaping of learners. Ultimately, however, the shaping potential of a curriculum can be realized only through teaching and learning.

Teaching and learning

Teaching and learning can be envisaged, respectively, as the unpacking and repacking of a curriculum storehouse. To teach, therefore, is to bring stored up experience to life in such a way that it can be grasped by the learner. The teacher's task is to unlock the potential of the curriculum whereas the learners' task is to reshape themselves in the light of the curriculum's potential. Unlike the learner, however, teachers conventionally have prior knowledge of the contents and layout of the storehouse. Typically, too, teachers have prior access to the cultural codebooks that govern the preservation (or codification) of human experience. Teaching and learning, therefore, are rather more than the handing on of experience. They are more complex activities. Teachers not only have to unpack the curriculum storehouse, they also have to translate experience into a form that is accessible to learners. Likewise, learning can only be accomplished if learners can find ways to link their own prior experience to the experiences offered by their teachers.

Although teaching was a recognized occupation in the Middle Ages, it was hardly a 'trade' or 'calling'. It was more of a transient activity than a permanent occupation. It was, for instance, an adjunct to monastic duties, or it was a task allocated to people forced (e.g. by physical injury) to abandon their chosen occupations. As a socially distinct activity, teaching presumably emerged when human beings gave thought to the collective and corporate reorganization of their economic and cultural activities. In turn, certain adults were charged with giving their time and attention to the communication of skills and knowledge. In classical Greece, this task often fell to slaves known as pedagogues. But, by the Middle Ages, teachers and teaching were closely bound up with the preparation of church officials and with the dissemination of craft skills through schemes of apprenticeship.

As described in O.J. Dunlop and R.D. Denman's *English Apprenticeship and Child Labour: A History* (1912), apprenticeship is a much older institution than schooling. Nevertheless, schools and schooling grew out of the organization and regulation of apprenticeship. Features of this transition can be seen, for instance, in the emergence of the oldest surviving universities – Paris and Bologna. From around AD 1150, students travelled from all over Europe to sit at the feet of lawyers (in Bologna) and theologians (in Paris). As foreigners, the students in Bologna were denied rights and privileges available to the established residents (or citizens) of that city. Accordingly, the visiting scholars banded together in the interests of self-preservation. The University of Bologna began life, therefore, as a guild of scholars. In Paris, by contrast, it was the teachers who banded together. They organized among themselves largely to counterbalance the power of the cathedral chancellor (who was also the local tax collector).

In essence, the universities of Bologna and Paris were like medieval guilds, or modern trade unions. As discussed in A.B. Cobban's *The Medieval Universities* (1975), they comprised people who shared an occupational identity and who, in turn, drew up their own rules, laws and statutes of incorporation. In Bologna, for instance, completion of an approved programme of studies became the basis for admittance into the local guild of lawyer–teachers. But admission was not a matter of open entry. Rather, it was carefully regulated by the established guild masters. As elsewhere, there was no guarantee that every apprentice would become a master. Many students, therefore, did not complete their studies. Instead, they merely attended lectures (e.g. on civil law) that met their practical concerns. The attraction of Bologna derived from the fact that local jurists (legal experts) were famous for the justifications they supplied for the transference of God's property into forms of outright – or freehold – ownership. Indeed, many students were sent to Bologna by land holders who wished to acquire the cultural power promised by such specialist knowledge.

The transition from apprentice to student took a new turn in the thirteenth century when Bologna obtained the right, ultimately from the Pope, to grant a new form of teaching licence. The *jus ubique docendi* (the right everywhere to teach), was not only valid in the territory supervised by the Archbishop of Bologna but also throughout the Papal domain. This papal privilege transformed the teaching at Bologna. Henceforth, the numbers of graduating students no longer need bear any relationship to the vacancies in the local guild. Equally, the prospect of being granted a *jus ubique docendi* gave Bologna students an incentive to complete approved programmes of study. Rapidly, therefore, universities began to take on their modern form. They began to function primarily as institutions of teaching rather than as institutions of apprenticeship.

Above all, universities became centres for the teaching of the liberal arts. These comprised a range of philosophical and logical techniques that, it was claimed, could be used to scrutinize – or extract the meaning – from past, present and future texts. The liberal arts, therefore, were a training in learning skills, a state of affairs reflected in the fact that the word art is the Latin equivalent of the Greek word for technique. An arts degree became regarded as a necessary prerequisite for entry into the higher realms of meaning (i.e. the faculties of theology, medicine, canon law and civil law). Indeed, this assumption has survived until the twentieth century: admission to schools of medicine and law in the United States is still based upon successful completion of a lower degree, often from a liberal arts college.

Typically, university teaching revolved around two kinds of lectures. The most important were 'ordinary' lectures which usually took place in the morning, and were given by one of the 'masters' of the university. Ordinary lectures comprised line by line exposition of an approved text, together with exploration of problems in the text. Students were expected to absorb the meanings, if not memorize the words, of such texts. 'Extraordinary' lectures – also known as 'cursory' lectures – were given in the afternoon by relatively junior members of the guild of teachers (e.g. 'bachelors'). They comprised paraphrases of the official texts and were, in effect, repetitions of the ordinary lectures.

Papal creation of the *jus ubique docendi* not only endorsed the teaching function of the universities, it also fostered a standardization of courses. As other centres of learning sought to achieve a comparable status, they adopted the constitutions of Paris and/or Bologna, and recruited teachers who had studied in those cities. Further, teachers from the older universities also set up on their own, offering private instruction in the liberal arts. Among other things, these private teachers prepared students for direct entry to the higher faculties. And, since they offered instruction in Latin – also known as 'grammar' – these teachers created the earliest grammar schools. Indeed, the preparatory function of grammar schools in respect of higher studies retained a measure of cultural currency until the twentieth century.

Additional standardization of courses, texts and teaching occurred in the Reformation, largely for political reasons. As noted earlier, Lutheran and Calvinist reformers aimed to put vernacular versions of God's word into the hands of every believer. Nevertheless, the preparation of suitable translations proved highly controversial. One of the earliest Protestant versions of the Bible, printed by William Tyndale in 1526, was a sell out in Britain, despite being publicly burned at the behest of the church authorities. They held that Tyndale's 'errors' of translation, made widely accessible by the technology of printing, would spread unwanted heresy among the common people. In fact, of course, the heresies proclaimed by the new Bibles were deliberate. As the reformers translated (or recoded) the ideas of the original texts, they played down certain allusions and emphasized others. For instance, Tyndale used the words 'congregation', 'elder' and 'knowledge' where the orthodox view would have preferred 'church', 'priest', and 'confession'.

Eventually, however, cultural and economic power resolved these disputes. Heretical printers were gradually brought under control, while favoured printers were granted monopolies in the production of approved and standardized texts. In Britain, the first official church primer appeared in 1534, the first *Book of Common Prayer* in 1549, the authorized *Bible* in 1611 and the *Shorter Catechism* in 1643.

Since the sixteenth century, the control of book production has remained a key element in the formalization and control of school instruction. The Society for the Propagation of Christian Knowledge (founded 1698) and the Sunday School Union (founded 1803) were deliberately established for the purpose of disseminating approved literature. Their efforts proved highly successful. Aided by subsidies and large print runs, they could sell religious and moral texts to elementary schools for half the price of competing texts.

The nineteenth century saw further formalization of teaching and learning. Approved texts began to be replaced by sets of 'graded' readers (e.g. the McGuffey elementary school readers published in the USA from the 1830s). In many ways, therefore, the craft production of schoolbooks became a highly mechanized and highly profitable branch of industry, an historical outcome discussed in Michael Apple's *Teachers and Texts* (1986). In the twentieth century, the production of graded texts has been combined with the preparation of student worksheets, filmstrips, teachers' guides, audio tapes, laboratory manuals, etc. If the late twentieth century is the age of the convenience food, it is also the era of the convenience curriculum.

Necessarily, then, the production of fully fashioned curricula has been a key process in the systematization of schooling. In their most elaborate form fully fashioned curricula are scarcely distinguishable from self-instructional programmes. They, too, are designed (or vernacularized) to give students personal access to the cultural prescriptions stored in the curriculum storehouse. Nevertheless, the production of such curricula, like the standardization of the Protestant Bible, tends to create a closed orthodoxy. As the curriculum is refined, so the possibilities of intervention by teachers and learners are reduced. In the extreme, teachers are envisaged as little more than curriculum minders. They are no longer encouraged to enter into, or comment upon, the curriculum storehouse. They are relocated in a subordinate position, as curriculum doorkeepers, curriculum customs officers and curriculum security guards.

Summary

Current educational theory tends to define curriculum as the 'what' of education; and teaching and learning, jointly as the 'how' of education. This chapter has been critical of such a strong separation. It suggests that there is a much closer relationship between the ways in which curricula are constructed and the pedagogic openings that they offer to teachers and learners. Every curriculum can be structured in many ways, each with a different educational potential. And, by the same token, the potential of every curriculum can be released in many ways (e.g. via lectures or seminars) and grasped in many ways (e.g. by rote learning or guided discovery). The bulk of schooling may revolve around only three basic processes – teaching, curriculum and learning; but these activities can express themselves in an infinity of different ways.

CHAPTER 6

Schooling and society

The school of experience is no school at all, not because no one learns in it, but because no one teaches.

(B.F. Skinner, psychologist, 1968)

Schools have changed since their early association with leisure. Over the centuries they have become more formalized and, in the process, schooling has broken away from other economic and cultural activities. This formalization has been associated with the division of labour. Communal experience was not only divided into different categories (e.g. subjects, faculties, disciplines), it was transmitted or communicated by groups of socially distinct teachers to groups of socially distinct learners. And if a person's curriculum of life was originally envisaged as a ladder leading to heavenly salvation, it was gradually recast as a branching tree or a journey that took each learner to a different location in the secular order of things. Throughout its history, therefore, schooling has been intimately linked to the wider structuring of society. Indeed, the organization of schooling and the structuring of society have close linguistic connections. Until the start of the Industrial Revolution (i.e. towards the end of the eighteenth century), the word *class* generally referred to a cohort of learners brought together for educational purposes. By 1820, however, class had taken on a new meaning. It began to refer to other groupings, most notably in the formulation 'working classes'. That is, older forms of educational thinking provided social theorists with new ways of conceptualizing the social world. In effect, the shaping of society took its cue from the shaping of schooling, not the other way around.

In the long run, of course, the trade in ideas is a twoway process. The realms of schooling, family life, the church, the military and factory production have repeatedly exchanged their images, terminology and practices. Sometimes, too, notions have travelled backwards and forwards between two specific institutions. For instance, early forms of schooling echoed family life. Gradually, however, schooling grew in cultural significance, cultural potency and cultural domination. By the late twentieth century, the ideological hegemony of schooling has become so great that many parents bring up their children according to strictures, or forms of discipline, that are more reminiscent of schooling than of the accumulated wisdom of family life.

Social change and schooling

As this suggests, schooling is never untouched by the broader fabric of society. But what, then, is the relationship between schooling and society? Should schools be regarded simply as a mirror or echo of society? Should they be treated as progressive institutions ahead of the rest of society? Or should they be presumed to take a conservative social role, preserving valued and stabilizing notions from yesteryear? Certainly, many schools operate to conserve pre-existing forms of life; and many accounts of schooling give priority to this aspect. But it may also be worth while to recognize that schooling is equally a transformative institution. Two related propositions – already outlined – support this argument: first, that schooling is a social tool, an instrument for changing human life styles; and second, that curricula can be agents of social production as much as they are agents of social reproduction.

Such a view of the transformative role of schooling was, as noted, very important in the Reformation. But it perhaps reached its height during the Enlightenment, a period of history that immediately preceded (and over-lapped with) the Industrial Revolution. From an educational perspective, the Enlightenment is notable for two political ideas; that the human condition could be greatly improved; and that such improvement would be assured if the law-like behaviour of the physical world could be extended to the social world. In many respects, therefore, the intellectual ferment of the Enlightenment was generated by a search for the natural laws that under-pinned the organization of society. Indeed, the term 'social science' first appeared towards the end of the Enlightenment, in the 1790s.

Enlightenment thinkers were motivated by a belief that God had passed responsibility for the organization of society to human beings. God's influence, however, was not entirely discounted. Adam Smith, for example, wrote of the 'invisible hand' that steered society. Nevertheless, the general tenor of Enlightenment thought was that, henceforth, the human species could begin to control its own destiny. Enlightenment perspectives, therefore, were intensely human centred. They paid less attention to the possibilities of human salvation and more attention to the science of human progress.

Towards the end of the eighteenth century, society was regarded as a hierarchical entity. Everyone had a natural and static place in the social order. Such a view, advanced largely by those near the top of the hier-archy, sought to justify the *status quo*. But, just as the Renaissance had seen the rise of merchant dynasties, so the eighteenth century witnessed the emergence of another historically important social grouping.

This comprised men and women who had acquired great wealth from a form of production – the factory system – that lay outside the normal orbit of the Merchant and Trades Guilds. Like the merchants before them, the factory owners were not readily welcomed into the existing elites. As before, some bought or married their way into positions of cultural power. But others took a more difficult route. They fought a battle of ideas, armed with notions gained from the teachings of Enlightenment social theorists, of whom Adam Smith (1723–1790) serves as a notable example.

Adam Smith's *The Wealth of Nations* was published in 1776. It was a text about the organization of society. For its preparation, Smith drew upon many of the ideas that circulated among the commercial and industrial classes of Glasgow and the west of Scotland. Smith advanced two economic propositions that were crucial to the new entrepreneurs: first, that the interests of the political state would be better served by policies of economic liberty (or free trade) than by the granting of commercial monopolies (restraint on trading); and second, that there was no contradiction between the self-interested pursuit of gain and the interests of society at large. Further, Smith implied that governments who followed these prescriptions would be acting more naturally (i.e. would be more in tune with the laws of nature) than governments who retained older economic assumptions.

In the thirty years before its publication, Smith had presented the ideas of *The Wealth of Nations* to a variety of audiences. In effect, these lectures projected a vision of the world that was yet to come. Nevertheless, these lectures resonated with the cultural assumptions of Smith's listeners, many of whom came from commercial backgrounds. Smith's teachings, therefore, served as improving devices. As discussed in R.H. Campbell and A.S. Skinner's *Adam Smith* (1985), they prepared his audiences for entry into new life styles and new social contexts. Given the fact that *The Wealth of Nations* was also translated into French, German and Danish during Smith's lifetime, it helped to articulate and consolidate a new outlook or worldview among aspiring members of future political and economic elites. The new industrialists, therefore, acquired an intellectual power that catalysed and greatly enhanced their economic power. In combination, these resources projected many of them into important positions of political power and cultural authority.

Like other European and American thinkers of the same era, Adam Smith played down the notion that the organization of society was beyond humankind's control. He pointed, instead, to the transformative potential of social (e.g. environmental) and personal (i.e. psychological) resources. Indeed, one of the most famous passages in *The Wealth of*

Nations was a direct challenge to those who held a static and immutable view of society. The 'difference of natural talents', Smith wrote, 'is much less than we are aware of'. Thus, the 'difference between a philosopher and a common street porter' arises 'not so much from nature' as from 'habit, custom and education'. And, in the same period, too, the French philosopher Claude Adrien Helvetius (1715–1771) found a more concise way of saying the same thing: 'education can do everything'.

Such Enlightenment rationales, documented in Merryan Williams's *Revolutions 1775–1830* (1971), were widely circulated. The ideas of Smith, for instance, not only entered the corridors of political and economic power, they also achieved extensive circulation through the schoolmasters and ministers who also attended his lectures. In turn, the popularity of notions about human potential and human freedom of action brought a new dimension to discussions about the organization of schooling. What was the purpose of schooling? Was it to produce pious and deferent adults? Or was schooling to be organized with the aim of releasing the newly identified intellectual talents of human beings?

There was another dimension to this Enlightenment debate about the relationship between schooling and society. How was the new-found potential of education and schooling to be channelled? In particular, how could the notion of human potential be accommodated with Enlightenment assumptions about human freedom? Was schooling to release the slumbering intellectual powers of young people, or was its purpose to integrate young people into the values of the state? Is schooling to promote learning? Or is it merely to promote approved forms of knowledge, approved cultural dispositions and approved cultural values?

During the eighteenth century, such issues were powerfully raised in two books written by Jean Jacques Rousseau (1712–1778). In *Emile* (1762), a book about upbringing, Rousseau argued that children were born in a natural or innocent state and that upbringing should be based upon the preservation and nurturance of a child's natural propensities. *Emile*, therefore, was an eloquent critique of earlier forms of schooling which, Rousseau claimed, were based on the 'crushing force of social conventions'. Accordingly, Rousseau believed that schooling, as well as upbringing, should be based unilaterally upon nature, albeit a nature already authored by God. 'Forced to combat either nature or society' he wrote in *Emile*, 'you must make your choice between the man and the citizen, you cannot train both'.

The other side of this argument – the status of citizenship – was pursued by Rousseau in *The Social Contract*, also published in 1762. Central to this book was a discussion of the conflict between the rights of the individual and the social responsibilities of citizenship. What, then, is the freedom and autonomy of the individual? Are citizens merely subordinates of the state? Is citizenship restricted to males, leaving females in a natural state of subordination and subjection? Or is it possible to resolve the interests of the state with those of the autonomous citizen?

Natural upbringing *versus* schooling for citizenship is an educational issue that has remained alive since Rousseau's time. Compare, for instance, two statements about the social functions of schooling. This first appears in John Holt's *How Children Fail* (1969): 'Schools should be places where children learn what they most want to know, instead of what we think they ought to know'. The second statement is the opening sentence of *Effective Secondary Schools* (1988) a discussion document produced by the Scottish Education Department: 'An effective secondary school is one in which pupils learn, to the limits of their capabilities, *what is deemed appropriate*, taking into account their personal needs and preferences' (added emphasis). The difference between these statements is perfectly consistent with the difference between education and schooling outlined earlier in this book. But what might Helvetius have made of the Scottish reference to limited 'capabilities'? And what might Rousseau have made of the emphasis upon 'appropriate' learning?

Differentiation and the allocation of pedagogic resources

Besides affecting the purpose of education and schooling, Enlightenment thought also had a major impact upon modes of instruction. In Glasgow, for instance, professors began to give extempore presentations (instead of dictating from prepared lectures); and students were encouraged to question their teachers immediately after the lectures. Two features of these new methods are historically noteworthy: first, that it was acceptable and legitimate for teachers to deviate from the recommended texts; and, second, that relatively junior learners might enter into dialogue with their teachers.

These new practices of the late eighteenth century were a direct expression of the political, social and psychological sentiments of the Enlightenment, when knowledge and ideas became more open to human scrutiny. Indeed, 'open-mindedness' would probably have been an alien, if not heretical, notion before the Enlightenment. During the Enlightenment, therefore, universities began to change their social role. University authorities gave less attention to the dissemination of God's unchanging and unchallenged word and instead began to see themselves as centres for the exploration and analysis of God's Kingdom. Put another way, universities began to be identified as research institutions for the pursuit of knowledge, a social purpose which, for instance, lay behind the establishment of Berlin University in 1809.

The traditional lecture (or reading) also underwent important changes as part of the Enlightenment reconceptualization of knowledge and learning. Teaching by means of tutorials and seminars began to appear in university circles, as described, for instance, in Ian Watt's article on 'The seminar' (1964). The term seminar comes from a Latin word meaning seedbed. Seminars, pioneered in Germany (e.g. at Halle University), embodied the notion that university teaching and inquiry should be based on the criticism rather than the memorization of texts. Indeed, such notions of pedagogic autonomy also spawned the concept of academic freedom for teachers and learners which, like many other aspects of Enlightenment thought, still continues to haunt the worlds of twentieth-century education and schooling.

Seminar instruction, like tutorial teaching, represented a major change in the organization of instruction. But it did not merely embody new ideas about teaching and learning; it also reflected changing notions about the allocation of pedagogic resources. Then, as now, one of the main differences between lectures and tutorials was their respective student/ teacher ratios. In a crude sense, then, the new thinking of the Enlightenment constituted a call for smaller teaching groups. But the adoption of smaller groups was hindered by two factors. Population increases at the time of the Industrial Revolution placed increased consumer pressure on the universities. Adam Smith's Glasgow University lectures had been attended by tens of students, whereas those of his successors were attended by hundreds of students. The increased fee income generated by new students could as easily be devoted to enhancing the earnings of the regular teacher as it could be used to reduce class sizes by employing more teachers.

Practices surrounding the distribution of teaching resources continue to be the subject of debate, and differences in teacher allocation continue to characterize different sectors of schooling. Current British student/teacher ratios are roughly as follows:

University	10:1
Secondary school	15:1
Primary school	20:1

Among other things, these figures confirm the fact that different sectors of the school system, and the different learners that they accommodate, are valued differently by those who distribute pedagogic resources. Yet, as suggested, the difference between small-group and large-group teaching is more than a matter of class size. It is also intimately related to different conceptions of teaching and learning.

In one sense there is no difference between large and small groups. It is as easy to lecture to a class of five students as it is to lecture to a hall of five hundred students. The converse, however, does not apply. A seminar or tutorial with 500 students is a contradiction in terms. Nevertheless, as class sizes decrease, certain possibilities arise. A change in the quantity of learners can be translated into changes in the quality of teaching. By comparison with large-group teaching, small-group teaching has the potential, above all, of enhancing the decoding efforts and activities of teachers and learners. A seminar or tutorial, therefore, can easily operate as an arena of guided *self-*instruction. Through dialogue with other members of the group (itself a form of self-instruction), learners find their own pathways through the curriculum storehouse. Moreover, given that the essential feature of a seminar is communication rather than transmission, there is no requirement that it contain a designated teacher (or transmitter).

These different emphases derive from the fact that seminars and lectures have different social roots. Ultimately, small-group teaching had its origins in the apprenticeship system. Learners were inducted into the mysteries of a craft on the presumption, above all, that they would eventually take over the master's position. Large group teaching, on the other hand, resonates with a different pedagogic precedent – expository forms of preaching. Within such a (pre-Reformation) preaching framework, there is no expectation that learners will eventually take the place of their teachers. Put another way, large-group teaching (i.e. lecturing) takes place across social boundaries whereas small group teaching takes place within social boundaries. In short, if a lecture is a 'them and us' situation, a seminar is governed more by a rationale of 'you and me'.

Medieval lecturing rested on the assumption that God's truth was to be found in the words of texts endorsed by church authorities. These texts were sacrosanct. If students or teachers questioned the authority of official texts, they left themselves open to the charge of heresy. In short, criticism represented a challenge to God's word. Necessarily, then, pre-Enlightenment pedagogic practices tended to promote social conformity and intellectual deference among teachers and learners alike. Nevertheless, many medieval teachers (e.g. Abelard, Thomas Aquinas) appear in history books because they did, indeed, break with tradition. Their fame derives from their efforts to reinterpret rather than to reproduce God's word. In effect, their commentaries constituted debates or dialogues with the official texts. They sought to extract, or clarify, the true meanings buried in God's word. And, in an important sense, their fame rests on the fact that, in their attempts at clarification, they produced rather than reproduced God's word.

The medieval university disputation is a further instance of a dialogic approach to the clarification of ideas. One party to the dispute proposed a thesis (e.g. 'There are eternal laws on earth'), and then repeatedly defended it against intellectual challenges mounted by other students or teachers (e.g. 'Every law applies to someone. No one, except God, has existed since eternity. Therefore no earthly law is eternal.'). Many of these disputations, however, were probably dialogic only in a formal sense. Students followed well-worn pathways. Disputations were scripts to be recalled and followed rather than methods to be selected and applied. Nevertheless, disputations were the hurdles that students tackled as they advanced through their studies. Proficiency in disputations, for instance, was one of the criteria for elevating 'bachelors' to the status of 'masters'. In the process, aspiring studies made a gradual transition from the outside to the inside of the university guild, from the ranks of 'them' to the realms of 'us'. And as students surmounted these intellectual hurdles and social divides, so the teacher–pupil relationships changed. Successful university students, like successful medieval apprentices, were taken into the immediate circle and confidence of their teachers. Not only did they learn from their teachers, they also began to think and behave like their teachers. Entering a guild was just as much a matter of adopting a life style as it was a matter of clearing intellectual hurdles.

But, as noted, not all students entered the teachers' guild. Many remained in a 'them' and 'us' relationship with their teachers. For this latter group, the lectures were, quite literally, instruments of indoctrination. Coming also from the Latin root *doceo* (I teach), indoctrination was indistinguishable from the practice of teaching. In the twentieth century, however, teaching and indoctrination are often evaluated differently. In part, this differentiation arises because the notion of indoctrination is suffused with medieval assumptions about the reproduction of received texts, whereas teaching is regarded more in the light of post-Enlightenment suppositions about the social and intellectual autonomy of learners and teachers.

Books and pedagogy

Although pedagogic variation is largely related to the distribution and allocation of human resources, other supplies are just as important. As noted in an earlier chapter, the increased provision of books in the immediate post-Gutenberg era heralded an important pedagogic revolution. Self-education was the central feature of this revolution. Nevertheless, two hundred years passed before book production ackowledged the existence of a mass reading public – a social development creatively discussed in Raymond Williams's *The Long Revolution* (1985). Lending libraries, for instance, did not appear until the eighteenth century. Likewise, university libraries were only gradually opened to undergraduates, previously being restricted to professors.

The importance of libraries to learning was reflected in the fact that, for the first time, university teachers could expect their students to engage in wider reading. Their lectures could, therefore, become 'reflections on' rather than 'repetitions of' contemporary texts. If the widespread use of books in universities dates from the beginning of the nineteenth century (aided, no doubt, by the gradual spread of steam printing after about 1815), a comparable influx of books into British primary schools did not occur until after the Second World War. A relative shortage of books tends to tilt pedagogic control towards the teacher (as was the case in the Middle Ages). Nevertheless, as books become available, students can follow their own interests and deviate from the approved curriculum, as happened in the Reformation. In more recent times, the replacement of identical class sets of texts with class libraries has also offered comparable curricular opportunities.

The provision of books opens up a welter of curriculum pathways. It broadens – or perhaps dissipates – the potency of approved curricula. Indeed, the provision of pupil texts as part of a curriculum may serve contradictory purposes. It may seek to keep the student on course (in both senses); but it may also provide teachers and learners with encouragement and opportunities to deviate from the approved curriculum. There is always the risk that something written as a textbook is read as something else.

Summary

One way to express the unity of teaching, curriculum and learning is to gather them together under the label pedagogy. Thus, to talk of the pedagogy of Hillhead Primary School, Eton College, Bologna University and the Bank Street School of Motoring is to refer, in each case, to a unique constellation of interrelated teaching, curriculum and learning activities. Every pedagogy is a form of life. And like other cultural and economic activities, every pedagogy is historically located. Above all, it is an expression of the wider circumstances – past, present and future – that nurture its day-to-day transactions.

In a sense, pedagogies are the mainsprings of schooling. They can serve, variously, as agents of social reproduction or as levers of social production. They can be in the vanguard of social change; or they can merely serve to protect the *status quo*. But pedagogies are not merely built around a vision of the future. They are also founded upon the investment of material and ideological resources. In the twentieth century, the state investment of economic and cultural capital (e.g. the recruitment and training of teachers) has struggled, not always successfully, to keep up with the growth of mass schooling and the rise of human expectations. The University of East Anglia (Norwich), for instance, was consciously founded in the

1960s as a seminar-based rather than a lecture-based university. But small-group teaching is more than a matter of investment. It also embodies and expresses new kinds of social relationships, new cultural alignments among teachers and learners, and new ways of conceptualizing indoctrination, education and schooling. It, too, is a comment upon the relationship between schooling and society.

CHAPTER 7

On becoming educated

'What would you have your son taught?', I asked an intelligent carpenter. 'Reading, writing, cyphering, drawing, algebra, Euclid – anything that he can learn until he knows his trade.' 'But', I said, 'What can be the use of such knowledge to your son if he means to be a working man?' To which the man answered with an air of considerable dignity, 'How do I know, Sir, what my son may become?'

(Education Commissioner, England, 1861)

In earlier chapters it was argued, first, that a curriculum is a structured set of experiences that are brought to life through the active engagement of teachers and learners; and, second, that patterns of teaching and learning are subject to the shaping influence of ideological and material constraints. This chapter takes a closer look at the realization and shaping processes that lie at the heart of teaching and learning.

Just as teaching takes different forms (e.g. 'showing how' and 'telling how') so learning can also be analysed in terms of different processes. For the sake of this discussion, learning is envisaged as an intellectual journey. To have learned something is to have moved progressively from a starting point, through a period of intellectual upheaval, to a finishing point. The starting point is reached when, for any given experience, the learner has achieved a state of readiness; the intervening journey comprises the assimilation of experience; and the finishing point is reached when the learner has achieved a state of understanding.

Readiness

Readiness is closely linked to the psychological concept of attention. Learners demonstrate attention when they are able to discriminate between the relevant and irrelevant demands of a task. Some forms of attention are innate and instinctive (e.g. the breast-seeking behaviour of new-born infants). But attention can also be cultivated. Indeed, the establishment of learner readiness has always been an important part of teaching.

A British radio programme called *Listen With Mother* is widely remembered for a famous example of readiness cultivation. The narrator of the programme's story introduced it with the invitation: 'Are you sitting comfortably? . . . [pause] . . . Then, I'll begin'. After a few episodes this formula was abandoned, only to be quickly reinstated after protests from the adult audience of the programme. They were quick to remind the producer that the programme had dispensed with one of its key pedagogic elements. Ultimately, these introductory remarks became a radio catchphrase, remembered and used by story tellers long after *Listen With Mother* had disappeared from the airwaves. Indeed, such rhetorical devices for encouraging, if not disciplining, the readiness of the listener are a deeply rooted element in story telling. Like the classic English language device, 'Once upon a time . . .', they both set the scene and settle the learner.

The concept of learning readiness can also be examined by reference to the word docility. Docile also comes from the Latin root *doceo* (I teach). Strictly speaking, therefore, a docile child is a teachable child, someone who exhibits a readiness to learn. This sense of docility, for example, can be found in the Scottish Calvinists' *Book of Discipline* (1560). It laid down that children who showed the 'spirit of docility' were to be 'charged to continue their study'. A docile child, therefore, was an intellectually promising child. However, by the time of the Industrial Revolution – 250 years later – the word docile seems to have lost its spirit. A docile child had become a 'tractable' (i.e. compliant) or 'biddable' (i.e. commandable) child; a person who has been tamed, if not accultured, to the rhythms and routines of factory production.

The Protestant reformers, for their part, had assumed that docility was an innate attribute – a gift bestowed by God. Yet, many of the arguments of the Industrial Revolution (as discussed in Harold Silver's *The Concept of Popular Education* (1965)) took the opposite position. They assumed that docility was an acquired rather than an innate propensity. And, in such a post-Enlightenment climate, they charged schooling with the task of promoting docility. For instance, Robert Owen of New Lanark cotton mill – a pioneer of the Industrial Revolution in Britain – proposed in 1812 that the inculcation of docility should take precedence over other goals of teaching. In a speech to factory owners and their supporters, he argued that 'The children [of the poor] must learn the habits of obedience, order, regularity, industry and constant attention, which are to them of more importance than merely learning to read, write and account'.

Unlike the sentiments of the *Book of Discipline*, Owen's strictures were directed towards a specific sector of society – the children of the labouring classes. Readiness, therefore, was recast as a class-biased notion. The teachability of middle-class children was identified in terms of their spirit and keenness, whereas the teachability of working-class children was identified with their passivity and deference.

States of readiness, or attention to learning, can also be communicated by body language. In so far as readiness is equated with keenness, it can be communicated by looking a social superior straight in the eye. On the other hand, readiness as passivity can be demonstrated by looking downwards (i.e. in a deferential direction). Equally, the body language of readiness may be gender linked as well as class related. Schoolgirls and schoolboys may be expected to demonstrate keenness in different ways (e.g. by different modes of eye contact). Likewise, the bodily dispositions or forms of attention associated with readiness may be deliberately cultivated (e.g. through assertiveness training for women) to help learners cross over cultural boundaries or break down cultural barriers. Nevertheless, attempts to cross social boundaries also carry social and cultural risks. Whenever working-class, female or black students display white, male, middle-class keenness, they are always vulnerable to the accusation of being forward, uppity, cheeky and above their true station.

Assimilation

The assimilation of experience relates to the absorption of knowledge, skills and dispositions. As part of their intellectual journey, learners go over the ground of the relevant stored up experience. Gradually, they begin to grasp the contents of the curriculum storehouse and, more important, are able to appreciate its organization and packaging. Further, they are also able to integrate elements of the curriculum storehouse into their own biographies. In an important sense, therefore, the experience of other people's lives becomes part of their own lives. Accordingly, learning is rather more than an accumulation process. The human mind and body do not act as a sponge: rather, learning is an active process. Typically, learners have to unpack, unlearn or disregard prior experiences before they can acquire new experiences. The human mind, therefore, is in a constant state of reorganization, upheaval, even turmoil. Indeed, the physiological and emotional consequences of these mental interruptions, dislocations and disturbances help to account for the fact that human beings are so different from other animals.

Overall, learning is a complex and poorly understood process. It can be described variously in terms, for example, of acquisition, accumulation, absorption, assimilation or appropriation. Accordingly, there is no more consensus about the workings of the mind than there is about the origins of the human species. Similarly, there is no agreement about how the mind may best be filled, stimulated, engaged, challenged, cultivated, etc. Necessarily, then, teaching is a highly problematic human activity. There is a world of difference between how teaching is conducted and how teaching should be conducted. The pedagogic maxim, 'There are no right ways to teach, only wrong ways' may be the only assumption shared by all educationists.

Historically, the promotion of assimilation learning entails taking learners repeatedly over the same terrain (e.g. a catechism). Repeated practice – exercise of the learner's mind and body – is a key activity. Learners are deemed to have successfully assimilated the designated experience when they can reproduce it (e.g. in the form of memorized facts and procedures). Assimilation pedagogies, therefore, shape the capacity of individuals to obey orders and to follow instructions. Thereafter, human rule-following propensities can be put to the service of institutions (e.g. bureaucracies) that value such human capacities. Assimilation learning, therefore, is the educational foundation of social reproduction.

Understanding

The third element in the intellectual journey of learning – the achievement of understanding – seems to be uniquely human. Somehow, human beings acquire the capacity to reach beyond the realm of recipe knowledge. They begin to stand in a new relationship to the curriculum storehouse. Persons with understanding have a heightened awareness of themselves and their circumstances. But, as important, they have a grasp of the relationship between themselves and their circumstances; and they can command sufficient power to change this relationship. Understanding, therefore, is the mother of invention.

Accordingly, pedagogies designed to promote understanding underwrite social production (i.e. social change). In the history of schooling, such pedagogies have been conducted primarily for the leadership strata of society. They prepare learners for all eventualities, even those that cannot be envisaged. If the test of assimilation learning is the regurgitation of secondhand knowledge, the acquisition of understanding is marked by a capacity to go beyond the information given.

This perspective upon teaching for leadership can be illustrated by reference to the work of the sixteenth-century Italian philosopher, Niccolo Machiavelli (1469–1527). Before Machiavelli's time, human affairs were assumed to be entirely under the control of two forces: God and chance. Machiavelli rejected this view and held, instead, that human destiny was also affected by a third force – the free will of human beings. Moreover, if human beings could take advantage of this third option, they could play a part in shaping their own futures. This celebration of human potential also had another consequence. It is one of the reasons why the Renaissance acquired an alternative title – the age of humanism. In an important historical sense, therefore, to understand a situation is to be in a position to take command of the future.

However, Machiavelli's analysis of human history raised a problem for subsequent humanists. If human affairs are not entirely determined by God or by chance, how are they to be regulated by Renaissance state officials? Was government to be left to the arbitrary exercise of the free will of unelected rulers and their political servants? Or was there a set of ethical principles, a code of conduct, that might be followed by all wise rulers? Without such a moral code to regulate their conduct, state officials would be no different from the despotic rulers of earlier times. How, then, could they claim to be humanists?

Machiavelli's allusions to the intellectual and moral attributes of state officials became an important element in the creation of the Christian gentleman. Humanist schooling, for instance, gave much attention to the examination of texts (e.g. by Cicero) which, in turn, modelled the values and principles deemed suitable to the proper pursuit of statecraft. Thus, Renaissance schooling of the kind offered at St Paul's School did not teach a set of skills so much as an outlook on life that stressed the importance of 'prudence', 'character', 'judgement' and 'virtue'. Guided by such forms of understanding, rulers were expected to invent political, diplomatic and, sometimes, military solutions to the dilemmas they faced.

Since Machiavelli, then, the training and education of civic officials has been based as much upon the inculcation of ethical deportment as upon the transmission of technical knowhow. In the nineteenth century, the application of such notions also spread to discussions of professionalism. In 1867, for instance, the philosopher John Stuart Mill echoed Machiavelli in his Rectorial Address to the students of St. Andrews University: 'What professionals . . . should carry away with them from a university is not professional knowledge but that which should direct the use of their professional knowledge.'

This humanist perspective on a university education is one of the reasons why arts degrees played such an important role in the training of professionals and state officials, even if the arts studied in the nineteenth century differed dramatically from the liberal arts taught in medieval universities. Nevertheless, there is an equally important sense in which both medieval and nineteenth-century students acquired a series of techniques (or arts). Confronted by uncertainty – the archetypal problem of colonial administrators and foreign missionaries – university-trained professionals could always draw upon a toolbox of ethical prescriptions (e.g. 'keep calm', 'moderation in all things', 'stiff upper lip', 'think of England'), even if such maxims could not tell them exactly what to do. Overall, then, education for understanding prepares people to make prudent judgements, or to deploy practical wisdom, in the face of new and unanticipated circumstances. Certainly, the training of professionals, then and now, has largely been concerned to solve the political problem posed by Machiavelli. It is designed to induct noviciates into a particular ethic of self-regulation. And, above all, professional training provides them with a practical framework to harness (in both senses) their powers of free will and understanding.

Learning by degrees

The model outlined above suggests that there is a general correspondence between the social and pedagogic divisions in society: that different kinds of teaching and learning serve different social purposes and different social constituencies. Viewed over time, such correspondences are constantly challenged and disrupted as new social groupings struggle to achieve cultural and economic ascendancy. Moreover, there is no guarantee that a pedagogy designed to promote recipe learning will serve such ends when it reaches the hands of teachers and learners (who may hold contrasting views).

Nevertheless, fossilized evidence of these social and pedagogic correspondences is preserved in the surviving categories of the guild system (i.e. apprentice, journeyman, master) and in the different types of degree awarded by universities (bachelor, master, doctor). The status of apprentice (i.e. learner) is equivalent to the status of a bachelor (i.e. undergraduate). To qualify for this status, candidates must demonstrate an aptitude or readiness to learn. They are expected to show, therefore, that they have acquired a suitable spirit of docility. And, typically, this readiness is vouched for in testimonials (verbal or written) offered to the admissions officers of the guild or university.

Having completed a designated period as a bachelor or apprentice, candidates are examined to establish that they have acquired (or assimilated) appropriate skills. Thereafter, they are eligible for admission to the status of master or to the privileges of a journeyman. With such privileges, they are entitled to practise their arts and crafts.

Finally, several years in practice are necessary before masters and journeymen can graduate to become university doctors and guild masters. At this stage, they acquire the right to teach as well as to practise their arts – note, again, the association between doctor and *doceo*. In university settings, therefore, doctors are permitted to supervise and examine research students; and in guild settings, masters have the right to recruit their own apprentices. By this stage in their intellectual journey, university doctors and craft masters are assumed to have a complete grasp, or understanding, of the mysteries (or ethics) of their craft.

States of readiness, therefore, are identified with general aptitudes rather than with specific skills. Learners are expected to have acquired an appropriate outlook on work, itself part of their general outlook on life.

Until the twentieth century, for instance, selection of apprentices and university students was based as much upon the civility, docility or character of applicants as it was upon identifiable and measurable competences or examination grades, if any. Indeed, the selection of entrants to the unskilled sector of the labour market is still governed largely by the apparent docility of candidates (e.g. their record of school attendance and timekeeping), despite the spread of examination-linked curricula for such school learners.

Assimilation learning differs from readiness learning in that it focuses upon competence as well as character. The learner is expected to absorb and regurgitate a range of skills and/or a corpus of knowledge. But from another perspective readiness and assimilation pedagogies are very similar. In both cases, the learner is very much under the direct authority of the teacher.

But teacher–learner relationships change fundamentally at the post-graduate or journeyman level. The acquisition of understanding is marked by the learner's ability to go beyond the teacher. Typically, learners are expected to be productive rather than reproductive. Their work, for instance, is expected to demonstrate imagination, originality and initiative. And regurgitation is neither expected nor rewarded. But what pedagogies promote productivity? And how do they differ from pedagogies of reproductivity? Productivity, like understanding, is a humanist outlook on life. It celebrates the ability of human beings to transform themselves and their surroundings. Historically, it was memorably demonstrated in the creativity shown by Renaissance thinkers, artists, inventors and architects. In late twentieth-century terms, however, the relationship between understanding and productivity (or invention) is more likely to be harnessed to the notion of enterprise than to the exercise of virtue. Much effort has been made in recent years to give students an enterprise-based outlook on life. But what are the acceptable limits of enterprise? How, in Renaissance terms, can enterprise remain humane and within the bounds of civility? Or will the enterprise culture of the twentieth-century revisit the realms of despotism eschewed by Machiavelli?

Summary

The forms of schooling associated with instilling docility and imparting information are, to use a Renaissance term, pedagogies of the 'closed fist'. Their aspiration is to fashion and sustain a conforming social order; and their methods include pedagogic techniques to bring dissident/uncivilized students into line. Such pedagogies treat knowledge as unambiguous, learners as passive objects, and teachers as licensed carriers of 'the word'. The medieval lecture – based on a cut and dried presentation – was the archetypal form of this pedagogy.

But there is another form of lecture, also with medieval precedents. This is constituted in a form that gives the learner access to the thought process of the teacher: the teacher thinks aloud, outlining arguments (e.g. relating to the frontiers of knowledge) rather than summarizing conclusions (i.e. the truisms of knowledge). Necessarily, however, lecturers who adopt this mode of teaching – the pedagogy of the 'open hand' – become socially vulnerable. By medieval standards they undermine established authority by discussing and questioning the boundaries of their own competence and knowledge. Very often, too, the separation of teacher from learners is disturbed (e.g. when the lecturer stops and solicits assistance from the students). In such circumstances, there is always a risk that discussion – as if among equals – will break out! The gulf between teacher and learner is bridged. Communication (i.e. sharing) occurs and the social context of the lecture is changed irreparably. Indeed, by analogy with the maxim 'give someone a fish and you feed them for a day; teach someone to fish and you feed them for life', the pedagogies of the closed fist and open hand are as far from each other as docility is from doctoring.

CHAPTER 8

Schooling and the economic order

A boy who had just left school was asked by his former headmaster what he thought of the new buildings. 'It could be all marble, Sir', he replied, 'but it would still be a bloody school'.

(British Government Report, 1963)

Recent arguments in this book have focused preferentially on the cultural domain; that is, on the relationship between cultural power, pedagogy and schooling. But the cultural domain is only part of a way of life. Matters of economic sustenance and survival are also important.

The connection between education, schooling and the economic system can be imagined in at least two ways. First, education and schooling can be regarded as preparatory to the economic activity of adults. For instance, they equip people for entry into the labour market; or they prepare adults to service the labour market (e.g. as mothers and house-keepers). To this extent, education and schooling are institutions of consumption rather than production. They are a drain on the exchequer; and they protect young children from the risk of over-exploitation.

The second perspective on education and schooling regards them more as centres of production than as institutions of consumption. They play a substantial role in producing and reproducing every new generation of adults. They are just as much part of a society's economic domain as its craft workshops or production lines. The language of education and schooling also reflects these assumptions about cultural production and reproduction. Teachers are 're-tooled'; curricula are 'delivered'; minds are 'equipped'; and 'raw' students are refashioned into socially accomplished citizens. Indeed, some learners even end up in a 'finishing' school.

This chapter, then, reflects upon education and schooling in the light of the second of these characterizations. It builds upon two assumptions: first, that education and schooling are productive processes; and second, that the organization of schooling can be examined with the same conceptual frameworks used to analyse other forms of production.

The labour process

Consider the following educational settings: a teacher and a learner sitting at opposite ends of a log, a Reformation catechism class, and an air-conditioned classroom filled with a network of microcomputers. Each is a work setting. None the less, each also embraces a different cultural and material milieu, and the forms of teaching and learning associated with these settings can be distinguished from each other. One way of highlighting these differences is to claim that each entails a different labour process. A labour process is not merely the physical activities of work. It also incorporates the context of such labour – the workers' tools, the organization of the workplace settings and, not least, the ways in which workers interact with other human beings (e.g. their cultural superiors, equals and subordinates).

Here is another illustration of teaching as a labour process. Until the 1980s, corporal punishment was extensively used in Scottish schools. Teachers curbed, coerced and kidded their pupils with the aid of a leather strap colloquially known as the belt. Threatened or actual use of the belt was an integral part of the labour process of many teachers. In a narrow sense, the labour process of belting is indicated in two prescriptions handed down from teacher to teacher (1) 'This is how you hold it' and (2) 'This is how you bring it down'. But such labour did not take place in isolation. Its cultural and educational significance cannot be appreciated in narrow, muscular terms. Corporal punishment was part of a much more extensive pedagogic machinery. And to understand corporal punishment or any other pedagogic activity, it is necessary to appreciate the origins, composition and workings of the wider machinery of schooling. Thus, the labour process that comprised the work of Socrates was not the same as that of a Renaissance teacher's in St Paul's School, nor was it the same as the work of a nineteenth-century elementary school teacher. In short, teaching is never a culture free activity nor, indeed, can teaching methods be unthinkingly exported across cultural boundaries.

As in other forms of production, a labour process typically revolves around four elements: (1) a worker; (2) a raw material; (3) instruments or tools for shaping the raw material; and (4) a vision or blueprint that steers the labour process in the direction of its intended outcomes. The raw material of schooling and education is not an inert substance like cast iron but, rather, a highly reactive substance – learners imbued with varying degrees of 'spirit'. It is this reactivity that helps to give education and schooling their distinctive flavours. It certainly provides much of the dynamism – and many of the labour relations problems – of the daily life of schooling.

Forms of schooling can therefore be studied in terms of static attributes

– the different components of the educational machine. Or forms of schooling can be examined in terms of their dynamics – the power relationships that also govern the machine's working. To attend to the labour processes of schooling is to attend, preferentially, to the dynamics of schooling. It is to ask such questions as: are the aspirations of teachers and learners subordinate to the political will of the curriculum? Under what circumstances can a teacher over-ride the authority of the curriculum? And what powers, if any, are conceded to the learner? Moreover, in so far as these power relationships have changed over time, there is an important sense in which the history of schooling is also the history of changes in the labour processes of schooling.

Tutoring as handicraft production

One of the earliest forms of educational labour can be described as tutoring. It accompanied the institutionalization of earlier practices of socialization and acculturation. Typically, tutoring was conducted by a family member or by a specialist servant (tutor, nanny, governess). And the tutoring activities were directly negotiated between the tutor and the family. Likewise, the blueprint for the tutoring was also derived from tutor–family negotiation. This kind of tutoring, therefore, was akin to small-scale, handicraft production. Just as the medieval tailor was hired to make up the owner's cloth, so the medieval tutor was engaged to shape up the owner's sons and daughters.

As this suggests, tutoring typically took place within the family circle. And, since its activities were negotiable, each product was (or could be) fashioned according to a different blueprint. Tutoring, therefore, was a form of one off, fee based production. It still survives in tailoring; but it remains relatively rare in education. Twentieth-century piano teachers or home-visiting mathematics tutors might qualify as handicraft producers, but only if their curricula are negotiated pupil by pupil. If, on the other hand, the visiting tutor is employed to assist learners through a course of externally derived graded lessons, their work differs fundamentally from that of the jobbing tailor or Victorian nanny.

Domestic production

Tutoring began to appear more like schooling in the late Middle Ages. Tutors did not hawk their wares from door to door but set up shop in rented premises or in their own homes (hence the adjective 'domestic'). In turn, they offered their services simultaneously to several families – often members of the same occupational group or religious sect. By comparison with medieval tutors, schoolteachers who adopted the domestic system tended to offer a fixed product for sale. They advertised themselves, and organized their teaching with reference to identified subjects and texts. Like tailors who produced garments for sale rather than at the behest of an individual client, such schoolteachers operated within a market economy. Unlike tutors, they did not create one off examples of their work, but, instead, produced multiple copies to a reasonably standardized pattern and at a reasonably fixed price. The domestic system, therefore, was the forerunner of mass (or commodity) production in schooling.

In Britain, private schools of this kind were particularly prominent in the seventeenth and eighteenth centuries, and are the subject of J.W.A. Smith's *The Birth of Modern Education* (1954); and Nicholas Hans's *New Trends in Education in the Eighteenth Century* (1951). Very often, such schools offered instruction in reading and, to a lesser degree, the rudiments of writing. Furthermore, many of them also offered more specialized subjects (e.g. algebra and fencing). Like all small businesses, however, such schools were relatively ephemeral features of the educational landscape. Nevertheless, such schools and their schoolteachers achieved national prominence in Britain and elsewhere for two specific reasons. First, they appealed to religious sects who wished their children to be educated in so-called 'dissenting academies' rather than in schools under the aegis of the established church. And second, they appealed to parents who, in the age of the scientific revolution, wished their children to receive tuition in subjects (e.g. natural philosophy) not offered by the established grammar schools. Some of these new subjects were marketable (e.g. navigation) for economic reasons; whereas others (e.g. dancing, elocution, French) gave young men and women cultural credentials that were the passport to more prestigious social circles. Indeed, boys might attend an established grammar school and also attend private 'schools' for extra subjects, just as twentieth-century girls and boys might combine regular school attendance with classes at a dancing, music or theatre school. Indeed, the viability of small private-schools was assisted by the fact that, very often, they worked in tandem with more established schools.

Although schools run on the domestic system can legitimately be classified as private schools, they were not necessarily restricted to wealthy families. On the contrary, many private-school teachers deliberately appealed to an impecunious audience by undercutting the fees of the established schools. As reported in Phil Gardner's significantly titled *The Lost Elementary Schools of Victorian England* (1984) such private schools retained their popularity among nineteenth-century parents who were suspicious of the motives that had prompted the provision of state schooling. Like seventeenth-century dissenters they, too, preferred to retain a greater measure of control over the upbringing of their children.

Schooling and batch production

In time, however, many private schools became 'lost' because they were rapidly hidden beneath a network of state-supported schools. In many ways, too, the network of state schools gradually became a system of schooling. If each private school had its own machinery and curriculum, state schools were increasingly expected to follow a standardized pattern – one that shaped both the administration and organization of the system. As documented in Malcolm Seaborne's *The English School: Its Architecture and Organization 1370–1870* (1971), teachers were expected to follow a curriculum prescribed by church and state authorities. Driven by the same forces, a new administrative stratum – male 'foremen' and 'managers' of schooling – emerged as schools grew in size and as women were recruited to fill the junior teaching positions. The most important pedagogic (or labour process) change in the nineteenth century, however, was the introduction of batch processing of learners. This development, closely related to the emergence of multi-teacher schools, culminated in the 1870s with the emergence of class teaching. In schools of sufficient size, children were moved through the curriculum in batches, a technique that came to be known as 'lockstep' teaching in the USA.

Through these reforms, the state rather than the teacher became the operator of schooling. In turn, teachers ceased to control the educational machine. Instead, they became more like cogs in its inner workings. Like the pupils in Calvinist schools, they too were subjected to an external discipline or drive system. Teachers neither owned their schools nor devised their own curricula, as they had done in the private schools of the seventeenth and eighteenth centuries. Likewise, parents ceased to retain overall control of the upbringing of their children. The dominant pedagogy of schooling became relatively mechanical, arbitrary and impersonal. Indeed, by the latter half of the nineteenth century, schooling had reached levels of systematization only dreamed about in the seventeenth century.

Continuous production

By the First World War, however, the batch mode of mass production was increasingly criticized as socially inefficient. It was claimed, for instance, that lockstep teaching paid insufficient attention to the peculiarities of the raw material that passed through the workings of the school system. Accordingly, it was proposed that greater attention to the individual child would inevitably improve the social efficiency of schooling. In effect, it was assumed that every child had a set of specific educational needs that could only be met through the differentiation (or individualization) of the school curriculum. In these terms, the philosophy of continuous production has close affinities with child-centred views of schooling.

In factories and schools, therefore, considerable attention was given to the reorganization of production. The most visible symbol of the new movement was the development of moving production lines by the Ford Motor Company (USA) in its Detroit factories shortly before World War One. The moving production line was an attempt to merge and maximize the joint production potential of machines and workers. Twentieth-century pedagogic reorganizations can be seen in a similar light and are the focus of Raymond Callahan's *Education and the Cult of Efficiency* (1962). Perhaps the most visible effect of the reorganization of educational production has been the changes that have occurred in the layout of schoolrooms. Desks have not only been unbolted from the floor, they have been rearranged (or replaced) in clusters rather than in rows of working surfaces.

The key educational presumption behind continuous production is that children should be allowed to work through a sequential and linear curriculum – itself a production line – at their own pace. But the individualization of schooling can also take other forms. For instance, a branching (or differentiated) curriculum may offer a range of pre-set routes to different categories of learners. From an historical perspective, however, the most significant variant of individualization occurs when the prescribed curriculum is discarded entirely. Instead, learners are encouraged to forge their own pathways or, to use a more fashionable phrase, follow their own interests through the storehouse of human experience.

Inevitably, the last view of child-driven production rests uneasily with the batch-processing presumption that children should follow school curricula devised, driven and controlled by the state. Taking their cue from Rousseau, many twentieth-century educationists have resolved this tension between the state and the child in favour of the latter. As documented, for instance, in Richard Selleck's *English Primary Education and the Progressives 1914–1939* (1972), many of them are remembered through the private schools they founded and maintained beyond the reach of state supervision. Nevertheless, attempts to sustain child-centred forms of schooling have also survived within the system of state-maintained schools. Modular curricula, for instance, are sometimes claimed to be more responsive to the variable interests of children. It is assumed that, if sufficient modules are provided, learners will be able to follow their interests and find a personalized pathway through the curriculum.

Yet it remains an open question whether a modular curriculum can, in fact, offer sufficient choices to learners.

Equally, it is not always clear that a modularized curriculum can also meet other canons of child-centredness. For instance, it is sometimes assumed that an individualized curriculum (e.g. a modularized curriculum) is also a personalized curriculum. But there is no necessary connection between individualization and personalization. There is always the danger that an individualized curriculum will treat the learner as a cipher rather than as a person. Pedagogies can be highly individualized, but they can also be highly depersonalized. To this extent an individualized curriculum may be scarcely distinguishable from the depersonalized curricula associated with lockstep teaching.

Historically, one of the most important manifestations of continuous educational production was the establishment of the Open University, a distance-learning institution started in Britain in the late 1960s. The organization of the Open University is based on the assumption that students work at home (i.e. individually); that they follow a pre-packaged modular curriculum largely at their own pace; and that their learning activities are regulated largely through a policy of continuous assessment. As in the factory system, there is an elaborate division of labour in the Open University between, for instance, those who encode the curricula (course teams); those who distribute the curricula (course managers), and those who decode the curricula (course tutors). Indeed, the machinery of the Open University also includes counsellors who, rather like personnel managers, tackle the industrial relations (or learning relations) problems that are thrown up by the workings of the entire system.

The Open University is, therefore, a very sophisticated machine. As a production line, it needs constant fine tuning, maintenance and renewal. When working, it is an enormous, efficient and accessible knowledge factory. But the systematization built into the machinery of the Open University is also its Achilles' heel. There is very little tolerance of error in the system. As with any moving production line, one small disruption (e.g. a postal strike) brings chaos. Moreover, Open University learners have very little control over the workings of the system. At times, no doubt, they feel they are the smallest of cogs in the largest of machines. In times of crisis, techno-deference – passivity and patience in the face of mechanical malfunction – is probably the only thing that they learn.

Beyond the factory system

As described above, the pedagogies of handicraft, domestic, batch and continuous production followed each other in chronological time. But each new form did not eradicate its predecessors. Rather, later forms emerged and bedded down alongside earlier forms. New forms of school-ing, therefore, arose in specific circumstances and did not necessarily spread effacing all earlier forms of schooling. For instance, batch produc-tion emerged in urban areas, leaving echoes of domestic production (e.g. one-teacher schools) to survive in rural areas, documented in Jon Wy-and's photographic essay, *Village Schools* (1980). Likewise, echoes of handicraft production survive in well-endowed institutions, like Oxford and Cambridge universities, which still pay a measure of homage to personalized tutorial teaching.

Schooling, therefore, takes many forms. It is not a unified productive process. Rather, it comprises a range of activities that, among other things, arose in different historical circumstances. As time passes, new activities come into prominence as others fade into obscurity. By the twentieth century, schooling may have become a unified and state-led system. But, throughout its history, it has never been a static institution. In recent years, for instance, there has been a dramatic change in the layout, furnishing and furbishing of schools. Open-plan designs, tannoy systems, telephones, television and photocopiers are now commonplace. Likewise, information technology – based on microprocessors, compact discs and video machinery – presages the same kind of revolution that print technology triggered after 1450. If Gutenberg's innovative system of production underpinned the educational upheavals of the Renaissance and the Reformation, what kind of upheavals are foreshadowed for the twenty-first century?

Summary

Like other human labour processes, education and schooling are goal-directed activities. They are conscious interventions in human affairs. They seek to transform the relationships that exist among human beings; and, as important, they seek to transform the relationships that exist between human beings and their natural and social environments. The form of such interventions varies from social context to social context and from historical epoch to historical epoch. Lectures, tutorials, seminars, practical work, library work, and so on, are not simply different styles of work – or styles of teaching and learning – they also embody different social and educational relationships.

A further reason for examining education and schooling in terms of labour processes is to explore their changing power relationships. In some settings, the labour (or pedagogic) processes of schooling are structured around a social divide that is as pronounced at the end of the interaction as it is at the outset. In other cases, a social division is presumed at the outset, but the pedagogy is designed and organized to reduce the separation of the teacher from the learner. And, in the final case, no social separation is presumed – the labour process is merely directed towards the redistribution (communication or sharing) of experience among persons of equivalent social, moral and intellectual standing. At the risk of oversimplification, these social relationships are exemplified, respectively, in lecturing (where the learner remains silent), in small-group instruction (where the learner is able to ask questions) and in research seminars (where the learner's questions are as frequent as the teacher's).

Finally, this chapter has tried to illuminate some of the social and historical differences between education and schooling, differences which, in certain respects, are akin to the differentiation between work as a physical and mental endeavour, and wage labour as a paid and regulated form of social life. Schooling was invented to control and to redirect earlier educational practices, just as the factory system was devised to control and redirect the fortunes of domestic producers. In both settings considerable attention is given to management, monitoring and control. Moreover, these administrative activities have coalesced into elaborate and highly sophisticated systems of production. Ultimately, the purpose of these systems is to contain, if not control, the reactivity of the human beings who work within their boundaries. Under such circumstances – sometimes described as Fordism – workers of all kinds have become subject to such high levels of external intervention, regulation and control that, in a profound sense, many of them no longer know what they are doing. Despite the early claims of scientific management, the productive efficiency of workers declines, along with their job satisfaction. In the light of these criticisms, considerable attention has been given, more recently, to the task of developing new systems of production – sometimes described as *post-Fordism* – that channel, rather than contain, human reactivity. It seems likely that the organization and management of large schools will receive the same kind of scrutiny as the organization and management of large factories. It is perhaps no accident that, since the early 1980s, proposals for the reform of the labour processes of schooling have often emanated from production-related agencies like the Organization for Economic Cooperation and Development (OECD) and, in Britain, from the government departments that embrace employment, trade and industry.

CHAPTER 9

Tools and pedagogic power

When the historians of education do equal and exact justice to all who have contributed toward educational progress, they will devote several pages to those revolutionists who invented steel pens and blackboards.

(V.T. Thayer, educationist, 1928)

The previous chapter analysed teaching and learning as forms of educational production. It assumed that educational production embraces more than the day-to-day labour of individual teachers and learners. It is a social and historically located process built around the coordination and harmonization of cultural goals, raw materials and various amounts and combinations of human labour. Extending the analysis of educational production, this chapter considers the tools of the teacher's and learner's trade.

As discussed earlier, tools serve to extend and amplify the mental and muscular power of human beings. In the early history of the human species, they contributed to the domestication of the natural environment and, since that time, they have also played a part in the shaping and organization of the social environment. In human history, therefore, tools have served two purposes. They have helped to keep the natural environment at bay and they have helped to bring forth (or produce) new social, cultural and economic environments. In short, tools both preserve and transform the life styles of human beings.

Educational tools can be regarded in a similar light. If our ancestors taught with their bare hands, contemporary education and schooling are high-technology institutions. They are awash with resources (e.g. books, pencils, blackboards, photographs, tape recordings) which, it is assumed, play an important part in educational production. But what is the educational purpose of these resources? In what sense are they educational tools? What is being preserved or transformed with the aid of such tools? And how has the leverage of such tools affected the power relationships of teachers and learners?

An educational tool may be home-made; or it may be part of a standard tool kit. It may be raw; or it may be fully fashioned. Further, a tool must, in some sense, be wielded by someone. A piece of wood is not automatically an educational tool. It only becomes an element of the production process when teachers or learners realize that it can be used to draw a straight line, to measure distances, or to stabilize a wobbling projector. A tool, therefore, may serve educational production in a variety of ways. Despite Thayer's observation, the adoption of steel pens and blackboards should not be seen as an automatic guarantee of educational advancement. Like most cultural artefacts, educational tools can be harnessed to a range of different social purposes and be deployed by a range of different social interests. A piece of wood can also be used as a tool of bodily chastisement. Indeed, the repeated retooling of schooling is as likely to reflect changes in pedagogic power as it is to prefigure linear advances in educational progress.

Pedagogic tools and educational change

Just as social change can be misread as social progress, it is also a common misconception that social change is prompted solely by technical innovation. Social histories, for instance, have been written around the invention and dissemination of the water mill, the bridle, movable type, the steam engine and artificial modes of contraception. Such histories, however, are often an overstatement of the argument that new technology automatically causes social change. In fact, there is a much more complex relationship between the invention of a tool and its incorporation into a production process. The history of school blackboards provides an illustration. Wall-mounted writing surfaces seem to have been invented by the middle of the seventeenth century; but they remained a relative novelty until the middle of the nineteenth century. Their full-scale introduction into the practices of schooling seems to have been contingent upon two post-Enlightenment developments: the replacement of teacher lecturing with extempore, question and answer teaching; and, the emergence of batch production methods of schooling. Together, these pedagogic reconceptualizations stimulated the use and widespread adoption of large display surfaces that could be seen by an entire class (or batch) of pupils sitting in rows.

By the end of the nineteenth century, these class-teaching methods were sometimes described as Socratic teaching, in honour of the questioning pedagogy attributed to the Greek philosopher. Socrates' methods, however, had little to do with class teaching. His dialogic pedagogy – built around the probing of learners' answers – was, in fact, a form of tutoring rarely conducted with more than one or two learners. Equally, Socrates' students were drawn from the ruling strata of Athenian society, not from the lower orders. In its original form, too, Socratic teaching sought to promote understanding, whereas nineteenth-century class teaching sought to exercise the memories rather than the minds of elementary school children. Socrates' teaching and class teaching were, therefore, radically different forms of educational production.

Class teaching came to prominence in the era of industrialization. The circumstances that prompted its introduction left their mark upon the activities of both pupils and teachers. On the one hand, children were expected to behave as an equalized class rather than as a group of individuals; and, on the other hand, teachers were expected to hold all the reins of pedagogic power. As an equalized batch, children were expected to focus their attention and vision upon relatively distant objects (i.e. the teacher and the blackboard). And, by analogy with machines that simultaneously powered banks of cotton spindles, teachers were expected to keep the simultaneous attention and maintain the motivation of rows of children.

Like comparable realignments of power in factory production, the advent of class teaching changed the productive capacities and rhythms of schooling. For example, larger class sizes increased the throughput of schools. Extension of the periods of time that the teacher commanded the attention of learners increased the potency of schooling. And increasing school enrolments without a comparable increase in the number of teachers enhanced the cost efficiency of schooling. Overall, therefore, the advent of class teaching was accompanied by many positive claims about its power and efficiency. Its introduction certainly served to lubricate the machinery of mass schooling. But, despite attempts to claim class teaching as Socratic teaching, it is an open question whether the pedagogic changes brought about through class teaching can also be described in terms of educational progress. It does not follow, for instance, that a tool in the service of a teacher or the state is also a tool in the service of the learner.

Similarly, it does not follow that the educational potential of a tool is always realized by the pedagogic context of its deployment. Late twentieth-century tools with educational potential include photocopiers, reference books, viewdata channels on television, and data archives stored on compact disks. But these devices may, in fact, be used merely to mimic older pedagogic procedures, as when an overhead projector is used as a blackboard or a microcomputer is used as an electronic catechist. Innovation without change is the outcome. Earlier relationships between teachers, learners and stored up experience are reaffirmed, not recast.

As this suggests, the full potential of educational tools may be released only through changes in the balance of pedagogic power. But such realignments are not easily accomplished. Schooling is a deeply rooted social edifice, bedded down with vast amounts of cultural hardcore. As discussed earlier, its ideological foundations, and its organizational structures, still owe much to medieval conceptions of indoctrination, Renaissance notions of civility, and nineteenth-century assumptions about the over-riding authority of the state. Equally, the conduct of schooling also owes much to views of professionalism, themselves forged through nineteenth- and twentieth-century struggles that took place between successive governments and various professional associations and trade unions of teachers.

Debates about teacher professionalism are also debates about the tools of the teacher's trade. Many disputes, therefore, have been conducted around proposals that teachers should be given greater command of the machinery of schooling and greater control over the selection and organization of curricula. But teacher professionalism or, more accurately, teacher autonomy, can also be construed in a different way: in terms of teacher individualism, teacher privatism and the freedom of teachers from outside interference. This latter view of autonomy regards teachers as craft workers who, like their seventeenth- and eighteenth-century forebears, occupy their own workshops and offer a specialist service to their clients. From this pre-industrial viewpoint, teaching is envisaged as a tool-based activity. Yet, as noted, by the nineteenth century teaching had become more like factory production. In these terms, nineteenth-century teaching was more of a technological than a tool-based activity. The elementary-school teacher had become less of a tool-user and more of an element in the inner workings of the machinery of schooling. Thus, debates about professionalism and autonomy need to be repeatedly updated. For instance, nineteenth-century views of professionalism assumed that professions were the sole preserve of male workers. They were like the Renaissance assumption that virtue (*vir* is the Latin for man) was an exclusively male characteristic. What, then, are the models and forms of professionalism appropriate to a twentieth-century occupation that is numerically, if not organizationally, dominated by women? And what forms of educational retooling would be adequate to the currently gendered status of schoolteaching?

Tools, technology and power

The changing circumstances of schooling have been closely linked to different forms of human autonomy and power. Indeed, technology and technological thinking have been central to the exertion of human power. Since the seventeenth century, important sections of the human species have been politically motivated by a vision of the human domination over nature. With the aid of science, the human species would elevate itself above the rest of nature and, at long last, would receive due compensation for the biblical fall of Adam and Eve. Nevertheless, human ascendancy was to be accomplished at nature's expense, by a shift in the ecological balance of power.

Gradually, this vision of the emancipatory potential of science spread to other areas of human concern, notably the organization of society. By the eighteenth century, it was believed that, in principle, the law-like behaviour of society could be deciphered in the same way that Newton had begun to unravel the law-like operations of the natural world. Indeed, it was this view of society's working that fuelled the rise of the social sciences. In turn, the belief that science and rationality would rule the world created a technocratic perspective on the governance of human life. It was assumed that, with the aid of the social sciences, society could make unimagined economic and cultural advances. Spiritual salvation would be replaced by human progress.

Such conceptions of the social sciences raised a major political and organizational issue. How was the leverage of the social sciences to be exerted? Would it be used for the benefit of all human beings? Or would there be an uneven distribution of social power? And at whose expense? Initially, 'them and us' conceptions of society were often invoked to reconcile the interests of those who found themselves at opposite ends of the balance of power. For example, women and non-white persons were always vulnerable to the claim that they were naturally inferior to white males. In this respect, and many others, the fruits of the scientific revolution were used both for and against the interests of human beings, outcomes documented, for instance, in Bridget Hill's *Eighteenth Century Women: An Anthology* (1984) and Peter Fryer's *Staying Power: The History of Black People in Britain* (1984). Eventually, however, arguments about natural inferiority, and the attendant denial of full citizenship, became less fashionable in political circles. It was assumed, for instance, that the benefits of the Industrial Revolution could more than offset the differences observed among human beings. Hence, differences between human and near-human forms of life were recast as differences between members of the same human species.

Nevertheless, the retooling of production in the eighteenth and nineteenth centuries did not always meet the aspirations and predictions of social philosophers and politicians. The post-Enlightenment spread of the free market produced unwanted social consequences: poverty, unemployment and disease. Gradually, it was argued and accepted that the state should intervene to offset these social problems, a movement examined, with much else, in Peter Gordon and John White's *Philosophers as Educational Reformers* (1979). The creation of the welfare state was the outcome of this reconceptualization of the role of the state. Essentially, the welfare state was designed and constructed as a state-powered and state-regulated instrument of social redistribution. But it was also a child of the social sciences, a system of social engineering run according to ideas supplied by the scientific as well as the landed and industrial aristocracies.

Schooling became an important arm of the welfare state. It was conceived both as a redistributive and transformative political instrument. As a redistributive technology, schooling attracted many teachers and educationists who had a comparable political outlook. They subscribed, for instance, to 'you and me' pedagogic philosophies and espoused, therefore, a commitment to social justice and the equality of opportunity. Yet many of the costs of the welfare state were met from profits repatriated from elsewhere in the British Empire. In other words, many Britons who sheltered under the umbrella of the welfare state received their protection at the expense of overseas citizens of the Empire.

But as the sun set on the British Empire, and as Britain lost its privileged position in world trade, the coffers of the welfare state began to run low. Since the late 1960s, the redistributive function of the welfare state has been trimmed back, largely through cuts in state expenditure on welfare. In schooling and elsewhere, a 'them and us' version of the welfare state has emerged. The welfare state has become more of an institution of political containment than a vehicle for economic redistribution and social transformation. But, whatever its priorities, the welfare state has remained a social technology – an artefact of power and social control.

In many ways, too, the natural sciences have reached a similar crisis. The prospect, raised in the seventeenth century, of humankind's domination over nature has led, nearly four hundred years later, to a recognition that the natural world is an overexploited, if not endangered, species. In the wake of the Chernobyl disaster, itself technologically and technocratically-driven, human progress has become a questionable concept. Human progress is held to be neither inevitable nor necessarily desirable. In an important historical turn around, technology, techno-thinking and, above all, techno-power have become a problem, not a solution, for the human species. Indeed, as the twenty-first century approaches, the word 'progress' is beginning to be about as unfashionable as its predecessor, 'salvation'.

Human beings as tools

Slavery represented a degradation (i.e. downgrading) of human beings. Deprived of their human rights, slaves could be grouped with non-human animals. In Roman times, for instance, an agricultural slave was designated an *instrumentum vocale* (speaking tool), one grade away from a livestock animal (an *instrumentum semi-vocale*), and two grades away from an agricultural implement (an *instrumental mutum*). Within such an etymological framework, slaves were recognzied as tools of production. But how,

exactly, do human beings fit into the production process? How, for instance, do they provide leverage? And what is the object of their leverage?

One approach to this problem is to regard the teacher as the tool of the
learner. The teacher, therefore, is an extension of the learner, someone
who provides the learner with leverage upon the curriculum. But teachers are special kinds of tools. They not only speak, they also think. Hence,
as thinking tools, teachers can operate in two ways. They can make
judgements about which elements, if any, of the curriculum are within
reach of the learner (who is also a thinking tool). And they can serve as
bridging devices – links between the learning potential of students and the
teaching potential of the curriculum.

In an educational context, the teacher-as-tool is placed at the disposal
of the learner. But teachers also serve as tools in another sense, one that is
more characteristic of schooling than education. Since the Reformation,
if not before, many teachers have been coopted by the political state, a
status exemplified in the title of Martin Lawn's *Servants of the State* (1987).
In turn, the labour of many teachers is incorporated into a machinery –
the school system – which is relatively remote from individual learners.
But where does this leave the lives and works of schoolteachers? Are they
tools of the state or are they tools of the learner? Above all, how do they
resolve their personal aspirations as educators with their political responsibilities as schoolteachers?

Summary

This chapter has examined the significance of tools in the organization of
education and schooling. It suggests that, as elsewhere, tools offer leverage
in the processes of education and schooling. But it has also suggested that
such leverage does not necessarily yield advantage to the learner or even
the teacher. In general, then, the successful introduction of a new educational tool – human or material – does more than merely enhance or
increase learning. It has much wider social ramifications. It affects not
only the power relationships between the learner and stored up human
experience, but also the power relationships among teachers and learners.
The provision of elaborately designed desks may have furnished
nineteenth-century learners with a writing surface; but it also provided
teachers with a device for putting learners in their place. Tools may be
levers in the learning process; but they are also pawns in a pedagogic
power game. Further, all technologies (in industry) and pedagogies (in
schooling) incorporate a human as well as a material dimension. And, in
recognition of this human presence, every pedagogy is more accurately
described as a socio-technology. Ultimately, therefore, its impact is contingent upon the docility or reactivity of those – teachers as well as
learners – whose lives it seeks to reshape.

CHAPTER 10

A time and a place to learn

No method's more sure at moments to take hold
Of the best feelings of mankind . . .
Than that all-softening, overpow'ring knell
the tocsin of the soul – the dinner bell.

(George Byron, poet, *c.*1819)

Schooling emerged as the processes of education became institutionalized. It gradually became a partitioned social activity, separate from the rest of life. Throughout its history, then, schooling has occupied distinct spatial settings and has been allocated distinct periods of social time. Indeed, as schooling sought to mimic the natural order of things in the seventeenth century, it adopted the organizational axiom that everything has its proper time and place.

This attention to the regulation of schooling also derived from the work of René Descartes (1596–1650) and Isaac Newton (1642–1727). Among other things, they popularized the view that the workings or machinery of nature and, later, civil society, could be exposed to rational investigation, logical understanding and conscious improvement. It was popularly assumed, therefore, that schooling would run smoothly and efficiently if all its elements could be suitably positioned in time and space. Indeed, such was the persuasive power of these notions that schooling was envisaged not merely as a machine but also as a friction free and self-regulating machine.

A place to learn

The notion that learning might be place specific is much older than the Scientific Revolution. The earliest schools were simply settings occupied by individual teachers and their disciples. As the teacher moved, so did the school. In its early usage, therefore, a school was not so much a place or building as a group of people. Moreover, this distinction survives in the phrase 'school of thought'. In this respect, school is like the word 'church' a term of comparable double meaning. A church can refer to a congregation of people (e.g. the church of Rome) or it can denote a more permanent structure (e.g. St Peter's, Rome). Early schools of learners, like early ecclesiastical congregations, were noted for their geographic mobility. Sometimes, however, a school or a congregation settled in one place and became known by its location. The School of Chartres, a cathedral town about eighty kilometres south-west of Paris, originated in this way. Its label, however, can be misleading. It does not necessarily follow that specialist school buildings were erected in Chartres. Nor does it mean that the School had a permanent and enduring existence. In fact, the School of Chartres waxed and waned in popularity as, for instance, its teachers migrated to live and work elsewhere (e.g. in Paris).

The early meaning of the word 'school', and its association with notable teachers, survived for centuries. Schools, that is, did not settle down until well into the Middle Ages, a fact reflected in the chronological starting point of Malcolm Seaborne's *The English School: Its Architecture and Organization 1370–1870* (1971). The establishment of relatively permanent and static schools seems to have accompanied the attraction of teachers to specific settings. From the twelfth century, for instance, cathedral churches (which were also the regional administrative centres of the Church) were expected to support teachers who assisted in the training of parish priests. Such teachers often became associated with specific locations in the cathedral princincts (e.g. a side chapel). Nevertheless, such schools were still known by their locations than by their association with architecturally distinct buildings.

By the Renaissance, however, teachers and teaching began to be tied down by additional factors. For instance, schools began to break away from the direct control of the Church. They were established in specific locations (e.g. market halls), often with monies left by local benefactors. Indeed, the fact that such legacies paid for a teacher's stipend often meant that they were known as free schools, even if the schoolteacher still charged fees! Sometimes, too, benefactors endowed funds for the erection of school buildings and left instructions about the topics to be taught and the procedures to be used by the teachers. Historically, however, such schools were exceptional, both numerally and socially. They catered for a small sector of the population and, typically as grammar schools, were closer to the universities than to the forms of domestic one-teacher schooling that served the rest of the population. Nevertheless, school buildings began to grow in size in the latter part of the nineteenth century. Schools that, previously, were based on a single schoolroom were amalgamated into multi-room, multi-storey, multi-teacher schools built with the latest innovations in structural engineering, heating, ventilation and illumination.

The multi-room school was to the single schoolroom as the factory was to the workshop. As noted earlier it embodied a new form of production. Each classroom was, in effect, a separate machine room. But how were the different machine shops to be coordinated? How were children to be allocated to their classrooms? How were they to be promoted from class to class? And were learners to be promoted (i.e. processed) as individuals or as batches?

Educationists struggled with these problems over several decades, just as a similar set of problems engaged the designers and managers of industrial production. One notable solution was the removal of classroom walls to create open-plan schools. Open-plan schooling solved the production difficulties associated with the box-like architecture and batch-based processing of classroom schools. Through its espousal of aspects of continuous production, open-plan schooling could be seen as an invention that allowed individual learners to progress at their own rate. From an industrial perspective, then, open-plan designs are to schooling as the moving production line is to industry.

But attention to learners' needs also points to another dimension of the open-plan story. The erection of open-plan schools was also prompted by a contrasting educational consideration, one that represented a conscious retreat from factory thinking. Many open-plan school designs reflect planners' intentions to make schools more like homes than factories. Areas of the school are carpeted; cosy quiet areas are provided for pupil privacy; and home bases are included where children can gather together in communal activities. In historical terms, therefore, open-plan schooling can be seen as an historical compromise – a convergence of different, even opposing, social rationales. Indeed, the fact that every open-plan design is a compromise may account for their notable variety.

Nevertheless, how do children (rather than architects) regard themselves in open-plan schools? Do they feel at work? Or are they at home? Are they working? Or are they playing?

Childhood: a time for work or play?

Before the Renaissance and Reformation, childhood did not exist. The transition from a state of dependence to the responsibilities of adulthood was very rapid. In this respect, human beings differed little from other animal species. As the centuries passed, however, the human species prolonged the period of infant-to-adult transition; and child rearing became a focus of social attention. Schooling, for instance, is one of the products of that attention, an institution designed to occupy young people during their transition from infancy to adulthood.

According to the pioneering arguments in Philippe Ariès's *Centuries of Childhood: A Social History of Family Life* (1962), childhood originally emerged after the thirteenth century. Children were previously portrayed (e.g. in paintings) as scaled down adults. Released from activities necessary to social survival, children in wealthy families began to occupy other social roles. For instance, they served as family playthings; and were sheltered and coddled rather like family pets. In a sense, too, children became symbols of family property and wealth, decorative elements of the household, polished and gilded by their tutors.

In time, however, children from less elevated backgrounds began to display the leisure attributes of childhood. In the sixteenth century, for instance, children from craft families took to the streets in search of enjoyment and recreation. Nevertheless, this substitution of child pleasure for child labour did not always receive universal approval. Then, as now, children who engaged in active forms of leisure were liable to be labelled as idle. Moreover, idleness was often held to be a form of sin. Accordingly, such children were to be censured rather than coddled; they were to be house-trained rather than gilded; and they were to be returned to work rather than equipped for play. In short, their sinfulness was to be exorcised through the medium of social discipline.

By the eighteenth-century Enlightenment, however, a new view of childhood emerged. It began to be claimed, for instance, that all children were born in a natural (i.e. innocent) state and that their subsequent fall owed more to the neglect of society than to a weakening of God's grace. The classic statement of this viewpoint appears as the opening lines of Rousseau's *Emile* (1762): 'God makes all things good; and man meddles with them and they become evil'. As noted earlier, Rousseau's protestations about the innocence of childhood, and about the value of natural (i.e. non-interventionist) upbringing were an important contribution to the canons of child-centred education.

Famous exponents of Rousseau's rationale include Johann Pestalozzi (1746–1827) and Friedrich Froebel (1782–1852). In Froebel's thinking, and in the language of natural upbringing, children were to be nurtured rather than decorated. They were to be trained, but as plants rather than as soldiers. Indeed, the word kindergarten (child garden) derives from Froebel and his followers. Froebel's essential assumption was that children need space and freedom to develop according to their true nature. Certainly, there was a strong biological element in the arguments of Rousseau and his followers. Child rearing, like horticulture, was the unfolding of a design already encrypted in the initial state of the organism.

Appeals to the inner nature of children have also survived in the writings of psychoanalytical theorists like Anna Freud, Melanie Klein and Susan Isaacs. There are many variants of psychoanalytic thought, but most protagonists adhere to the view that education and schooling should provide children with physical space, material resources (e.g. playthings) and intellectual freedom to resolve their early (if not innate) emotional and intellectual difficulties. Indeed, psychoanalytic theory has offered strong support for free play in schools for very young children. It is assumed, for instance, that good play is a psychoanalytic ground-clearing prelude to good learning.

Nevertheless, the ghosts of John Calvin and John Knox also police the social freedoms made available to young children. Today, therefore, discussions of childhood and schooling are driven by different views of childhood and, as important, different class-based conceptions of childhood. Since the Second World War, for instance, these different views of childhood have informed discussion of the relative merits of playgroups and nursery schools.

The playgroup movement initially arose as a self-help movement closely associated with the professional and middle classes. Playgroups were intended to service the early – and natural – upbringing of members of those classes. Playgroup parents, therefore, were the linear descendants of the coddlers of the late Middle Ages and of the many upper-class adults attracted to Rousseau's and Froebel's ideas in the eighteenth and nineteenth centuries. The nursery school movement, on the other hand, began by paying much less attention to natural upbringing. It stressed the disciplinary value of organized activities, not the emancipatory (or therapeutic) potential of play. Its aim was more to civilize than to nurture young children. Moreover, nursery schooling typically adopted an interventionist stance. It was more likely to receive state funding, and to be organized by one social group for the children of another social group (i.e. the working class).

But cross-fertilization has occurred. Many playgroups were established in working-class housing schemes and many nursery schools have adopted the rationales surrounding children's play. Nevertheless, this recent attention to pre-schooling is also a response to the world of work rather than to the world of play: the extension of school provision for young children has been seen as a means of increasing female participation in the labour market. It seems quite likely, therefore, that pre-schooling in the twenty-first century will be driven as much by the artificial rhythms of work as by the natural rhythms of child development.

A time to learn

The nineteenth- and twentieth-century development of pre-schooling can be seen as an extension of the length of state-sponsored schooling. For many children, therefore, the time to learn (or, more accurately, the time to be schooled) starts earlier in their lives and finishes later. But there are also other ways in which the 'time to learn' has changed since the invention of schooling.

Like the rest of life, schooling originally followed a solar timetable. Most activities, that is, were organized between dawn and dusk. Under solar influence, schooling also followed an agricultural rhythm. For instance, children began school early in the morning and returned home for their breakfast during a morning interval. It seems, too, that the agricultural timetable also influenced the structure of the school year. In Britain, if not elsewhere, the school year was conventionally divided into four quarters; and the quarter days (e.g. Lammas, Candlemas) were occasions when rents were paid, servants were hired, and school fees given to schoolteachers.

Schooling seems to have been conducted throughout the year. Yet even if a school was open all the year, it does not follow that pupil attendance was equally an all-year phenomenon. Typically, children attended school until they could read – a course of study that might last only a few months. Similarly, it was by no means unusual for one set of fees to be used by more than one child. Robert Burns and his brother, for instance, attended on alternate days. School attendance also responded to the agricultural year in other ways. For instance, the demands of harvest-time lowered summer attendance, while a poor income from the harvest could reduce winter attendances.

The introduction of summer holidays of more than two weeks seems to have been a fairly late development. It may, in fact, have been associated with nineteenth-century attempts to increase and prolong school attendance. In effect, longer school holidays at harvest-time was the social price paid to compensate for the increased school retention of child labour during the remainder of the year.

British institutions of higher education have also conventionally followed a quarterly pattern, as demonstrated in the quarter names (e.g. Lammas, Whitsun, Michaelmas) used to label university terms. In Glasgow, for instance, the summer quarter remained an important period of university life until at least the end of the eighteenth century. Students left the university precinct at the end of May taking with them academic tasks to be completed over the summer. And they returned to Glasgow in September for the annual diet of examinations.

During the first part of the nineteenth century, however, Glasgow University examinations underwent two changes (as they did elsewhere). For centuries, examinations had been conducted orally, with the students being examined one at a time. Expansion, however, put pressure upon these arrangements. In Glasgow, for instance, it became difficult to examine several hundred students in the latter part of September. Pressure was eased by moving examinations to May and June and by introducing written examinations which could be taken simultaneously by batches of students. Together, such innovations reshaped the academic year into a form that has survived to the present day.

Arguably, British higher education still follows an agricultural rather than an industrial pattern of production. Each year, a crop of students is harvested and a new crop is planted. And each year, too, there is a fallow quarter which allows for the recovery and refurbishment of the university's plant and personnel. To this extent, universities have lagged behind industry, which began to abandon seasonal and diurnal rhythms of work at the beginning of the nineteenth century. Steam power could, in principle, be maintained all the year round and, unlike water power, was not dependent upon variations in rainfall. Further, the introduction of artificial gas lighting also assisted all-day production by reducing the incidence of factory fires triggered by unattended candles.

In the twentieth century, however, certain new universities have tried to make a break with agricultural rhythms (e.g. by abandoning quarterly forms of organization). The Open University is the most notable example. Unlike most other institutions of higher education, its annual cycle begins in February rather than October and the student year continues without a break until October. The Open University vacation (October–January) exists not so much to rest the students but, as before, to provide sufficient opportunities for the harvesting of one generation of students and the replanting of the following generation.

The practice of annual harvesting suggests that continuous production has rarely been implemented in British higher education. Nevertheless, there is a sense in which continuous production has made a backdoor entrance in recent years. Most notably, its ideals have been expressed through the introduction of continuous assessment, and by the associated decline of written examinations. Student effort is evaluated constantly, not merely on the basis of a single outcome. The introduction of continuous assessment can be regarded as an attempt to introduce an industrial discipline (i.e. a new drive system) into an agricultural enterprise. Given this convergence of agricultural and factory rationales, certain forms of late twentieth-century schooling (e.g. cubicle-based learning stations and all-night opening of libraries) are the educational equivalent of factory farming. A social rhythm ultimately derived from the daily and seasonal patterns of the earth's orbit has, in part, given way to a greenhouse educational tempo – one that is consciously shaped and continuously monitored through a new pedagogic discipline.

Summary

The patterns of education and schooling that have emerged and persisted over the ages can be understood as attempts to intervene in the natural (or innocent) processes of child rearing and socialization. Such patterns have unfolded through the gradual differentiation of the tasks of upbringing. In an important sense, changes in the institutionalized fabric of schooling derive from attempts to impose new rhythms on the lives of human beings. For these reasons, schooling is not a natural process shared with other animals. Rather, it is a social activity that has been created, in effect, for unnatural purposes – to efface the animality of *Homo sapiens*.

CHAPTER 11

Epilogue

Teach your children well . . .
And feed them on your dreams.

(Graham Nash, Troubadour, 1974)

The human species has an unusual history. Humanity exists in its present form because it broke away from nature. It began to communicate, accumulate and transform its experience through social rather than biological mechanisms. In the process, it acquired a measure of economic, cultural and intellectual autonomy.

In an important sense, too, the human species has evolved eugenically rather than naturally. The social practices of infanticide, castration, sterilization, contraception and abstinence have interrupted biological (or Darwinian) evolution. In their turn, such intervention practices have also changed substantially. Most notably, humankind has recently begun to rewrite the codebook of life – the chromosome. Social engineering has been joined by the cultural and political practices of genetic engineering. What, therefore, do these interruptions and interventions mean for the future of education and schooling? Earlier chapters, for instance, have suggested that schooling has had a beginning and a middle. But will it also come to an end? Or is schooling an endless institution?

The endless view of schooling dates back to the Scientific Revolution. Teaching and learning began to be claimed as sequential and linear activities; and these claims were underpinned by Cartesian and Newtonian assumptions about re-establishing, for perpetuity, the natural order of things. But how do notions about the order of teaching and learning resonate with post-Newtonian conceptions of knowledge? How has Einstein's relativity theory informed the organization of twentieth-century curricula? And have contemporary versions of chaos theory any pedagogic relevance? Will schooling shortly find a place and purpose for the carefully planned chaotic lesson?

These questions are not easily answered. Indeed, it is unlikely that any useful purpose is served by trying to answer them. Nevertheless, they are important to this book because they affirm that, in R.S. Peters's terms, education is, indeed, a chancy business. If the educational record remains open ended and unfinished, so must this book.

In fact, this book also aspires to be unfinished in two additional senses. First, few of the chapters are fully fashioned. Instead, attempts have been made to acknowledge the rawness of their disparate ideas and assumptions. But has it, in fact, been possible to do textual justice to the debates, disagreements and discoveries that currently exercise students of early humankind? Likewise, has it been possible to honour the historical sensitivity – and semantic diversity – of the term *curriculum*? Above all, is it possible to render an account that is both unfinished and accessible?

Second, this book is also intended to be open ended in so far as certain tensions are deliberately left unresolved. Under what circumstances, if any, is it possible to reconcile the 'needs' of the learner with the 'needs' of the state? Similarly, should tax-funded institutions of teacher training focus upon the skills and competences of teaching or should they, by contrast, address a different set of practices – schoolteaching? Or can they do both?

This last issue – the relationship between teaching and schoolteaching – is one of the most important themes in this book. Yet, paradoxically, it is rarely examined in the educational literature. Indeed, many texts that occupy the education shelves of libraries even fail to acknowledge the possibility of its existence. By default, they seem to presume that schooling is for horses, not humans. As a consequence, such texts not only mask the diversity and complexity of pedagogic practice, they also mask the minds of those schoolteachers whose practice they seek to influence. Very often, too, they promote doubt and confusion among intending teachers. Having read extensively about the mysteries of education, noviciate teachers rapidly find that schooling is something else. Not surprisingly, many of them begin to question whether they can survive as teachers in a world of schoolteachers.

Perhaps this book will only add to their alienation. Throughout, it implies that, in its post-Enlightenment sense, education cannot readily be reconciled with pre-Enlightenment conceptions of schooling. At the same time, however, this book has also identified and explored a contrasting possibility. If nothing else, the history of schooling is an eloquent testimony to the self-conscious and reactivity of human beings. Moreover, it was the reactivity of human beings – learners as well as teachers – that helped to turn education into schooling, and teaching into schoolteaching. For the same reason, therefore, human beings retain the capacity to challenge and reverse these processes. Who knows, therefore, what education and schooling might become?

Bibliography

Apple, M. (1986). *Teachers and Texts: A Political Economy of Class and Gender Relations in Education*. London, Routledge.

Ariès, P. (1962). *Centuries of Childhood: A Social History of Family Life*. London, Jonathan Cape.

Arnot, M. and Weiner, G. (eds) (1987). *Gender and the Politics of Schooling*. London, Hutchinson.

Attenborough, D. (1987). *The First Eden: The Mediterranean World and Man*. London, Collins.

Brand, S. (1988). *The Media Lab: Inventing the Future at MIT*. Harmondsworth, Penguin.

Callahan, R.E. (1962). *Education and the Cult of Efficiency: A Study of the Administrative Forces that have Shaped the Administration of the Public Schools*. London, University of Chicago Press.

Campbell, R.H. and Skinner, A.S. (1985). *Adam Smith*. London, Croom Helm.

Chalmers, G.S. (1976). *Reading Easy 1800–50: A Study of the Teaching of Reading*. London, The Broadsheet King.

Clamehy, M.T. (1979). *From Memory to Written Record*. London, Edward Arnold.

Cobban, A.B. (1975). *The Medieval Universities: Their Development and Organisation*. London, Methuen.

Corrigan, P. (1979). *Schooling the Smash Street Kids*. London, Macmillan.

Davies, F. (1973). *Teaching Reading in Early England*. London, Pitman.

Davies, L. (1984). *Pupil Power: Deviance and Gender in School*. London, Falmer.

Delamont, S. and Duffin, L. (eds) (1978). *The Nineteenth Century Woman: Her Cultural and Physical World*. London, Croom Helm.

Dunlop, O.J. and Denman, R.D. (1912). *English Apprenticeship and Child Labour: A History*. London, Fisher Unwin.

Eisenstein, E.L. (1979). *The Printing Press as an Agent of Change: Communications and Cultural Transformations in Early-Modern Europe*. Cambridge, Cambridge University Press.

Elias, N. (1978). *The Civilising Process*. Oxford, Blackwell.

Fanon, F. (1965). *The Wretched of the Earth*. London, McGibbon and Kee.

Febvre, L. and Martin, H.J. (1976). *The Coming of the Book: the Impact of Printing 1450–1800*. London, New Left Books.

Fryer, P. (1984). *Staying Power: The History of Black People in Britain*. London, Pluto.

Gardner, P. (1984). *The Lost Elementary Schools of Victorian England*. London, Croom Helm.

Glenday, N. and Price, M. (1974). *Reluctant Revolutionaries: A Century of Head Mistresses 1874–1974*. London, Pitman.

Gordon, P. and White, J. (1979). *Philosophers as Educational Reformers: The Influence of Idealism on British Educational Thought and Practice*. London, Routledge.

Gould, S.J. (1981). *The Mismeasure of Man*. London, Norton.

Gow, L. and Mcpherson, A. (1980). *Tell Them From Me: Scottish School Leavers Write About School and Life Afterwards*. Aberdeen, Aberdeen University Press.

Graff, H. (1987). *The Labyrinths of Literacy: Reflections on Literacy Past and Present*. London, Falmer Press.

Grafton, A. and Jardine, L. (1986). *From Humanism to the Humanities: Education and the Liberal Arts in Fifteenth- and Sixteenth-Century Europe*. London, Duckworth.

Hans, N. (1951). *New Trends in Education in the Eighteenth Century*. London, Routledge.

Harris, M. (1978). *Cows, Pigs, Wars and Witches: The Riddles of Culture*. New York, Vintage Books.

Havelock, E.A. (1976). *The Origins of Western Literacy*. Toronto, Ontario Institute for Studies in Education.

Hill, B. (1984). *Eighteenth Century Women: An Anthology*. London, Allen and Unwin.

Holt, J. (1969). *How Children Fail*. Harmondsworth, Penguin.

Humphries, S. (1983). *Hooligans or Rebels? An Oral History of Working-Class Childhood and Youth 1889–1939*. Oxford, Blackwell.

Huppert, G. (1984). *Public Schools in Renaissance France*. Urbana, University of Illinois Press.

Illich, I. and Sanders, B. (1989). *The Alphabetization of the Popular Mind: The History and Impact of Literacy from Homer to Huxley and from Univac to Uniquack*. Harmondsworth, Penguin.

Ingold, T. (1986). *The Appropriation of Nature: Essays on Human Ecology and Social Relations*. Manchester, Manchester University Press.

Karabel, L. and Halse, A.H. (eds) (1977). *Power and Ideology in Education*. New York, Oxford University Press.

Karier, C., Violas, P. and Spring, J. (eds) (1973). *Roots of Crisis: American Education in the Twentieth Century*. Chicago, Rand McNally.

Koestler, A. (1964). *The Sleepwalkers: A History of Man's Changing Vision of the Universe*. Harmondsworth, Penguin.

Kozol, J. (1968). *Death at an Early Age*. Harmondsworth, Penguin.

Lawn, M. (1987). *Servants of the State: The Contested Control of Teaching 1900–1930*. London, Falmer.

Lewin, R. (1989). *Bones of Contention: Controversies in the Search for Human Origins*. Harmondsworth, Penguin.

Mangan, J.A. (1981). *Athleticism in the Victorian and Edwardian Public School: The Emergence and Consolidation of an Educational Ideology*. Cambridge, Cambridge University Press.

Mangan, J.A. (1985). *The Games Ethic and Imperialism*. Harmondsworth, Penguin.

Moore, T. and Carling, C. (1988). *The Limitations of Language*. London, Macmillan.

Morgan, J. (1986). *Godly Learning: Puritan Attitudes Towards Reason, Learning and Education*. Cambridge, Cambridge University Press.

Sacks, O. (1986). *The Man Who Mistook His Wife for a Hat*. London, Pan Books.

School of Barbiana. (1970). *Letter to a Teacher*. Harmondsworth, Penguin.

Seaborne, M. (1971). *The English School: Its Architecture and Organization 1370–1870*. London, Routledge.

Selleck, R.J.W. (1972). *English Primary Education and the Progressives 1914–1939*. London, Routledge.

Silver, H. (1965). *The Concept of Popular Education: A Study of the Ideas and Social Movements in the Early Nineteenth Century*. London, MacGibbon and Kee.

Simon, B. (1960). *The Two Nations and the Educational Structure 1780–1870*. London, Lawrence and Wishart.

Simon, J. (1966). *Education and Society in Tudor England*. Cambridge, Cambridge University Press.

Simon, J. (1970). *The Social Origins of English Education*. London, Routledge.

Smith, J.W.A. (1954). *The Birth of Modern Education: The Contribution of the Dissenting Academies 1660–1800*. London, Independent Press.

Strauss, G. (1978). *Luther's House of Learning: The Indoctrination of the Young in the German Reformation*. Baltimore, Johns Hopkins.

Tawney, R. (1942). *Religion and the Rise of Capitalism*. Harmondsworth, Penguin.

Thompson, E.P. (1968). *The Making of the English Working Class*. Harmondsworth, Penguin.

Watt, I. (1964). 'The seminar', reprinted in Musgrave, P.W. (1970). *Sociology, History and Education*. London, Methuen.

Williams, M. (1971). *Revolutions 1775–1830*. Harmondsworth, Penguin.

Williams, R. (ed.) (1981). *Contact: Human Communication and its History*. London, Thames and Hudson.

Williams, R. (1985). *The Long Revolution*. Harmondsworth, Penguin.

Willis, P. (1977). *Learning to Labour*. Farnborough, Saxon House.

Wyand, J. (1980). *Village Schools: a Future for the Past?* London, Evans.

Index

LET ME OFF
at the TOP!

LET ME OFF at the TOP!

My Classy Life & Other Musings

RON BURGUNDY

CROWN
ARCHETYPE
NEW YORK

Text by Ron Burgundy
Doodles by Ron Burgundy

Library of Congress Cataloging-in-Publication Data
is available upon request.

ISBN 978-0-8041-3957-1
eBook ISBN 978-0-3853-4932-1

Book design by Elizabeth Rendfleisch
Illustration on page 154 by Fred Haynes
Photography credits appear on page 224
Jacket design by Michael Nagin
Jacket photographs: Emily Shur, TM *& © Par. Pics. All rights reserved*
(front and author); TM *& © Par. Pics. All rights reserved (spine).*

10 9 8 7 6 5 4 3 2 1

First Edition

DISCLAIMER

Every word in this book is true. You can fact-check most of it but much of it lives within my brain. Fortunately for you my memory is infallible. With the exception of people, places, situations and dialogue, I'm like a walking encyclopedia of facts. You might as well chisel this baby in stone, because what you are holding is a perfect unchallengeable chronicle of American history and personal narrative. You are welcome.

AUTHOR'S NOTE

It took me eight years to write this book. The research alone—fact-checking, reading the source materials, asking questions—was endless and I didn't care for it that much. I just didn't. But I persisted because I knew what I was doing was truly very important. A book is never the work of one man. Many people contribute to its failure, or as in this case, its success. Dorathoy Roberts at the Harvard Widener Library was instrumental in recovering so many facts and nautical terms. Janart Prancer aided my work immensely with her near-encyclopedic understanding of rare manuscripts in the Herzog August Library, Wolfenbüttel, Germany. Esther Nausbaum, head librarian at the prestigious Kirkland School of Dinosaurs, was instrumental in tracking down indispensable paleoecological records for chapter 15 in this book. Herb Kolowsky was ever watchful and patient, reading over many drafts of the manuscript as well as cleaning my gutters. I consulted with my dear friend and lover Doris Kearns Goodwin over many breakfasts in bed. Her sharp intellect and sharper teeth found their way into practically every page. Although we are no longer lovers because I don't know why, her knowledge of presidential history is the basis for chapter 12. Her dogged enthusiasm for the project was only outpaced by her enthusiasm for lovemaking, which I could barely equal. I don't know what to say about Doris really except if she's still out there and she would like another bounce, I would be game. Johnny Bench was an invaluable spell-checker. Lars Mankike brought an artistic eye to the project and a kind of European nihilism that was completely unnecessary. We fought often and he got what he deserved, so I'm not even sure why I'm thanking him here, but it's too late now. Sandy Duncan is full of boundless energy. What can I say about Veronica Corningstone, the love of my life? We've had our ups and downs for sure, and usually the downs were because of something stupid she said or did while losing blood. You really can't fault women for being irrational. Blood drips out of them willy-nilly and there's nothing they can do about it. It's like being a hemophiliac. I suspect science will one day cure them of this blood-dripping disease but until then, *Vive la différence*. Finally Baxter, my dog and best friend, saw me through many tough hours as I struggled with my emotions during this project. His love and support sustained me through extremely difficult excavations into my past. Only Baxter knows the pain I have lived. Our nightly talks formed the basis for what you hold in your hand now.

WHY WRITE THIS BOOK?

Does mankind really need another book dumped onto the giant garbage heap of books already out there? Is there some pressing desire for the wisdom of a humble News Anchor in this world? Will it add to the great literary achievements throughout time or will it be lost in a swamp of trivial scribbling like pornography—devoured and then destroyed out of shame? I stand here (I write standing up) and I say, "No!" No, this book will NOT be lost! This book is necessary. It's an important work from an important man. I was the number one News Anchor in all of San Diego. My name is Ron Burgundy and what you have in your hands is a very big deal. It's . . . my . . . life. It's my words. It's my gift to you.

If the truth be told, I've wanted to write a book for a long time, but how? How do you write a book? Oh sure, I know you get paper and pencils and make yourself a pot of coffee and you stay up all night and write one. Seems simple enough, but it's not. There's a very long tradition of book writing going back through history all the way to Roman times, and if you know history like I do you understand that book writing is NOT EASY! Rule number one sayeth the bard, "To thy own self be truthful in regards to yourself." I knew from the beginning, before even purchasing the paper and the pencils and the cans of coffee, I would have to spend a little time getting to know me. I've been so busy being Ron Burgundy the legend that I never stopped to really get to know Ron Burgundy the man. Before I wrote one word of this masterpiece I took long walks through the streets of San Diego trying to make friends with a guy I barely knew: myself. I talked to myself, that's right, in bars, at bus stops, in laundromats, wherever my muse took me. I recommend it. Go out and talk to yourself. Record the conversations like I did. I had a small lightweight twenty-pound Grundig reel-to-reel tape recorder with a built-in microphone. A typical conversation went like this:

    Ron
Hey, good friend of mine.

    Ron
Hey right back at you.

    Ron
What's it all about?

Ron

It's a good question, Ron. You ask tough questions.

Ron

It's my business, I'm a News Anchor by trade.

Ron

No kidding, that's important!

Ron

Yeah, it's really nothing. I'm kind of a big deal around San Diego.

Ron

It sounds damn impressive.

Ron

It is in a way. It's pretty impressive. Are you hungry?

Ron

I could definitely go for some fish-and-chips. Do you know where they have the best fish-and-chips in San Diego?

Ron

I do. There's a one-of-a-kind sea shanty called Long John Silver's that fixes up delicious fish-and-chips at a reasonable price.

Ron

Man, that sounds yummy.

Ron

Why don't you join me? I'm heading over there now.

Ron
How far of a walk is it?

Ron
About six miles.

Ron
Do you want to discuss life some more while we walk?

Ron
No, let's shut it down until after we eat.

Night after night like a ghost I walked the streets of San Diego holding conversations with only myself. Sometimes the conversations were trivial, like the time I got into an argument over which dog breed, Labrador or collie, was better at learning tricks, but sometimes they reached a sublime level of deep thinking, like this conversation I recorded while sitting on a transit bus.

Ron
What's it all mean, Ron?

Ron
Sometimes I think we're all crazy.

Ron
I know what you mean. I feel crazy myself sometimes.

Ron
I mean, what's to stop me from lighting this bus on fire?

Ron

I know! But keep your voice down, okay?

Ron

I mean it! There's nothing. What holds us together, Ron? Very little. VERY LITTLE!

Ron

Ron, you're in your head too much. Breathe.

Ron

No but listen to me, Ron, the world is made of strands of particles and atoms that commingle without meaning, taking form momentarily, decaying, finding new form— senseless activity without a guiding center. How can we make sense of it? Burning down this bus with all these people holds the same value as giving birth to a child. Don't you get it?

Ron

Keep it together, buddy.

Ron

I WILL NOT BE TALKED TO IN THIS WAY. I AM NOT A CHILD! I MIGHT JUST BURN DOWN THIS BUS TO PROVE A POINT!

Bus Driver

Do we have a problem?

Ron

Cool it, Ron. You're making people nervous.

Ron

I DON'T CARE! I DON'T CARE! I'M GOING TO BURN DOWN THIS BUS!

Unidentified Male Voice
Get him. Hold him down.

Ron

I'M RON BURGUNDY! Ow, come on. CHANNEL FOUR NEWS!

Ron

He's okay. Stop hitting. He's okay . . . he's okay, let him breathe.

I have over a thousand hours of recorded conversations with myself. What was I looking for? What was I trying to get at? I knew if I was going to write a book I would have to call on all of my powers of concentration. I would have to dig deep into the man, not the myth but the man, Ron Burgundy. To begin with I climbed Mount San Gorgonio, the highest peak in all of Southern California, and I called on an old friend, mighty Athena, the goddess of wisdom and courage, to guide me in this noble endeavor.

There I stood naked to the stars and the great gods above and yelled out, "My name is Ron Burgundy and I call on you, Athena, for inspiration! I am going to write a book. It shall be the story of my life, a great novel! I'm not sure *novel* is what you call a life story. There's another name for *life story* and I have forgotten it. For it does not matter! Brobalia! It's called a Brobalia! No, that's not it but it starts with a *B*. It is of no importance, mighty Athena! I stand here alone, naked on this mount with these tourists from Germany"—it's true, there were some tourists from Germany up there as well—"to ask for your guidance and wisdom while writing this Binocular. Nope, that's a word for something different. NO MATTER! Bisojagular! Still not right but I'm getting closer, fair Athena, and thanks for your patience—let all the gods know, Zeus, Apollo, Poseidon and Hestia, to name only a few, that I will ask for their strength in writing this Braknopod. Way off! My old pal Doris Kearns Goodwin would surely know the name you give a life story. She was a real egghead, among other things. Anyway, Athena, just help me write this thing. I swear to you that I will remember the name people give to life stories the minute I get down from this mountain! Thank you, brave Athena!"

Judging by what I have written here I can say with all confidence she heard my plaintive cries that raw night up on that tourist trap of a peak in the San Bernardino Mountains.

Now, I'm not going to lie, a searching evaluation of who I am has been an ordeal, not just for me but for those closest to me. It's been hard on my wife, Veronica, and Baxter, my dog, and for anyone who lives within screaming distance of my house and for law enforcement personnel. I went all in on this quest for self-discovery. William Thackeray Thoreau once said, "Desperate men lead lives of quiet songs that are left unsung when they do end up in their cold tombs." Something like that. Anyway, the point is you only go around once and you really need to go for the gold!

I can tell you this: There were a lot of people out there

who didn't think it was such a good idea to write a book. I know stuff about certain people and let's just say that sometimes knowledge can be dangerous. When word got out I was writing a "tell-all" book there were attempts made on my life! This is serious business. Most men would have run for the hills. Not me; I welcome the challenge. There is a chance I may have to go into hiding after this book comes out. I can't say where I will disappear to but more than likely it will be my cabin I purchased with George C. Scott's cousin. Its location can never be known. Scott's cousin is never there and it's less rustic than you think, with a pool table and full bar as well as a washer-dryer combo, and it's within walking distance to the Big Bear Lake general store.

Death threats are an occupational hazard of course for us anchormen. I'm very comfortable living each minute with the expectation of being attacked. It's been many years since JFK told me he used to enjoy Marilyn Monroe from behind while Joe DiMaggio looked on in the corner. The main players have all left the stage, so perhaps now is the time to speak out without fear of reprisal. Maybe telling the truth is more important than any danger I may face. Then again, maybe the truth has nothing to do with it. Maybe I just don't like it when people say, "Ron, you can't write a book, you don't have the courage," or "Ron, you can't write a book, you don't know how to type," or "Ron, have you ever even read a book?" It's the naysayers who get me. I like surprising people. I always have. I think everyone in the world took it for granted that I would not have the balls to write this book. I've got the balls, big hairy misshapen balls in a wrinkly sack. This book is a testament to my giant balls. If you want some feel-good story about how to live your life, then go look elsewhere. This book is a hard-hitting, no-holds-barred, unafraid account of my exceptional life with some words of wisdom thrown in for good measure. You won't find a lot of fluff here. If you're looking for fluff to take to the beach, check out the Holy Bible. This ain't that book.

So who am I? That's what this book is about. Over the next eight hundred pages (unless some bitch of an editor gets ahold of it with his clammy hands and snotty nose) I will let you in on a very big secret: my life. Of course some of it isn't such a secret. Some of it you know already. I'm a man. A News Anchor. A lover. Husband. A friend to animals on land and at sea. A handsome devil. A connoisseur of fine wine. I have one of the classiest collections of driftwood art in the world. I can throw a Wham-O Frisbee if I have to, but I prefer not to. I love the outdoors. Nature drives me nuts. I make pancakes for anyone who asks. I take long nude walks on the beach. I play jazz flute, not for business but for pleasure. I'm a world-class water-ski instructor. I don't care a lick about the fashion world, although they seem to care an awful lot about me. My best friend is a dog named Baxter. I'm quite famous. I'm a history buff. I collect authentic replications of Spanish broadswords. I smoke a pipe on occasion, not for profit but for pleasure. I've been known to sing out loud at weddings and funerals. I'm a collector of puns. I have over three hundred handcrafted shoes of all sizes. I don't give a damn about broccoli. I believe all men have the right to self-pleasure. I carry a picture of Buffy Sainte-Marie in my wallet and I'm not even Catholic. My favorite drink is scotch. My second-favorite drink is a Hairy Gaylord. I'm affiliated with at least a hundred secret societies; some of them, like the Knights of Thunder, will kill you just for printing their name. I adore tits. I will never be persuaded to try yogurt. I'm allergic to fear. Other men have fallen in love with me in a sexual way and that's okay. I have mixed feelings about bicycles. My handmade fishing lures are sought after by fly-fishermen the world over. I've never been one for blue jeans. Sandals on another man have been known to make me vomit. My Indian name is Ketsoh Silaago. My French name is Pierre Laflume. I can never tell anyone about what happened in Youngstown, Ohio, one January night. There are no other people who look like me on this planet; I've looked. Babies, bless their souls, give me the creeps. I own a chain of hobby stores in the Twin Cities I have never seen. I once ate a ham dinner and then realized it was not ham. People tell me I look like Mickey Rooney. Woody the Woodpecker cracks me up every time. That's the basic stuff; now prepare yourself for the journey—the journey into an extraordinary life.

THE BOY FROM
HAGGLEWORTH

The story we were told as children went something like this. . . . On June 27, 1844, Joseph Smith, the great Mormon martyr, and his brother Hyrum were killed by a mob in Carthage, Illinois. In the middle of the mob was a smooth opportunist named Franklin Haggleworth. Haggleworth was on his way to Keokuk, Iowa, and the Mississippi River to cheat people out of money. As the mob grew outside the jail where Smith and his brother were held, Haggleworth stirred up the crowd with anti-Mormon slogans and songs. Up to that point the crowd had been a peaceful assembly of reasonable people willing to discuss whether Smith or his brother had transgressed any laws. Haggleworth saw an opening. With his honey-tongued skill for oratory he was able to cajole the law-abiding citizenry into a frenzied pack of murderers. Within minutes of his opening his mouth, the crowd stormed the jail and shot the two brothers. Haggleworth ran off to the Mormon camp to report the sad news that their leader had been shot. Feigning sympathy with the now-distraught Mormons, he produced a dirty dinner plate and proclaimed Joseph Smith himself had given it to him right before his death. According to Haggleworth it was the last plate given to Smith by the angel Moroni. But unlike the plates Smith "translated," this new plate had never been translated. Pretending to read the plate, a fairly crappy piece of pottery that sits in the Haggleworth Museum to this day, he told the crowd that a new religion would be born out of Mormonism—a new religion dedicated to worshipping the penis of Mr. Franklin Haggleworth. He went on to explain that this new religion required up to twelve but no less than three women "who didn't have to be virgins because that seemed kind of overused" to frequently see to the needs of his ever-demanding penis. For the most part the men and women in the Mormon settlement were not convinced of Haggleworth's "vision." But try and remember—this was a strange part of American history and folks were dropping everything to follow men with heaven-born plates. There were nudist colonies and polygamist silverware-making colonies and people going to séances left and right—not like now, when reason holds sway. This was a wildly superstitious time and so it should come as no surprise that eight women of various ages believed the plate and followed

Haggleworth up the river to worship his penis. He landed on a bald, shale-covered scrap of earth not far from the river in northeastern Iowa. Because it could not be farmed Haggleworth was able to buy the property for a dollar and fifty cents. Three days into the new colony, tragedy struck. A great famine overtook the settlers, so the angel ordered Haggleworth to send some of his women to the river to worship other men's penises for money and food. It worked! Haggleworth was in business! A steady stream of boatmen beat a path to Haggleworth's church of penis worship over the next thirty years. Haggleworth lived to the ripe old age of forty-eight and died with a boner. That's what we were told anyway growing up in Haggleworth.

About ten years after Haggleworth's death, the Valley Coal and Iron Company bought the town for seventy-five cents and began mining for coal. Although the company changed hands many times over the next fifty years, Standard Oil of Iowa took over the operations in 1922 and successfully mined forty miles of intersecting tunnels of coal beneath the town. In 1940, the year I was born, Latham Nubbs flicked a half-chewed, still-lit stogie into the street outside of Kressler's Five and Dime and the town of Haggleworth caught on fire—a fire that still burns to this day. Deadly carbon monoxide gas and plumes of hell-spawned black smoke appear and disappear at random. The smell of sulfur, literally the smell of Satan himself, permeates the air, sending visitors and lost strangers to emergency rooms all over the state. In 1965 the governor of Iowa, Harold Hughes, condemned the town and relocated its remaining twenty-eight residents.

I was born into a simpler time. Environmental concerns wouldn't come into play until hippies and weirdos started crawling the earth. For us, growing up in Haggleworth, the fires were a way of life, a hazard like any other. The smell went unnoticed because it's what we knew. The black smoke rising from the hot earth was a daily reminder of the hell pit below the surface. I was born into this town of three hundred hardheaded Iowans whose only way of life was mining, and of course drinking and burning to death. Mining was especially hard because of the fire, and drinking wasn't any easier, also because of the fire. The more you drank alcohol, the more likely your chance of igniting yourself. It was a cruel irony, but the only way to stave off that horrible impending feeling of one day burning to death was to drink more . . . a vicious circle, really, but one we enjoyed with gusto.

In this carefree community the Burgundys were a proud clan. Claude and Brender Burgundy had eight boys. I was the last one born. The plain fact of the matter is we all hated each other equally. There were no alliances within the family. It was every man for himself. The day I was born was the day I received my first sock in the face. My brother Lonny Burgundy smacked me the first time he saw me. I couldn't speak yet, as I was only a few minutes old, but I do remember thinking to myself, "So that's the way it is." I grew to like the uncertain anticipation of being pounded on by my older siblings and by the occasional explosion of fire that jumped up out of the earth. In grade school, my best friend, Cassy Moinahan, and I were walking home when a sinkhole opened up and down he went into the fiery pit that was Haggleworth just below the surface. His screams of pain could be heard coming through the floor of the hardware store for two days. I came to recognize a kind of fluidity to life that has stayed with me from those early days. Every man takes a beating and every man gets dumped back into the earth . . . so why cry about it? Right?

My father, Claude Burgundy, was a learned man, educated in Oxford, England. He came to Haggleworth out of a deep respect for its unlivable conditions. His wife, and soul mate for life, Brender, was all class with tits out to here. I didn't much care for either of them but they were my parents and I loved them both dearly. On Saturday nights they went dancing over at the Elks Lodge. They never missed a Saturday night at the lodge. Just as soon as they were out the door it was every Burgundy for himself. Fists, chair legs, frying pans, railroad spikes—whatever was lying around the house we used to pummel the other guy. We all had our tricks. Horner set traps all over the house. Lonny carried a whip. Bartholemew welded himself a whole medieval suit of armor. Jessup had attack dogs. For me it quickly came down to Jack Johnson and Tom O'Leary, the names I gave my left and right fists respectively. With Johnson I was able to fend off most of the blows, but with O'Leary I could mete out my own share of pain. By the time I was ten years old even my oldest brother, Hargood, knew to keep away from O'Leary's leaden punishment. Johnson had them on their heels quick but O'Leary was the one that put them to sleep. Even to this day I've been known to call on O'Leary to clear up an argument or end some nonsense.

Years back I was in New York City and I found myself in a tricky situation with professional blowhard Norman Mailer. He and I had occasion to mix it up from time to time and I always had no problem stuffing his face back in his shirt. But he caught me off guard on this occasion. We were at Clyde Frazier's place on the Upper West Side of Manhattan. Mailer must have been waiting in a broom closet for me for more than an hour when he jumped out and began whacking at me with a hammer. I took as many blows as I could until I unleashed the Ole Doomsday from Dublin, Tom O'Leary. That was all she wrote for Norman. He probably took the nightmare of my knuckles to his grave. No sir, I've never been afraid to resort to fisticuffs. Not my first option, mind you. I've stepped on too many loose teeth to want anything to do with violence . . . but if it comes my way I know what to do.

It wasn't all fistfights and terror in Haggleworth. There were many days and nights of pure unabashed fun. For instance, for some unknown reason that really makes no sense at all, Haggleworth had the finest jazz supper club west of Chicago. It was called Pinky's Inferno. It made very little sense—it's almost unbelievable really—but there it was, a jazz club in a town of three hundred in the middle of nowhere. At age eleven I got a job as a busboy in Pinky's and a passion was born in me—a passion so strong I feel it to this day whenever I make love to a woman or see a sunrise or smell thick-cut Canadian bacon cooking, or whenever I report the news. It's a passion for jazz flute. It all started for me in 1951 at Pinky's Inferno. Diz, Bird, Miles—they all came through Haggleworth, unbelievable as that sounds, to play at Pinky's.

Even typing it now seems stupid. I was there at the time and I still want to fact-check this. I made my first flute out of a length of steel pipe my brother Winston tried to beat me with. Winston was my least-favorite brother, and that's saying a lot. He would beat you while you slept—clearly against the rules, but he didn't care. He was a union strike buster for many years before he was brained by a rock. Now he sells pencils in a little wooden stall in downtown Omaha. I buy twenty every Christmas. They say hatred and love are two sides of the same golden coin.

THE END

I loved that homemade pipe flute. Dizzy Gillespie used to make me get up onstage with him and play that thing until my mouth would bleed. Maybe I'm misremembering this part. I'll fact-check it one more time before I finally commit it to paper though. Dexter Gordon, Art Blakey, even the older guys, Louis Armstrong and Sidney Bechet, came by. Hey, I get it, if you don't want to believe any of this I can't blame you. Anyway, I picked up a little something from each one of these jazz masters—you know what? I think the whole "jazz flute" stuff should stay out of the novel, come to think of it. It's too ridiculous even if it did really happen. I will simply say this: Chet Baker and Gerry Mulligan taught me, an eleven-year-old boy, the rudiments of jazz improvisation in the alley behind Pinky's Inferno one night in Haggleworth, Iowa. That's solid enough information that is very believable. (I have no idea if this is going to hurt or help my credibility here, but just down the alley from us Jack Kerouac was getting a blow job from Allen Ginsberg. More than likely this can be corroborated in their own writings. Those guys wrote an awful lot.) With all these hep cats coming through Haggleworth in the fifties I became the source for their drug habits. I had an in with some of the dealers in the area and I would score smack for the musicians in exchange for music lessons. I quickly learned to cook it so they could fix up before their sets. Forget it. This sounds impossible to me. I know what happened but none of this reads real. I'm just going to go with this: I have a passion for jazz flute. I got it from somewhere. It's part of who I am. There.

When my brothers and I weren't beating on each other we would roam the streets looking for any other kind of fun we could get into. These days you would call us a "street gang" but in those days it was just considered horsing around. The regular folks of Haggleworth, when not scared of falling into the hot ground below their feet, were quite comically terrified of the Burgundys. There was a saying around Haggleworth that mothers told their children. It went something like this: "Eat your vegetables or the Burgundy boys will beat the living shit out of you." Silly really. Men would sometimes refer to a black eye as a "Burgundy." Derrick Burgundy, the second-oldest of my brothers, did do acts of violence that transcended the usual fun boy stuff and he was gunned down by a posse, which absolutely nobody had any objection to . . . but that was only one Burgundy in eight who was a bad egg. Our reputation as town bullies didn't mean much to us. We just laughed it all off and had a good time. The only townsfolk who were not scared of the Burgundys were the Haggleworths. They were the only other prominent family in Haggleworth and because of their last name they felt they owned the whole town. It was non-sense of course. Shell Oil owned Haggleworth. (That's why there was no real government or police or any order whatso-ever. It was the reason why my father, a strict Darwinist, loved the town.) But the Haggleworths erected a museum in honor of their founding father. Some of them still practiced their pious religion of penis worship, but for the most part they were an uncultured, rangy bunch of derelicts who ate cat food and lived in caves. Some others lived on Willow Street in large Victorian houses. They did manage to build one impressive building downtown, a great big marble and granite Roman-looking thing. It was a sort of clubhouse and harkened back to a more forward-looking time in Haggleworth when money was flowing into the city from foreign investors and sex per-verts. They called this huge building "the Courthouse." They even carved the name "Courthouse" into the stone above the door. No one recognized it as an actual courthouse unless you had to pay a ticket or get a marriage license. Shell Oil certainly had no use for it. And no Burgundy ever stepped foot in it as far as I know.

The Haggleworths really stuck their noses up at the rest of us . . . which was laughable really, because they were descended from whores mainly. A Burgundy, upon encountering a Hag-gleworth in the street, would make a point of reminding the

Haggleworth of his or her ignominious lineage with something pithy like "How's it going, son of a whore?" To which a Haggleworth might come back at a Burgundy with something like "When was the last time you took a bath?" (It was a fair blow as we never took them growing up.) Then a little boxing might ensue and depending on the number involved in the conflict some more pushing and shoving, and then usually a kind of riot would break out with fires and broken glass and such. Totally predictable small-town-type stuff. A bygone era really. Apple pie. Fishing villages. I had a lot of respect for the Haggleworth boys and girls. They could fight like devils. Many nights after a riot I would find myself limping home because they had gotten the best of me. I can laugh about it now. Heck, I laughed about it then.

And then there was Jenny Haggleworth. She was simply a dream. Every boy in town was in love with her. She was the kind of girl that if you saw her at the malt shop, your heart just stopped—fiery red hair, long legs, the softest hands, like two dove wings. Her eyes were like enchanted emeralds. She was a cross between Rita Hayworth and Grace Kelly, and me being twelve years old I was head over heels in love with her. She was twenty-eight and had a job in the mining office.

Because she was a Haggleworth and I was a Burgundy it was a forbidden love but one that I knew I would risk. I also knew that if ever my secret was revealed the whole Haggleworth clan would chase me down and throw me into Dutchman's Dungeon—a fire pit so deep and terrifying that years later when the Army Corps of Engineers were called in to cap it off they turned tail and ran out of there faster than baboons running from a ghost lion. To this day its location isn't on any map and is a well-kept government secret. I know how to get there, of course, as does anyone who grew up in Haggleworth, but we have all signed a presidential oath of secrecy demanding that we never reveal its whereabouts. Among many others over the years I took noted tennis legend and feminist Billie Jean King up there one night with the intent of throwing her in. I was steaming mad at her—I still am but I'm not a murderer. Billie Jean King knows the whereabouts of Dutchman's Dungeon; so do famed quarterback Roman Gabriel and legendary funnyman Dicky Smothers and many more. Jenny and I would meet in a small clearing in the woods that was unknown but to her and me. The sunlight splashed through the leafy canopy of maple and oak, dappling spots of light on a quiet glade no bigger than a bedroom. It was our hideaway. We talked and held hands, and occasionally I was rewarded with a kiss from her soft lips. I lived for those kisses. I saved our correspondences, which one day I will publish as *The Love Letters of Ron Burgundy and Jenny Haggleworth*. I think mankind would benefit greatly from reading them, with the disclaimer that these are the simple yearnings of a twelve-year-old boy addressing his love sixteen years his senior. Here are just a few exchanges.

Dearest Jenny,

Each hour I spend away from you is another hour in torment. I cannot bear the distance our hearts must suffer! Purgatory knows no pain like the agony of our separation. My minutes are filled with anxious longing for a mere glimpse of your beauty. The ruby ringlets in your hair, like ribbons adorning a Christmas gift, await my unfurling! A poem I write to you! "So soft the cheek, so smooth the shoulders, the liquefaction of your clothes rippling over your huge boulders." Ron Burgundy, Haggleworth, Iowa, 1952.

I must see you. Until then, my heart beats only for your answer.

    Your love servant, Ron Burgundy

Ron,

Got your letter. Meet in make-out woods after work.

    Jenny

PS: Bring gum

Sweet Jenny,

I am beside myself with joy! Your encouraging words of our anticipated reunion and our innocent pleasures have placed me in a transcendent mood! God surely works a spirit through every living being and only love can open the window to its ebb and flow. I shall wait upon the hour in joyous anticipation. Your thoughts of shared love shall remain forever locked in my bosom awaiting a key that only you possess. Oh, Jenny Haggleworth! How the name itself floats and flutters like a butterfly over the fields of flowers. Our reunion cannot come fast enough. Not even Mercury himself with winged foot could bring about our conjoining with the speed my heart so desires. I am forever at your mercy and your undying worshipper, Ron Burgundy.

Ron,

Might be late. Gotta get some oil for my car. See ya.

Jenny

PS: Bring gum

Pages and pages of suchlike correspondence poured forth from the two of us. Volumes of letters, enough to fill at least forty leather-bound books. Some years back I saw an advertisement in the popular fashion magazine *Jiggle* for a bookbinding device. It came with leather sheets, needles, high-test threading and plans for a build-your-own press. I don't know what I was thinking! I'm all thumbs when it comes to crafts! Many of you may recall I did the news with my hands bandaged for a three-month stint. I explained on air that I had rescued a child from a hospital fire. We found a baby and a mother who needed a couple of bucks and set up a story, all in good fun. What really happened was that I tried to bind those letters with that complicated binding setup! I tore up my hands pretty good. I got a chuckle out of that.

Eventually the lovers were discovered. In a town of three hundred it's hard to keep a secret. The Haggleworth clan found out I was diddling their sister and I was jumped and roped and dragged behind Jenny's car as she drove through the streets of Haggleworth. These were lawless days when men took it upon themselves to impose justice. Jazz great Erroll Garner was in town doing a two-week stint at Pinky's Inferno. He saw me being dragged through town and went off to get my brothers. I guess their hatred for the Haggleworths was greater than their hated for me, because pretty quickly all eight of the Burgundy boys were in town. A verbal back-and-forth rapidly escalated to a situation where the National Guard was called in. Some people were burned pretty badly, that I do remember.

After the bloodiest day in Haggleworth history, Jenny and I agreed it was best to take some time off. She left town one night with jazz great Thelonious Monk and then was married to Jack Paar for a while. I can't say for sure why Jenny Haggleworth, a twenty-eight-year-old model and Miss Iowa, was so infatuated with a twelve-year-old boy, but I had a couple of theories. One was pretty basic. At twelve I was already beginning to show signs of the future girth for which I would become somewhat legendary. I could see, looking down into my pants, something I would enjoy looking at and talking to for many years to come. Some women have called it Pegasus, after the winged horse of Greek mythology. The Lord Jesus Christ works in mysterious ways when he hands out lower body parts! Some men are blessed with extraordinary length but not much girth. Others have been awarded great girth but less length, and then . . . there are a select few who are granted the whole wonderful package, girth and length. I'm one of those guys who got just the girth. I wouldn't trade it for nothing—except more length. I know for a fact Jenny was transfixed by my reproductive parts because in some of our more tender and romantic moments she would yell out, "Show me that stack of pancakes!" or "Gimme that can of beans!" My understuff was and has been a source of great pride for me but not my greatest. If I had to guess at what body part Jenny Haggleworth and a million other women were attracted to most I would have to say it was my hair.

MY HAIR

First of all I'd like to dispel the nine most popular myths about my hair.

MYTH NUMBER 1: My hair is called Andros Papanakas. It is not. I have no name for my hair.

MYTH NUMBER 2: My hair was bestowed upon me by the gods. This one is hard to dispel. It would have been just like Zeus to make such a gift, or Hermes, but even though I have called on these two gods many times I have never been told specifically by either one that I was given my hair, so I have to say no to the gift-from-the-gods theory.

MYTH NUMBER 3: My hair is insured by Lloyd's of London

for one thousand dollars. Nope! It's fifteen hundred, thank you.

MYTH NUMBER 4: My hair won't talk to my mustache. This is basically true but I would hardly call that a myth.

MYTH NUMBER 5: My hair starred in the movie *Logan's Run*. It was definitely up for the part of Logan but that eventually went to Michael York. He did an excellent job in the film and to this day it's still considered the best film of all time.

MYTH NUMBER 6: My hair on my head is the exact same as the hair on my crotch. Don't I wish!

MYTH NUMBER 7: My hair was the principal cause of the overthrow of the Chilean government in '73. This one is true. Look it up.

MYTH NUMBER 8: Each strand of my hair carries the DNA for not only a complete Ron Burgundy clone but also a duck-billed platypus. This is incorrect. Scientists at Georgetown University studying my hair strands have detected the DNA from eight different semiaquatic mammals. The platypus is nowhere in sight.

MYTH NUMBER 9: I wear a toupee. Sure, I wear a toupee, and women don't have vaginas and cats don't have dongs! Seriously, this is not a myth, just an insult. Stop it. This is my hair. You can't have it. You can't buy it. You can't burgle it, but you can enjoy it on top of my leathery oversized head.

I would love to be able to report to you that my hair is the

work of many hours of teasing, combing, conditioning, dye-
ing, fluffing and whatever else men do for vanity's sake, but
it's simply not the case. I was born with my hair and that's
that. I could be cruising down the road in a new convertible
sports car with a topless beauty queen at my side. She could
be feeding me a thick New York strip steak and pouring me a
tall glass of scotch as I drive. In the backseat of the car there
could be a stuffed bear and Johnny Carson, but as that car
sped by, most guys on the street would look up and say to
themselves, "Man, I wish I had that hair." It's just a simple
fact. My hair is great. I've always had it, literally, from the day
I came out of the womb. From what I was told, on first seeing me come into this world the doctor and the nurse stood
dumbfounded and then ordered the entire hospital into the
delivery room because they thought perhaps they had witnessed the second coming of Christ! NO, they hadn't! It was
just me, Ron Burgundy, and my perfect hair.

Ed Harken, my boss at Channel 4, once joked that if anyone ever cut my hair, like Samson I would lose my power. I
laughed deeply and heartily for many hours and lost no sleep
at all over his wit. Several days later, a little more anxious, I
went to the San Diego Public Library and asked if they had
any books on this Samson guy. Little-known fact, turns out
he's mentioned in the Bible. It's just a blurb really but that's
pretty cool to get a mention in the Bible! It wasn't a well-
written story but I got the gist. It was comforting to know the
whole story and I was able to function without much incident
having this new knowledge of what happened to Samson's
hair. Knowing all about Samson and his girlfriend Delilah

did not make me nervous and I hardly spent any time thinking about what would happen if someone cut my hair off. It
was fairly easy to not think about it, although at night for a few
hours I would give it a thought. Why did he tell her? It made
no sense! I guess women always want to know the source of
our power. That's why they sleep with us, right, guys?

Anyway, I know that it calmed me immeasurably to know
all about Samson and what happened to him. That's why I was
surprised a few weeks later during our production meeting
when I yelled out very loud, "Ed Harken, if you touch my hair
I will cut your face up like a root grinder and your friends will
spend the rest of their lives too terrified to look at the mess
I left behind. Do you understand me! DO YOU!" I believe I
had a twelve-inch hunting knife in my hand at the time I said
it. Long story short: My hair is not mythological or magical
in any way. It's very simply a great gathering of hair strands
formed in such a way as to be undeniably perfect, and I am
not nervous at all about someone cutting it off someday. That
doesn't make me nervous.

Now, I know in the past you've seen pictures of me in the ad
section of the *San Diego Union-Tribune* endorsing this or that
hair product but I'm here to tell you it's all a lot of horse crap.
I say and do a lot of stuff for money. One thing I've always
stayed true to even if it meant never compromising is that Ron
Burgundy is for sale. I'll endorse anything if there's money on
the table. Seriously, if some dirty grease bag flies into town
with a bottle of cat urine and pays me enough money to say it
will make your hair look like mine, I'll do it. Just know your
hair will never look like mine. That's not to say I don't on

occasion use product. All anchormen use product. Most of the better hair products have either lost traction with today's youth or been discontinued by the EPA. Over the years these were the products I came to trust but that now no longer exist for one reason or another.

FRED MACMURRAY'S MAN GUM

One of the best ever. Was the "go-to" hair product growing up. It came in a one-gallon bucket and had the consistency of axle grease. You could use it as axle grease in a pinch but at a quarter a gallon, why waste it? In the sixties they discovered that lead chips were not safe and Man Gum lost favor with hair lovers.

HARMON KILLERBREW'S HEAD GOO

If you were a sports nut like me you couldn't wait to squeeze out a tube of Killerbrew's Head Goo before heading out to the movies. More like plaster of Paris than a malleable gel, it went on wet and minutes later you had a rock of hair on your head that no force could change for days. We just loved it. Like all plaster-based products in those days, the lime content was pretty high. One day it disappeared from the shelves with an offer to join in a class-action lawsuit. No harm no foul, I've always said. Baseball legend Harmon Killerbrew took the *r* out of his name and became "Killebrew." It was enough of a name change to hide him from the lawsuit and any culpability relating to all the seizures.

EXXON HAIR TAR

This stuff was everywhere and it really did the trick. It was the only hair product with the words *Completely Edible* on the label. Not that you would eat it, because it tasted like farts and clams, but it got thrown into a lot of pastry recipes around where I grew up and no one cared a lick. It took a while to work it into your hair as it was pretty sticky stuff, but once it was applied, look out, James Dean. It also helped if you had black hair because that's the only color it came in. A shipment of Exxon Hair Tar spilled out on Route 66 in Indiana in '56 and they closed down the highway for half a year. Every animal and piece of vegetation was annihilated within ten miles of the spill. Sad, when you think about it. In a gesture of true American courage Exxon owned up to their goof by saying they were sorry for what the truck driver did and that truck driver would have been fired if he had lived. Gosh darn it! Sometimes I wish we all could stand so tall in the face of our failure!

DR. LON'S LOVE SAUCE

Frankly this was the best of the bunch. It could only be found in adult bookstores and the backs of gentlemen's magazines, but if you got your hands on a tub of this creamy sauce it made all the rest look like turds. No one knew anything about Dr. Lon except that he was a real doctor who specialized in hairology and that he had discovered his sauce while hiking in Tibet. It smelled a bunch like socks and yeast, so you had to keep your distance from other people, but the glow it gave your hair was worth it. I liberally put this on my head three times a day for four years but then decided I needed human touch and I put it away. Years later I did a story on Dr. Lon, only to discover he was not a real human at all but just a made-up name. The real Dr. Lon was a bunch of researchers at Exxon Oil! Ingenious!

In the end, because I'm such a hobby lover, I concocted my own special hair formula through trial and error. It took six years to get the perfect balance but here it is, my gift to those of you who honor your hair with love and affection.

Eggs (six to eight)
Bourbon (half bottle)
Beer (Schaefer, four cans)
Maple syrup (bottle)
Rotten apples (four)
Coconut milk (one gallon)
Paint thinner (two cups)
Shoe polish (two tins)
Bouillon cubes (twenty)
Cat urine (bowl)
Wet newspaper (two to six pages)
Cream of broccoli soup (one can)

To prepare, throw all the ingredients into a large lobster pot and stir vigorously; add paint, color optional, when necessary. Cook till boiling and then let cool. Recipe makes enough for one or two applications. Your hair will look shimmery and stout all day. Hey . . . I'm just pulling your chain. My hair looks this way when I wake up and stays the same all day long. It's just something you're going to have to come to terms with. Unless your last name is Hudson, as in Rock, or Goulet, as in Robert, you won't even come close to hair like mine in your lifetime no matter what you plop on your head. Ron Burgundy.

One other quick story about my hair. In 1971 I was awarded the prestigious *Action-Man Magazine* award for best hair. It's quite an honor. Past winners have been Lorne Greene, Bobby Sherman, and professional golfer Johnny Miller, among others. So yes, it's a very big deal. The big shots over at *Action-Man Magazine* and Brunswick Bowling Balls fly the winners first-class to Hawaii for an all-expenses-paid weekend of fun and sun at Eros Hotel and Spa. Beautiful mixed-race nude women parade around with colorful drinks, sashaying between ice sculptures of scenes from the *Kama Sutra* and live exotic animals on chains. It's a first-class operation all around. Although I'm not the biggest celebrity at the gathering (Buddy Hackett and Agnes Moorehead are both in attendance!), I feel pretty at home surrounded by all this class and style. I plant myself at the Outrigger Bar and enjoy a whole menu full of ice-cream drinks while feasting on shrimp and hot dogs. I will admit straight up I'm doing my very best to put out some Burgundy sex signals. From the hotel gift shop I've purchased a bold new swimsuit and robe that are most definitely working. I am getting more than my share of looks! (That swimsuit was hands-down my favorite for years until my associate Brian Fantana told me it was a pair of women's underwear. Carpe diem!) Sure enough I lock eyes with a sultry temptress with a name tag that reads "Kimberly Gropff, Brunswick Bowling."

(For her protection—she is a married woman with children from Sterling, Illinois—I will call her "Tanya Lambkin." We later had relations in many different positions and styles, but that's not where this story is going, although it's hard not to think about it.) As "Tanya Lambkin" is making her way over to me at the bar and Sir Roderick Hainsworth is peeking out of my swimsuit (women's underwear), a sudden burst of crashing plates and general commotion explodes out by the pool. From where I'm perched I can barely make it out but someone is sing-yelling my name: "Roooooon Buuuuuuurgundy! Yooooou are an imposterrrrr!" I think I've made it very clear I abhor violence of any kind but when it comes looking for me I sleuth out my chances and decide if I need to run away or stand my ground. "Roooooon Buuuuuurgundy! I knoooooow you're at this hoooooooteeeeel!" Almost more singing than yelling really. I stand, still uncertain if I'm going to take off or get ready for some boisterous action, but I've run out of time. Moving at me like a charging rhino is Hollywood legend and world-class singer Jim Nabors. I quickly sidestep his attack and give him a karate chop to the back of his head. Unfazed, he turns on me and swipes a bear-paw-sized fist at my head, which I fend off with my left (Jack Johnson, as you may recall). No time to lose! I bring Tom O'Leary from down below and come up strong on Nabors's chin. The big man hardly rocks back at all! Too much man there. I lay into him with some rabbit punches to his bread basket—nothing. Something like Thor's mighty hammer comes down on my head and I start to wobble. Jim Nabors, television's Gomer Pyle, is about to take me down. Time to get tricky. Like a boxer just trying to make it through a round, I dive at the big fella and grab on for dear life. I need to catch my breath—we dance like this for a few minutes. It starts to dawn on me that Nabors is enjoying the close contact with another man. He relaxes for a second and pow! Tom O'Leary right to the nut sack. Down goes Gomer in a Pyle! (Just too hard to resist. It's a chuckle for sure.) Once he's down I get into his mug. "Hey, what's the big idea?" He gives me a confused look for a second and then sheepishly admits, "Ahhh, someone said your hair was better'n mine and I got sore." Then he smiles and starts laughing. It's an infectious laughter so I start giggling too. Pretty soon we both are chuckling up a storm. We became friends. "Tanya Lambkin" invited the two of us up to her room along with Hawaiian lounge singer Don Ho. A lot of beef got passed around that night, if you know what I mean. Anyway, I thought I'd share that story about my hair.

OUR LADY QUEEN OF CHEWBACCA

If the town of Haggleworth, with its burning streets and ash heaps and high murder rate, was a grim place to grow up, no effort was made inside the walls of Our Lady Queen of Chewbacca High School to make us think otherwise. The hallways of the high school were some of the most dangerous thoroughfares in town. Grown men didn't like walking those halls. Because of the town's mining tradition, much of the school was dug underground. If you weren't careful, one wrong turn and you could get lost for days. Rumor had it that somewhere in the deep, past the teachers' lounge and further down into the subbasement, there was a Minotaur. It seems almost too mythological to believe but this Minotaur, which did in fact exist, came from the deepest recesses in the earth. Minotaurs are born of fire and anger. No man can kill one unless equipped with the arrow of Theseus. Ahhh, now I'm just listing Minotaur facts to show off! You got me! Anyway, there probably was a Minotaur in the basement of my high school but it's one of those unconfirmed facts. There were, however, some classrooms that kept a canary in a cage in the corner. The oxygen could get pretty thin on some days, and if that canary dropped it was an unorganized scramble to see who could get out alive.

Carrying my flute through the halls with my impossibly beautiful hair put a fat bull's-eye on my back from the beginning. I knew if I was going to make it through those four years I needed to find the toughest guy in school and show him I was not one to be trifled with. On my first day I went right up to Han Solonski, a big lump of a Pole, and I beat him within an inch of his life. The poor dumb lug didn't know what hit him. (It was a brick. I used a brick.) After that day no one dared bother me. I was number one. No one ever officially declared that I was number one, but I knew it. I had posters made. It was pretty obvious.

I can't say I was much of a student. The good sisters, bless their hearts, showed a lot of patience with me but it just didn't take. A word about the good sisters, and all nuns for that matter. I'm no Catholic; in fact I have an irrational and unexplainable dislike for the Catholics. They're a grubby bunch of sour sacks if you ask me, but even the Catholics I talk to hate nuns. I mean, you're always hearing about stone-faced old hags rapping kids on the knuckles for not paying attention or stern old maids pulling children through the halls by their ears. First of all, if any nun would have tried any kind of nonsense like that in Haggleworth they would have gotten socked in the puss. I would have been the first in line to do the socking. I've socked old ladies before and believe me, it's not pretty. But the nuns at Chewbacca who tried to put education in me were nothing like the repressed old maids we all think of when we think of nuns. No, I don't know why—maybe it was a papal order from the Vatican—but the nuns we got at Our Lady Queen of Chewbacca were very sweet and very, very gorgeous. The whole lot of them across the board could have been *Playboy* centerfolds for sure, but they gave their lives over to Jesus Christ. There were about twenty-five of them there in the high school and they ranged from age eighteen to twenty-two. Jesus was their lord and master, and what a lucky guy he was, because these ladies were absolutely stunning. Maybe God sent the very best to Haggleworth because it was so close to hell. Who knows? All of them were five foot seven inches tall and built like Raquel Welch, with legs that went on for days.

Of course, we never saw the nuns out of their habits and hats, except when they taught wrestling or during swim class, but other than those two hours every day they were as buttoned up as Eskimos in a snowstorm. I'm gonna admit it: When one of those nuns showered with us after wrestling practice there were more than a few boners on display. It wasn't very respectful of us but it was hard not to think of them as just ordinary women even though they had given over their lives to serve only Jesus Christ. Heck, we were all just boys with very little understanding of religious conviction. Lando Calrissian, the only African American (still getting used to saying it like that!), made a play for Sister Honeytits (I'm not making that name up. Why would I make that name up?) but that was the only instance I knew of such fiddling about. Lando was the star shooting guard for the Chewbacca Stormtroopers, so he was basically immune to punishment anyway. One of the sisters, Sister Vicky Vaginalicious (real name), did leave the faith and took up with my good buddy Wedge Antilles, but it was rare. These women respected the church too much to let carnal desire interfere with their calling.

Every year as part of a charity drive for the local hospital the nuns would do a fun pageant for the students and the parents. The students would make animal costumes and put on a show with singing and some kind of story. Most of the time I was a friendly raccoon or a squirrel and I showed off my flute playing. It was really a great night for the proud parents. Then the auditorium would start to fill up with mine workers and out-of-towners and we children would be asked to leave. The rest of the show was performed by the nuns, who would, for charitable reasons, strip off their habits for the night and, because they had sacrificed their lives to Christ, put on six-inch heels and colorful lingerie and do up their hair and look like real Italian movie stars! Most of them could have been Italian movie stars! Not one of them was less beautiful than Sophia Loren in her prime. Imagine twenty-five basically naked young women in lingerie and heels walking back and forth onstage in a wonderful show of faith and charity and religious servitude. If they weren't nuns you would have thought they were strippers! But of course they were nuns and no one could see them as anything else. For my own part, it was almost enough to make me a convert if my hatred of the Catholics had not been so irrational and visceral. Between the two shows we would sometimes get twenty to forty thousand dollars for the night in donations. The principal, Monsignor Morty Grossman, would sometimes have the sisters do the same "act," as he called it, up in Chicago, where they would make even more money! The kids were never invited to Chicago or Memphis or Kansas City but the monsignor would always tell us it was a huge success when he would roll back into town in his limo. I may not look back on Haggleworth with much fondness but whenever I see a nun, despite my almost limitless and completely unfounded hatred for Catholics, I do remember those sweet, innocent and, I'll say it, ridiculously sexy nuns at Our Lady Queen of Chewbacca.

Here's something you might not have known about me: I was a joiner in high school. Flag Folders Club, Glee Club, Drama Society, Taxidermy Society, Friends of Jazz, Society of Mineral and Rock Collectors, Jolly Jesters, United Socialist Party, Freudian Study Group—I did just about everything. I went out for all sports and I loved them all, but basketball was to me what horses are to twelve-year-old girls—some weird transferred sexual energy that really is more physically fulfilling than actual sex. Which is to say I just loved basketball. I did! I wasn't too good at it though. I was a brawler more than a player. "Five Fouls Burgundy" is what they called me. I got put into games for one reason and one reason only—to foul and to foul hard. I wanted guys on the opposing team to look across half court and worry about whether I was coming in the game. Sometimes opposing teams did their best to eliminate me way before game time, because if they didn't they knew I was going to come in and start throwing elbows. A team from the Quad Cities once tried to run me over in a parking lot a week before game time. If teammate Darth Blortsky wasn't there to push me out of the way I wouldn't be here today. Believe me, they ended up paying for their little prank on the court with some hard, hard, completely legal fouls. I got thrown out of the game that night! I was thrown out of every game, but not before I got my five in. I still hold the Iowa state record for most technicals in a season. Look it up.

We had a great team in '57: a big Swede named Swen Vader at center; a nimble power forward named Luke Walker; Brad Darklighter was our small forward; a lightning-fast little Italian, Vinny Cithreepio, ran the point; and Lando Calrissian shot the lights out as our number two. Obiwan Kanobi, an exchange student from Japan, was always good for six points as well. We won state that year but were later disqualified, as a lot of those guys had played semi-pro ball in Brazil; some of them were in their thirties. Nowadays people check that kind of stuff out, but back then we had a lot of thirty- and forty-year-old men posing as high school students. It was just something you did.

QUICK SIDE NOTE

Okay, here's something completely unrelated to this book but I'm not writing another word till I get this off my chest. It's literally paralyzed me. I can't work. I can't sleep. I can't do anything. My neighbor Richard Wellspar came over here last Wednesday and borrowed my leaf blower. It's a Craftsman, so you can't go wrong there. Anyway, I'm a good guy so I let him borrow it. I go back in the house and start writing again. I don't even think about it for two or three hours, but then I see Richard out in his driveway and yell over to him, "Did you get a chance to use that leaf blower?" To which he says, "No." If that's not weird enough, it gets weirder. He then proceeds to talk about his new clients instead of keeping the leaf blower conversation going. He's some kind of high-end pool sales- man and he's always talking about his customers as "clients." Okay, so I go back in the house but I'm kinda miffed. I'm thinking, "When is he going to use the frickin' leaf blower so I can get it back?" Sure enough, the whole day goes by and I don't hear the leaf blower—then the next day, same thing. Well, now I can't work. I'm just sitting in my living room in silence waiting to hear the leaf blower. The anticipation is unbearable. Why did he ask to borrow it if he's not going to use it? Several days go by and now here we are! He hasn't even used it. He borrowed it and never used it! It's not about the stupid leaf blower. I could go buy ten of them tomorrow! I'm doing very well thank you. I'm the kind of guy who will walk into a Sears and buy three suits, a vacuum cleaner and four new tires and think nothing of it! It's about integrity! Being a good neighbor. The social contract. Anyway, I simply had to get that off my chest and now back to the writing! Not another thought about it.

A FAMILY
OF ANCHORMEN

My father, Claude Burgundy, was a natural-born News Anchor, as was his father and his father before him. Of course there was no television or radio station in Haggleworth, Iowa. Instead, every Friday night he would set up a desk in the Tight Manhole, an Irish bar where the mine workers drank and sang songs of misery. The oil company paid him to report on all the charitable and civic-minded projects they had in the works as well as hard-hitting news stories happening in Haggleworth. Because of his honest face and gifted speaking voice, men and women would come in from all the other bars in Haggleworth—the Dirty Chute, the Mine Shaft, the

Rear End, the Suspect Opening, the Black Orifice, the Poop Chute, too many to list here—all to listen to *The Shell Oil Burgundy Hour*. In Haggleworth it was the most popular show on Fridays at ten P.M. for years. It consistently beat out *Dragnet* and Ernie Kovacs in the local ratings. He would report high school sports scores, weddings, divorces, births, who was diddling who, but mostly good news about the oil company and their interests. I would come and watch from the front row and be transfixed by his smooth delivery and sharp tailoring.

One day, the fire that continued to burn under Haggleworth leaped over into tunnel 8, the most profitable tunnel in the whole coal operation. Unlike the fire that occasionally shot up from the earth and burned cars or dogs, this fire was getting in the way of profit and had to be contained. Men were sent down into the shaft to try and stop the fire, but it was no use. Eleven men died. The whole town was in a somber mood when my father got up to deliver the news. "Good evening, I'm Claude Burgundy and this is how I see it." (That's how he started every *Burgundy Hour*.) The bar was quieter than usual as they hung on every word. "Today, the Shell Oil Company of Iowa announced a new plan to bring multicolored blinking lights to downtown Haggleworth for the upcoming holiday season." On a day when eleven miners had burned to death, and husbands and fathers of people sitting in that bar had died, the Christmas-light story was the lead. A woman in the back shouted something at my father. Another man called him a coward. He just sat there, taking insult after insult as he bravely continued on with a story about a precocious little dog that wore a hat around town that everyone loved. He reported a story about a planned two-hole golf course. There was an in-depth interview with a woman who had won second place at the state fair for her lemon bars. It was great news and slowly people began to smile. When he got to his sign-off ("And that's what happened this week in Haggleworth") they were sad to see him go and could hardly wait for the next week's news.

In a candid moment as we were walking home that night I asked my old man why he didn't talk about the eleven men who had died or the culpability of the oil company or the environmental impact of this new deadly fire or the emotional damage many deaths could have on a small community like ours or even the plain fact that without tunnel 8 most of the town would be out of work. "Ron, sometimes people don't want the truth. They just want the news." I'll never forget these sage words from my father. Up until that point I made no distinction between "truth" and "news." I had thought they were one and the same! I was a boy of course and the world was just a kaleidoscope of butterscotch candies and rum cookies. I didn't understand the reason for news until that day.

I knew from a very early age that I would be a News Anchorman. I had great hair, for one, which is 70 percent of the job. I also had the pipes. I was blessed with my father's golden tones and melodious speaking voice. By the time I left Our Lady Queen of Chewbacca High I could read a document out loud from forty feet away without ever stumbling over a word. A photograph from shortly after my graduation shows me looking much the same way I do now. In fact at age eighteen I looked exactly as I do today. Women found me irresistible.

They still do find me irresistible. It's worth mentioning but not so important to the narrative at this moment. I mention stuff like that not for vanity's sake but because it simply needs to be said.

It was all lining up perfectly. Every year the National News Association of Anchormen, NNAA, sends out over a thousand representatives to find fresh new anchorman talent across the land. Prospects are invited to a brutal six-day camp to test their mettle through grueling challenges and photo shoots. It's a make-or-break week for young anchormen. An anchorman scout traveling through Haggleworth noticed me in the eighth grade but was not allowed to talk to me until I graduated. (After it was discovered that Edward R. Murrow was paid illegally by CBS as a four-year-old without his parents' consent, new guidelines were put into place to protect children from getting money.) By the time I graduated several scouts were interested in me. I was invited to Williamsport, Pennsylvania, to the anchorman camp—the "Gauntlet," as it's known in news circles. The field that year was tough—my class alone had News Hall of Famers Peter Jennings, Ted Koppel and Jim Lehrer. Vance Bucksnot, who became the number one anchor for the Quad Cities, was there, as was Punch Wilcox, the legendary anchor for Salt Lake City's KPAL. There was also Snack Reynolds (Austin), Brunt Harrisly (Columbus), Tink Stewart (Butte), Race Bannon (Minneapolis), Hit Johnson (Albany), Kick Fronby (Charlotte), Ass Perkins (Mobile) and Lunk Brickman (Boston). All of these men distinguished themselves with long careers for their respective stations, so yeah, it was very competitive.

The main goal of the Gauntlet was to test if you had the avocados for anchorman work. Could you hold your liquor? Could you tell the difference between bespoke and off-the-rack suits? Could you seduce women through a camera lens? Test after test of skills. Could you turn your head sideways to other news team members when speaking? Could you manufacture a laugh after reading a lighthearted story? Could you muster a knowing, disapproving head shake after a story of sadness? On and on for two, sometimes two and a half hours a day! If it were not for the fun diversions to be had in Williamsport I would have gone crazy! But fortunately Williamsport, Pennsylvania, is one of the wildest places I know. The key parties alone—and this is way before they had caught on around the rest of the country—were almost too decadent. I'm just going to assume that most people who live in Williamsport, Pennsylvania, to this day moved there to engage in terrifyingly adventurous sexual activity. I mean, how else could you account for the reckless bacchanalia that happened in that town every night? As a small-town boy in a big city for the first time I was warned of some of the dangers, but no one prepared me for what went on in that town. Maybe it's because it's not on the main east-west highway, Interstate 80, or maybe because the town is sufficiently surrounded by vegetation, lending itself to an isolationist mentality. Whatever has caused the town to feel cut off from the rest of civilization has also ensured its disconnect from the laws of man. It is a town of pleasure-seeking animals only gratified by buttery foods and genital friction. It's a wonderful place to be for a week and provides great relief from stress, but if you lived there, as was borne out by the people I met, you were little more than a skin-wrapped blob of insatiable carnal urges. Many people in Williamsport, Pennsylvania, walk around town with their mouths open, their pants down and their dicks flopping around.

At the end of the week I had distinguished myself enough at the Gauntlet to receive six promising offers for News Anchor. I leapt at Tucson. In a real show of Burgundy independence I stole the family car and never looked back. Good-bye Haggleworth, Iowa, hello Tucson. The drive east was delicious. I drank up the scenery like a man freed from prison. Two straight days I drove until I overheard two truckers outside of Washington, DC, say that Tucson was in the West. I should have looked at a map but in those days they didn't have maps, so off I went to the West. I felt like a young Horatio Alger traveling west to make my fortune. A few days later I was in the middle of Florida and getting kind of frustrated. I sometimes wonder how long-haul truck drivers even do it. How do they get from one destination to the next without getting lost? The stars? Anyway, once I got straightened out of Florida I was on my way. I went through Alabama, then Mississippi, then Arkansas, then Missouri and back through Iowa, up through Minnesota into Canada and then back into North Dakota and South Dakota and over into Wyoming, down through Colorado and Utah and Nevada and up through Idaho and back into Wyoming and Montana and into Idaho and Washington, down through Oregon to California and over to Arizona and over to New Mexico, where I had one of those "hey, wait a minute" moments where I thought maybe I had gone right through Arizona, so I turned around. When I landed in Tucson I hadn't slept in three weeks, and I hadn't shaved or showered. My suit smelled like eggs and butt and was stiff from all the sweat and dirt I'd built up on the road. Big problem: I was due on the air in five minutes! It was my first time on camera . . . and I knocked it out of the park. The station got hundreds of calls claiming a caveman had just reported the news. I got a chuckle out of that one. I worked for that station for about half a year until I found out it was in Albuquerque and not Tucson, and then off I went again until, about a month later (it's like twenty thousand miles from Albuquerque to Tucson if you take the direct route through Maine), I finally arrived at my first real job as the nightly News Anchor for WKXM Tucson.

BREAKING HORSES
THE BURGUNDY WAY

I've owned many horses over the years. I've had racehorses, plow horses, trick horses—you name it, I've owned it. I once bought a whole herd of wild horses up in Wyoming from a man in a big cowboy hat. He had no right to them at all but I bought them. I guess you could say I was conned out of six hundred bucks in that case. You could definitely say that! Anyway, breaking a horse can be a challenging but rewarding experience. Through very long and patient study it's a skill that I have mastered through my ability to whisper to horses.

I start off by gently whispering in their ear, "My name is Ron Burgundy and I respect you, great and proud animal.

Your lineage from winged Pegasus on down to Trigger is well-known to all. I too am well-known. I am a very popular News Anchor and I do quite well with the ladies, if you know what I mean. What else . . . oh, here's something—you, sir, are a piece of shit and I own you. Did you hear me? I own you and you are basically my bitch. So you might as well stop dicking around, okay? I need you to stop dicking around, 'kay?" Remember, all this is whispered so gently in the horse's ear. I continue with "Know this: I represent one thing and one thing only to you, and that is death. You are living on this earth because I choose to let you live, so you better get your shit together fast or you will be dog food. Got it, friend? Good. Good horse." Horses respond in a myriad of ways but I find, like children, if you can break them down fast to a place where they are nervous and uncertain about everything, building them up is more fun. It doesn't always work but I would say I have about a 5 percent success rate.

For about a two-month period I rode a horse to work in San Diego. It was an ordeal. I would whisper stuff in that old gal's ear every day but she never quite got the point. Finally, the traffic and honking, the fast food and always being stuck inside my office took their toll. I ended up dumping her on my friend Mac Davis for a few bucks, and wouldn't you know it, that horse went on to win the Santa Anita Derby two years running and showed up in the movie *The Wild Bunch*! It was as if the horse had a new lease on life and made a conscious decision to enjoy each and every day. Horses, you just gotta love 'em!

MY NEIGHBOR AGAIN . . .

The Richard Wellspar ordeal continues. You'll remember that he's the deranged neighbor who "borrowed" my Craftsman leaf blower. We made eye contact as he was entering his house this evening. I just happened to be sitting in one of my dining room chairs on my front lawn very casual-like so he wouldn't suspect anything. He gets to his door, checks his mailbox and then turns his head and looks right at me! I give him a little wave and he nods his head. Nothing! Nothing about the leaf blower! I would laugh if it wasn't so serious. This is becoming a tragedy on an epic scale. I sat motionless for about an hour and then went back inside.

Anyway, Baxter and I have decided it's time to ratchet up the stakes in this game of chicken. Tonight I'm going to take my garbage can and unload the contents—old food and junk mail mostly—into his pool. Wish me luck!

ABOVE: The Burgundy family, 1942. We didn't have much but we had each other. Unfortunately we hated each other. The boy in the dress is my brother Horner. BELOW: Is it wrong to say I was a very sexy baby? I know I felt it. How could that be wrong?

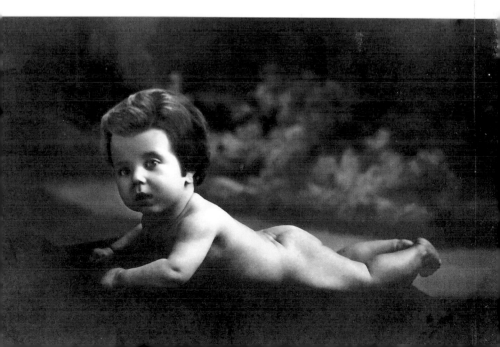

1958 graduating class of Our Lady Queen of Chewbacca High
School.

My first sweetheart, Jenny Haggleworth.

Me, Miles and Bird at Pinky's Inferno, 1952. Had I not found this photographic evidence I'm not sure people would have believed me. Whew.

Brokaw with a double-breasted suit! The guy had a knack for beating me to the punch.

At the top of my game with Barbara and Walter. They were tons of fun when they stopped talking.

Sir Humphrey. The greatest gamecock that ever entered a cockpit.

Lucretia. My finest broadsword.

THE BEST NEWS TEAM
OF ALL TIME

When I got to San Diego there was nothing. The station was a washed-up losing affiliate sharing space with a bakery. Rats walked across the floor in the middle of the day for no other reason than being bored. The station had no original programming to speak of and the news team consisted of an old lady who read the newswire and then made up stories. It was known all around San Diego that Channel 4 lied about the news every night. The lead story was often a story about the racetrack, because that's where the news team spent most of their time. There was no sports desk and no field reporting. The anchor was a man by the name of Chalk Munson. He was not a handsome man, nor was he well-spoken, nor could he hold his liquor. He barely made it through a broadcast without the aid of a four-letter word. He was beloved by no one in San Diego. When Ed Harken broke the news to him that he was getting fired he collapsed on the floor and started bawling—he had been praying for the day but thought it would never come. Every night, being forced to read the news was torture for him. He just assumed he would be doing it until he died. He frequently dreamed that he would be hit by a bus. It was his only escape he thought. I never met Chalk Munson but I do know that a large population of News Anchors feel trapped by their own chosen line of work. It's a lot of pressure to deliver the news night after night and some guys can't take it. Current newsman Wolf Blitzer hates his job and you can tell it every time he opens his mouth. Talking on camera for him is like one giant exhale, like he's trying to empty all his oxygen out of his body so he can die and free himself of the terrible pressure. Chris Wallace would rather live in a hobo camp than deliver the news, but he's up there, taking his lumps like a man. You can tell Brian Williams hates his job, but what's he going to do? He'd make a great pharmacist in my opinion. He should go to pharmacy school and bone up on drugs and get a job at CVS or Duane Reade. Being a News Anchor is not a job for the faint of heart. I took the job at Channel 4 because I recognized a challenge. That's me! I'm driven to be the very best.

The first order of business was the news team. Every one of the big stations was getting news teams in the sixties, and I knew we needed a great one. Ed Harken informed me that he too had been thinking about a news team and he was already looking for the guys to help me. I stopped him right there and told him I didn't want anyone but me putting together my team. We fought. No lie; we fought hard. Suits were ruined and coffeepots were broken, but in the end I won the fight. Little did he know I had already found one member of the team.

As it so happened I met Champ Kind my first week in San Diego. I came in from Denver on the bus and found a flophouse across from the station with rooms to let for one dollar a week. This was the early sixties, mind you, and San Diego has cleaned up its act since those rough-and-tumble days, but back then it was no place for honest Americans. I spent my first night out on the fire escape trying to stay cool in the midnight air, playing my flute as police sirens and gunshots went off all over town. It was a lonely time for me. After that first night I spent my evenings in some of the dirtiest lowdown bars in town. Bars with names like the Filthy Slug, the Rusty Axe, the Toothless Sailor. Tough guys and loose ladies drank themselves to death in places like these, and I felt right at home.

One night I was stumbling back to my cold-water flat when four thugs jumped me in an alley. It was a real boisterous scuffle. I got hit everywhere, in the head and neck and ribs, but I gave back as good as I got. I put three of them on the ground pretty quick but the fourth guy was a real tangler. We beat on each other for a good half hour, circling and striking like two spotted hyenas. When it started to look like there wasn't going to be a clear victor I yelled *uncle*. We both put our fists down and had a good hearty laugh. He introduced himself as Champ Kind. I could tell we were going to be fast friends right then and there. In a loveless town full of empty souls and desperate men, I had found my first buddy. We tore it up. Some of our bar fights are now part of San Diego legend. They are the only bar fights I know of that have been given names: "the Punch-'Em-Up of '66," "the Black-Eye Derby," "the San Diego Bone Bonanza" and many more. I will tell you this: Champ has no scruples whatsoever. He will kill a man, probably has, for no reason at all. Well, I asked Champ why he jumped me and he said he just likes to throw his fists around from time to time and get knocked about and punched, and then he yelled out, "Whammy!" and that was that. He said *whammy* way too much. Every time he finished a drink, "Whammy." Ordering a sandwich, "Whammy." He had sad whammies and happy whammies and sometimes he would throw a whammy into a sentence where it made absolutely no sense, like "This Texas barbecue whammy so delicious, whammy." It might have been Tourette's. A lot of doctors told me it was Tourette's. Whatever it was, it was pure gold on air. I asked him if he knew anything about sports and he said he didn't but that he knew how to read and get excited. Well, I brought him in to Ed Harken and we both agreed that the best sports announcers are the ones who know how to read and get excited. If you had a young Jewish kid or a Chinese kid or college kid good with statistics, they could write the copy, but you needed a big dumb American male to yell out the sports. Champ Kind was perfect. "Whammy" became a household word in San Diego. Several restaurants offered "the Whammy," which was nothing more than ham on white bread, but it sounded fun. The Padres had "Whammy Day" at the park, where the first five thousand got Champ Kind bobbleheads. Every year some poor soul was trampled but they still do it to this day. It's worth the trade-off. If you ever get a chance make sure to pick up a copy of Champ's self-penned autobiography, *Whammy!* It's not always the most fun read. There's more darkness than light for sure, but still, it lets you in on a fascinating life of ups and downs. I wouldn't read more than twenty pages at a clip. It can really darken your mood for the day. It's definitely too revealing but that's Champ.

The next step was finding a field reporter. I've known a few in my time. Geraldo Rivera comes to mind. He's probably the best there is behind Brian Fantana. Of course no one is smoother and more professional than Brian Fantana. In my opinion he is the very best. It takes a special man to hit the streets and investigate stories, interviewing people while also being on camera. It's no easy job and it demands a certain kind of sex appeal. Geraldo had it. Brian Fantana had it in spades! He hooked up with women every time he took a camera crew out of the building. His secret: Only go after the best! That's what his secret was. I sometimes questioned what he meant by "the best." I mean, he basically went after anything with tits. I think maybe he thought women, just women in general, all women, were "the best," but that translates on camera. You can see it in Geraldo too. You just know he's rolled around with some homely fatties for sure and I'll bet you he didn't love them any less for the fun. That was Fantana's approach as well. Women just liked him because he never judged.

Anyway, before we found Fantana, Champ Kind and I were inseparable. After work we hit the bars and then went home. We roomed up together in those early days to save on bills. A lot of nights we would invite some of the guys from around the station or over at the bus depot to watch some nudie flicks. Champ had boxes and boxes of eight-millimeter film strips with all kinds of romantic action going on. Well on one such occasion the whole lot of us were struck dumb by an actor in one of the films. It was a short ten-minute thing called *A Lonely Girl Calls Up for Room Service.* If you're over fifty you know how these films go. So when the room service guy comes into the room—even before the pants came off— we were all just staring at the most handsome man with the greatest face for film ever. We never even got to the sex part. There were about ten guys and one lesbian and a he-she in the room and we just kept going back to the point in the film strip where this handsome devil entered. We did it over and over again until it hit me: "This guy needs to be our new field reporter." Ed Harken was in the room and he says, "What if he's an idiot or can't read?" Champ wasn't convinced either: "Hold your horses, Ron, most of these films are made in Sweden. We can't hire a Swede!" Well, I was hooked. I didn't care what these guys said; I had to find this guy and make an offer even if it meant going to Sweden.

The box the film came in said JACK PEPPER PRODUCTIONS on it and with a little quick calling around I discovered a business by that name up in the San Fernando Valley area of Los

Angeles. Champ and I took the bus up there and several buses
to North Hollywood out in the Valley. It was hotter than shit,
that I do remember. Jack Pepper Productions was a house out
on Saticoy Street. Nothing fancy, just a little stucco prefab
deal. The kind you see all over Southern California if you're
not careful. Jack himself was in the back, by his pool, shooting
a movie. He didn't exactly welcome our intrusion but Champ
and I can be pretty persuasive with our fists. Pretty quickly
everyone making the movie took a ten-minute break while we
talked to Mr. Pepper. We showed him the film. He confessed
it was one of his but he had no idea where the actor was. His
name at the time of shooting the movie was Cyrus Court. Pepper was quick to tell us that these guys changed their names
faster than Esther Williams changed costumes in *Million Dollar Mermaid*. Well, that's what he said. It's not like I'm making
any of this up. He went on to say, "Cyrus Court could be any
number of guys out there, Tony Oakland, Wayne Duke, Kevin
Dangle and a lot more. The plain truth is most of these guys
end up on Hollywood Boulevard hustling for tricks." Well,
it was a pretty sad picture really. Here we thought this guy,
Cyrus Court, had it made being in the movie business and
having sex and all but Jack Pepper painted a different picture. Pepper's world was one of broken homes, drug use and
loose morals. We went back outside by the pool to watch some
filming but sitting there in the 110-degree heat, watching two
people have sex like that, took all the spirituality out of it for
me. It was as close as I've ever come to understanding what ex-
istentialism means. I lost sight of whatever theological center
there is that holds us together, however loosely, while watch-

ing two very beautiful people with perfect anatomies go at it like dogs. In his defense Champ Kind turned to me and said quite simply, "Let's go, Ron. This ain't love."

We gave up on finding the actor in the film. If Pepper was right the kid was probably one pill short of an overdose, if not already dead. Before heading back to San Diego we decided to take in some music along the Sunset Strip. It was the midsixties and the Strip was where it was happening. We must have looked like a couple of old fuddy-duddies at the Whisky a Go Go but we paid our five bucks to see Johnny Rivers and forget our troubles. I don't have much use for long-haired people and man, there were a lot of them in the Whisky that night. The band that opened for Johnny Rivers was called the Practical Figs. They came out dressed in eighteenth-century garb with some guitars and started making noise—a lot of noise, really too much noise. Champ got disoriented and started swinging his arms around hoping to hit someone. I started yelling and then singing and then yelling. It was a crazy mess! If that's rock and roll then no thanks! They were barely into their first "number" when I grabbed Champ and said, "There he is!" It was Cyrus Court or Tony Oakland or whoever he was—the guy from the film up onstage as the lead "singer" of this "band." Champ rushed the stage and tackled him right away. It was the wrong thing to do and we acknowledged that. We did a bad thing. The crowd of hippies and drug addicts pounced on us and called us "the fuzz" and "narcs" and "Dad"—hurtful stuff, really, since we were none of those things. I might have been a dad but I certainly didn't know it. Anyway when the melee was over and the cops had gone I got a chance to talk to Tony Oakland. Right out of the gate he told me his name was Lance Poole. It wasn't his real name but the name he'd had for the last two months fronting the Practical Figs. He did the porn thing and scraped up enough dough to get through UCLA as a journalism major. The whole rock thing was a goof—just good college-guy fun and a great way to score chicks. I had him! I told him about the gig down in San Diego, where he could not only use his journalism degree but he could score all the chicks he wanted. He was looking to get out of that scene anyway and he agreed to give it a try for a few weeks. A few weeks became thirty years in the news game—eight Peabody Awards, a Mr. San Diego Award, six day-time Emmys, and a *Playgirl* spread. His real name was Brian Fantanofskavitch, which sounded too commie for comfort, so we changed it to Fantana and the rest is history. Ratings at the station went up the very moment he came on camera. Women wrote in to the station to complain they were having spontaneous and uncontrolled orgasms when he spoke. It was a real problem. For about a three-year period from '72 to '75 the news van was nothing more than a traveling bedroom for Fantana. We did way too many breaking stories from the suburbs. Real news might have been happening downtown or over at the harbor but Fantana liked trolling the suburbs for bored housewives. I would lead in with a line like "And Brian Fantana with a special report on crime in the suburbs" or maybe "Backyard barbecues, are they safe? Brian Fantana weighs in!" I mean, there were nights when I would throw to him with nothing and he'd make up a story standing outside a house he'd just come from. "Ron, I'm standing here on the corner of Mountain View and Grove, the virtual epicenter of a frightening new trend in exercising called 'jogging.'" Back at the station we had a hard time keeping a straight face. We knew what Fantana was up to. We supported it. It was good for ratings and frankly speaking it was good news. Veronica Corningstone, my wife and massage partner, ruined all that fun male stuff for us—in a good way of course.

The last member of the news team was our weatherman. We knew to really put us over the top we needed a great weatherman. It wasn't going to be easy. A team is about chemistry and a bad weatherman can ruin the mix. I've seen it happen before. A weatherman named Len Front was added to the number one Channel 2 news team in Denver back in '68. The team had been number one for at least ten years. Their longtime weatherman, Jerk Watson, was hit by lightning, which burned a red and blue mark across his face, making him virtually impossible to look at. I'm not going to hide my feelings when I say I never could forgive David Bowie for stealing the only thing Jerk had left, his red and blue streak, for his *Aladdin Sane* record. People would see poor Jerk Watson on the street where he sold wind-up toys and tease him about the terrible David Bowie impression. Jerk Watson was the first person with a red and blue streak through his face and he never saw a dime for it. Anyway, Len Front replaced him; the chemistry was wrong and the station dropped in the ratings faster than the Octomom drops babies. (NOTE TO SELF: Is there a better line for that? Probably not but give it some thought. Maybe put a clock on it. If you can't get a better line in three hours, then just leave it. It's really extremely funny but maybe a little too hip.) It wasn't Len Front's fault that the ratings dropped. He went on to become one of the great weathermen of all time over in Laramie but the chemistry was off in Denver and it tanked the whole operation. I don't think the importance can be overstated: If a news team makes a mistake in its weatherman they might as well change their names and leave the country or face the consequences of a life of shame.

We canvassed the country for just the right guy. He had to know meteorology. He had to be nice—a little too nice and too happy. He had to be clean. Most important, he had to come across like a simpleton or a village idiot. A lot of guys came into the station, mostly overweight guys who had clowning skills and useless meteorology degrees from tech institutes and third-tier colleges. Guys with names like "Hap" and "Doc" and "Cappy" came through the door but none of them had the mettle for the kind of team I was putting together. I think we looked at well over a thousand laughing idiots. We were just about to give up when it hit me—we needed to be active in the search. Where do weather guys come from? How can you spot one? We all got in a room and came up with a scientific list of what to look for.

THE PERFECT WEATHERMAN

Must be nice.
Should carry lunch in a kid's lunch box.
Should live with mother.
Remembers the birthday of everyone he's met.

Listens to transistor radio at bus stop.

Likes watching softball games in park.

Enjoys petting rabbits.

Has rigid daily routine.

Should smile too much.

Will try any food.

Cannot resist waiting in lines.

Only has tighty-whitey underwear.

Buys shoes from nursing supply store.

Is best friends with old people.

Must have name tags sewn into his clothes with address and phone number in case of an emergency.

Someone in the room then asked about meteorological understanding but I said no. It was important but not vital, not like these other qualities on the list. A guy could be whip-smart with meteorology skills but what's that got to do with being a weatherman? It's a little like saying a smart news reporter makes a great anchorman. Let's also consider the very real possibility that meteorology is nothing less than wizardry handed down to us from Arthurian times. Was Merlin the first weatherman? I don't think there's enough evidence to point to the contrary. If that's the case, then we have to assume that anyone who studies meteorology is really a wizard. I don't know about you but I think having a wizard on staff is not very professional. Is it neat? Of course it's way cool, but is it safe? Wizards are notorious for meddling in affairs they should not meddle in—using potions and spells in harmful ways and just generally engaging in mischief. In my opinion the safety issue outweighs the cool benefits of having a wizard around. I struck meteorology off the list and we went looking for our man.

The guys spread out, going to city parks, drinking fountains, bus stops, places where there were ducks—no stone was left unturned. Champ brought back a guy who on the surface looked pretty good, but when he was fully vetted it was discovered he had been working in a petroleum refinery and had been exposed to way too many gas leaks. Ed Harken found a timid-looking fortysomething man feeding bread crumbs to ducks out of an Aquaman lunch box but every time he tried to approach him the guy ran away like a scared deer. Brian just took off looking for tail and wasn't much help at all.

Turns out lady luck was with me again. She has always favored Ron Burgundy and I have honored her with many burning sacrifices. I found Brick Tamland sitting on a park bench listening to a baseball game through a tiny transistor radio. I knew he was our guy from the moment I saw him. I asked him about the game and lo and behold, he produced a turtle from his pocket and told me his name was "Turtle." The rest of the conversation went something like this:

Brick
I have a head and feet too.

Me
What's that?

Brick
I am inside my head and outside my head.

Me

My name is Ron Burgundy.

Brick

My name is name.

Me

I'm a News Anchor.

Brick

I know one thing for sure. . . .

Me

What's that?

Brick

It's a funny sunny funny day.

Truer words have never been spoken. In fact, since the very first days on record, there never has been anything but a sunny day in San Diego. Every day in San Diego is exactly the same as the day before. Here was the perfect guy. When I asked him where he lived his first response was to point at me and yell, "Stranger! Danger!" But when he saw I wasn't going anywhere he checked inside his elastic underwear band and read where it said "Brick Tamland, 410 Meadow Lane, San Diego, California, USA."

The man was a natural. He stood in front of a map and smiled and told everyone that today was sunny and tomorrow was also going to be sunny. He did fun segments with elementary school kids and old people. He went to petting zoos and raffled weather maps for charity, and every day he did the birthday list off the top of his head. Was he mentally challenged? Sure. Did we know it then? Of course not. We had mentally challenged people playing football, working in aviation, appointed secretary of agriculture. Mentally challenged folks taught high school shop, made excellent nurses and wrote television shows. It was a simpler time. Have we progressed since then? It's a good question. Brick Tamland is my friend and he's a retard.

With Brick in place we had it. We had the entire news team. Our domination in the San Diego area went unchecked for years. We were beyond legendary. We were gods. No statement of fact has ever been more factual than this one: We were the best news team that ever lived.

THE NIGHT I MADE LOVE TO BRUCE LEE

Here's a quick story that I just have to tell. In 1973 martial arts champion and actor Bruce Lee came to San Diego to promote his new film, *Enter the Dragon*. I've always been a fan of the martial arts. I love the kicking and the flipping and the hitting. It really gets the heart pumping. I can't say I've mastered martial arts. I've taken karate classes and I do have a green belt. The problem for me is if I get into a fight I tend to improvise a lot. The karate goes out the window and I end up throwing O'Leary and Johnson around like a drunken idiot. I wish I were a karate expert like Bruce Lee. Sometimes I imagine myself in a situation with a briefcase full of important top secret documents and seven Asian guys have surrounded me in an attempt to steal the briefcase. I then pretend that I must fight them off using martial arts. I usually win, but not always.

I was a little nervous about meeting Bruce Lee because I am such a fan. His nunchuk work alone is simply legendary. Nunchuks, or "nunchaku," as the Chinese call them, are two sticks connected by a chain and used as a weapon in martial arts. If I'm in a room with nunchuks you might as well forget it. It's like putting down a plate of peanut butter cookies, I cannot resist picking them up. I will invariably grab those nunchuks and start flipping them around, whirling them through the air and within seconds my whole face is bruised and bleeding. I can't work 'em. I just can't. Don't even let me hold them. I will start swinging them all over the place and bonk. "Bonk" is the wrong word. You can't get taken to the hospital when you are "bonked." It's like a team of horses has trampled me.

So I go to meet Bruce Lee in the lobby of the Hilton in downtown San Diego. Sure enough, as soon as I'm seated across from him for an interview I notice the nunchuks. I remember reaching for them. I remember Bruce Lee smiling at me and the next thing I know I'm lying in a room at the Hilton with welts on my face. Those darn nunchuks! Apparently I hit myself five or six times in the head and then went down. Bruce Lee, the perfect gentleman, suggested I be taken to his

room until I came to. When I finally regained consciousness
it was well into the evening and frankly I was a little embar-
rassed to be lying in bed in his hotel room. It's not important
to say it at all but the Hilton has the finest bedding, the best
thread count and firmest pillows of any of the hotel chains.
Oh, and the service is excellent.

When I came to, Mr. Lee was washing my feet in the tradition of a Japanese samurai warrior. It's traditional for the
samurai to sponge the feet of honored visitors. I noticed that
all my clothes had been removed. Mr. Lee was also naked—in
the tradition of the samurai warrior. Humility, respect and
hospitality are some of the traits of a true samurai along with
courage, quickness and strength. Their ability to move gently and stay secretive, striking at the opportune moment, is a
result of hours and hours of disciplined study. I respect these
ancient Japanese warriors and their customs so when Mr. Lee
explained to me in his broken, frankly awful English that he
needed to make love to me, I understood the cultural significance. Historians tell us that the samurai warriors would seek
out village men for a night of lovemaking before heading into
battle. It was a great honor to be chosen thusly. I didn't know
this historical fact at the time but Mr. Lee explained this to
be the case. I pointed out that he was Chinese not Japanese
but he brushed this aside saying it didn't really matter. Our
eyes locked. He was, without a doubt, a beautiful man. The
musculature alone was something to behold but the eyes were
where he got you. Those dark pools were just too enchanting,
like two warm baths, you could not but be enticed to take a

dip. There was a part of me that wanted to look away but I knew that would be a sign of great disrespect.

The lovemaking was lightning quick, like his fighting style. His efficiency and flexibility were stunning. There were hands and feet all over the place. With all the biting and scratching it was like wrestling with three hairless wolves. Keep in mind this was 1973 and long before homosexuality was invented. I've made my stance pretty clear on how I feel about that and how I'm A-OK with the whole business but this had very little to do with anything of that nature—this was two warriors going at it with great respect and admiration for ancient traditions. Was there tenderness? Of course there was. Was it sexually gratifying? Yes. Did fingers find their way into places reserved for baser functions? You bet. But all of it happened in the fraternal spirit of male bonding, just like in olden times when men did stuff like that all the time. It was very manly.

When it was over we both felt the triumph of having worshipped at the altar of heroes. We were two proud warriors: he, the ancient Chinese samurai, and I, like some noble Greek champion of yore. We enjoyed a couple of cigarettes and lay next to each other in the quiet peace of a job well done. We were just a couple of guys.

As I left the room that morning he turned to me and said in his terrible English, "Mr. Burgundy, we like golden boat in river that have no current."

"Huh?" I said.

"My feewings to you are like night bird afwaid of light."

"You feel for me like a bat? Okay. See you."

I walked out never to see him again. He was to pass away two weeks later in Hong Kong. I miss Bruce Lee—he was a great fighter, a decent actor and a great lover. Anyway, that story gets told at least once a day, sometimes twice, to just about anyone I meet.

MY LOVE FOR THIS COUNTRY

I don't often talk about it because I don't like to brag but I am a real patriot. It's a pretty controversial opinion, I know, but I love the United States of America and I'm not afraid to say it. There was a time, from about 1967 to 1974, when I would make phone calls to people I didn't know all across this land and tell them that I loved the United States. Imagine you're sitting in your home, lying in bed or in the kitchen enjoying a meal, and the phone rings. Now imagine picking up that phone and the first thing you hear is "I love the United States." It must have been great. My phone bills were through the roof! I didn't care. It was my way of giving back. Some guys went off to war, some gave to charities and still others had red, white and blue belts. I called people at any hour of the night in cities all across this nation to let them know how I feel.

If you don't love this country you need to go and spend a half an hour in Canada or Mexico. Here's two countries, literally right next to us, that really blew it. I get down to Mexico from time to time. San Diego is a just a short way from the border and it can be a fun day to drive down, hit Tijuana, take in a show, maybe watch a bullfight, and eat some tacos. I'll usually also have a drink or two. Here's what always happens. After the show or the bullfight I'll have a couple more drinks. Well, that just about does it. The rest of the night is a circus blur of colorful piñatas and distorted toothless laughter. I don't know how it happens but somehow, after the bullfight or the show, I get drugged. It happens every time. Some sneaky Mexican puts something in my drink and good-bye, Ron Burgundy. How long am I out? Sometimes weeks. Ed Harken, my good friend and station manager at Channel 4, sent a team of navy SEALs into Mexico one time to see if he could find me. In the end they did find me but what they found was a surprise to all, including myself. I wasn't even Ron Burgundy. My name was Señor Big Jones and I was the mayor of a fishing village on the Baja Peninsula. I had been mayor for almost a month, establishing new literacy programs and public works projects, giving the town a real sense of pride. I worked like the devil, pushing through important legislation not just for well-heeled residents, of which there were none, but for the simple man in the street. I think I could have easily won a second term—I had plans for a new light rail transit system—but Ed had me airlifted back to San Diego and the town fell back into the hands of the shitbird who ran it before. Maria, my wife during this period (go figure!), tells me that the Big Jones Library still stands, with one of the finest collections of original incunabula in the world, including two complete copies of the Gutenberg Bible, whatever the heck that is. Oh well, I have been known to do some pretty dumb stuff when I'm on a bender.

In general, and this is only part of the problem with the country, Mexico is not a place to go on a bender. Apart from my colorful time as a mayor and the year I was a hill bandit, the usual Mexican bender ended with me in jail. Traditionally I'd wake up and some squat *polistero* (Spanish for "policeman") would be pointing his pudgy Mexican finger in my face yelling something about me throwing punches. I don't doubt it. I have thrown a lot of punches in Mexico. When you get the whole news team down there, Brian, Champ and Brick, you are talking about a human tornado of irresponsible fists. We don't go looking for fights, but gosh darn it, those Mexican guys down there can't take criticism. I mean, you open your mouth about how their food smells, or how they speak American worse than children, or how there isn't one of them with blond hair—reasonable and fair criticism—and they just go crazy! Do I love Mayan art? Yes. Do I love Cortés? Yes. Do I love Herb Alpert and the Tijuana Brass? Of course I do. I love the Mexican peoples but they can be a proud, fiery race. One theory, which I believe will one day be taken as fact, explaining why their passion often outstrips their reason is related to brain size. Due to a bean diet and other environmental factors, like their proximity to the sun and its powerful shrinking rays, their brains are just not that big. Has this theory been proven? No, but sometimes it's not prudent to wait for all the facts to come in. You have to quickly sign up for a theory so you can say, "I was there first."

There are many great things about Mexico. If it wasn't a huge waste of time a guy could write a whole book about Mexico. They got history. I mean, somebody made those pyramids, right? (I'm revealing stuff I said I never would, so I would prefer it if you read this next sentence after I'm dead. Those pyramids were built by aliens. That's a fact. The pyramids in Egypt were built by the British in the seventeenth century and the pyramids in Vegas were built by my good friend Steve Wynn. These are all facts. They are disputable for sure but facts just the same.) Mexico is very rich with history. If I were to write such a book, a gigantic waste of my time mind you, but if I were to write it I would bind it in sumptuous Corinthian leather and illustrate it with paintings by my very best friend, LeRoy Neiman. The book would weigh at least twenty-five pounds and would make a great addition to any fine library, and if you're into pressing flowers between the pages of books this would be the one. I have a book of poems by Henry Wadsworth Longfellow, the undisputed champion of American poetry, that I purchased in an old curio shop called B. Dalton for thirty-six dollars with beautiful etched illustrations and golden pages bound in the most expensive absolutely real leather available. It's probably a first edition and I own it. I make sure people see it and talk about it when they come in my house. You can't miss it. The display case I built for it makes it impossible to open the front door all the way but it's worth it. I'm sure this Mr. B. Dalton is pretty steamed I walked off with a first-edition Longfellow, our greatest poet, for thirty-six bucks! Guess what? He's not getting it back! Anyway, if I was to write a history of Mexico, meaning if I was willing to take time away from picking my nose or watching *Jeopardy!* or sitting on the toilet, it would be that kind of book—a big luxurious book with old-timey Spanish-style letters. I would call the book *The Fabulous Fables and Rich Tales of Olden Mexico and Its Regal Peoples.* I would like to see that title written in gold! I'm beginning to think I may just write this book. I bet everyone in Mexico would appreciate it—to have a book written specifically about you by a legitimately important American! Who wouldn't want that? The Mexicans may not deserve such a book but I'm going to give it some serious thought. Can you imagine waking up one morning in that godforsaken, dust-blown country and then hearing that Ron Burgundy has taken the time to write a book all about you and your land? Incredible. It would be incredible. I'm going to do it.

The fact is the United States of America is better than Mexico not for all the reasons above but for this simple fact: The Mexican people are THE most self-centered people I know. Here's a little test I throw at your average Mexican. I have five questions locked and loaded that I will spring on them just to prove my theory from time to time.

Question 1. Who signed the Declaration of Independence first?

Question 2. How many original colonies were there?

Question 3. Name three Hostess baked-good products.

Question 4. Order these five cities by population, highest to lowest: Toledo, Mobile, St. Paul, Salt Lake City, Orlando.

Question 5. Sing the national anthem.

As you can see, no tricks here, just plain simple questions anybody on this green earth should be able to answer, especially Mexicans. Notice I don't just ask culturally specific questions. These are questions to which everyone in the world knows the answer. Of course in this country children can answer these questions! In Mexico hardly anybody knows the answers. Who doesn't know the original colonies? Who can't say three Hostess products? Cupcakes! Twinkies! Ho Hos! Easy! It's not like I'm asking some poor Mexican guy off the street to recite the Constitution. Heck, *I* can't even do that. But really? You grow up a few miles from the greatest country in history and you don't even know "The Star-Spangled Banner"? That's either stupidity or willful ignorance. I go back and forth on this one. I used to only believe it was willful ignorance, which got me into a lot of fights and a lot of jail time. Now I see the Mexican as a simple man without much capacity for learning. It goes back to my theory on brain size. In some ways I feel sorry for him. As a great nation we should do something, but what? What can you really do if the people themselves don't want to learn American history so they can better themselves? What can you do! It's terribly frustrating! Goddamn it, I just threw my typewriter out the window! It gets me so frustrated though. You're not going to believe this; I threw another typewriter out the window. That's two that have flown through the air while I've been writing about Mexico. I gotta cool down. Typewriters are heavy and could cause a lot of damage down below. I took a shower. I shouldn't get so worked up. Anyway, I challenge you to find a nation wallowing in its own stupid patriotic pride more than the Mexican nation. Everywhere you go idiots are waving flags and bragging about how great they are. Okay, if you're so great, how is it you can't even sing the national anthem? Grrrrrr! Hard to believe but I threw out my last typewriter. Luckily Sears was open, where I have a card, and I was able to purchase THEIR last typewriter. No more writing about Mexico!

Canada is a whole different ball of wax. Imagine sitting in an airport lobby for three days. The only food you can eat is raw potatoes and water. The whole time you're being forced to listen to babies crying and the hits of Sha Na Na. Also there are no bathrooms. This is the kind of insufferable boredom one feels the moment you enter Canada. Your whole body begins to physically decay. The spiritual life drains out of you. Suicide constantly enters your thoughts. Being awake in Canada offers nothing more than watching the sands of your own mortality pass through the hourglass until it is empty. There is nothing to be hopeful about. There is no projection of something better, only existence in the rawest form.

A Canadian might tell you he is happy. Don't be fooled. He is living within a sickening paradigm that defines happiness as joyless existing devoid of those qualities that make us human. Almost any Canadian you meet in our country and who has been out of Canada for a while can tell you that he now lives in a magical land. That's why so many of the Canadians you meet in this country are so creative and pleasant. They have escaped a prison worse than any concentration camp ever constructed.

I've done news stories in Canada. I don't like to go there but sometimes duty calls. Within about five minutes of entering the country I start having suicidal thoughts. The prospect of death seems like a better alternative than being in Toronto or Vancouver. I usually start drinking, which is what the whole country does. They make their beer with a higher alcohol content so they can numb out the pain faster. Most of them don't drink beer though. Most of them drink gasoline. The Indians around Medicine Hat drink turpentine thickened with rat poison every night hoping they won't wake up in Canada the next day. Go there. You'll see. Of course, drinking is a two-edged sword. It can lead to great sadness. Combine that sadness with the naturally depressed state of everyday living in Canada and you will want to lie down on a railroad track. I have done this. I was covering the winter Olympic Games in Calgary. I was trying everything in the book to stay positive. I made sure I had friends around. I packed a pamphlet of daily affirmations, along with puzzles and games. I played flute every morning. I hung out in the ski lodge by the fire and read children's books to Baxter. But it was no use.

Slowly Canada worked its way into my bones. I lost focus. I was told to cover the women's biathlon, normally a very exciting sport with skiing AND rifle shooting and women, but I became more and more aware I was standing in Canada. My stomach became heavy, like I had eaten mud. My shoulders stooped. I lost any bounce to my step as I trudged through the snow. Life lost all meaning until a light of hope guided me. I followed the light, a beautiful blue ray, for what seemed like days. The light sang to me. It sounded like the voices of Karen Carpenter, Debby Boone and Olivia Newton-John combined into one welcoming, nurturing symphony. I was in a near-blissful trance and when I saw where it had led me I was euphoric. It was a railroad track. My escape from Canada was only a nap away. I lay down and fell asleep. Luckily for me a big Swede came along. The Swedish people have a great capacity for boredom. Although they are not boring themselves, they can withstand boring situations and boring people with great skill. The Swede took me to a McDonald's, where I was nursed back to believing I was in America. I stayed in the confines of those golden arches for a full week before I even had the courage to step out into Canada again. In the hundred or so steps I took to the helicopter that was waiting to take me to the United States and safety, I contemplated strangling myself.

Again, I don't want to disparage any Canadians here. Outside of their own country they can be simply delightful. I've met some very playful ones. I do however keep my guard up. If someone is introduced to me as a Canadian I instinctively fortify myself for the torrent of soul-crushing boredom to come plunging out of their mouth. I even cover my ears if I suspect them of not having been properly Americanized. I once had to interview singer-songwriter Joni Mitchell. She's from Canada. I very was hip to the new music scene and she was a real up-and-comer. Here's a transcript of the interview. Notice how quickly my mood changes.

Ron

So tell me about this new brand of folk and rock.

Joni Mitchell

You know, it's hard to put a label on it.

Ron

Uh-hum.

Joni Mitchell

I think a lot of us, those of us who came out of the Trou-badour up in L.A., consider ourselves songwriters first.

Ron

Uh . . .

Joni Mitchell

My good friend Carole King started out as just that—a songwriter. She really didn't have ambitions beyond that.

Ron

Please stop.

Joni Mitchell

I'm sorry.

Ron

I'm trying. It's hard. So . . . go on. What else?

Joni Mitchell

Are you okay?

Ron

No. No I'm not okay. You are boring the shit out of me. Every word coming out of your mouth is like another pillow to my face, suffocating me to a cold mute death. STOP IT, RON! BE PROFESSIONAL! What's it like being a singer?

Joni Mitchell

I'm confused.

Ron

Answer the question! NO, DON'T! Pleeeeease don't answer the question. Come on, Ron! Be a professional. Whatsitlikebeingasinger?

Joni Mitchell

Um, well. I enjoy the intimacy of performance.

Ron

Stop it! I know what you're doing. You're trying to kill me. This woman is from Canada! WE HAD A RULE. WE HAD A RULE, DAMN IT! I CANNOT TAKE IT!

Joni Mitchell

What's going on? Should I sing something from my new album, *Clouds*?

Ron

**Lady. If you sing one note in this studio I will hang myself
from the lights. Did you hear me? I will step up on this
news desk, undo my tie and hang myself from the lights!**

What a laugh! Thankfully Joni Mitchell moved to the U.S.
and settled with us here in Southern California, where she
became more American and less Canadian. Her unorthodox
chord changes and haunting voice frequently can be heard
coming forth from the cassette deck I have in my bedroom.
I've almost forgotten she is Canadian. No, I would say across
the board when I was challenged with an interview of a Canadian talent, be it world-famous writer Margaret Atwood,
funnyman Rich Little or rock musician Neil Young, I ended
the interview always threatening to kill myself.

What is so surprising about this is that Canada, except for
being colder and maybe having more pine trees and lakes,
is basically the same, geologically speaking, as Minnesota
or Michigan. It really should be as exciting and prideful as
America. It just isn't. I mean, both Mexicans and Canadians
can express pride in their respective countries but it's a false
pride. It's like the kind of pride someone has in being a loser
or an artist instead of a businessman. Everyone knows you
wanted to be a businessman but then you became an artist.
You have no choice but to take pride in it. That's just not the
case with our great country. We are number one. We take
great, truthful and honest pride in being number one.

Sometimes when I'm driving the freeways of San Diego I

will put on my national anthem tape. It has no words, just the music. I had the tape made for the day when I would be asked to sing the anthem before a World Series game. It hasn't happened yet, some sort of mix-up I'm sure, but when it does I will be ready. However, I've listened to our beautiful anthem thousands of times and I must say I've never liked the words. I've never felt they captured the true feeling of how much I love this country. Over the years I've played around with my own lyrics and I must say, should I ever get the chance to do the national anthem at a World Series, or anywhere for that matter, I would probably do my own new and better words. I almost hesitate to share it with you now because I just know it will get ripped off and then IT will become the new national anthem and I won't see a dime. Not that I'm in it for money, but you know.

My New National Anthem (To the tune of the old one. I'm very happy with the old tune.)

This is a great land,
with awesome majesty.
Nobody does it better
over land or even sea.
It's got all the right moves
for being the best.
You've got the cities in the East
and the mountains in the West.

The women here are gorgeous.

Not all of them but many.

It's got a lot of class,

from the dollar to the penny.

So make mine a double

and drinks are on the house.

For those who love their country

I am buying the next round.

Needless to say I'm pretty proud of this baby. It was a struggle but all poetry is pain sayeth the bard, right? I tend to get poetic when waxing on about my country. My love for the country knows no bounds. This land has given birth to the blues down in the deep delta, jazz born out of the struggles of the Irish immigrants who settled in Chicago, the hot dog, the old Mississippi rolling through the vast plains of Kansas and on down to Louisiana. America is the birthplace of Mark Twain, Oscar Wilde, Humphrey Bogart, the Dust Bowl, the Hollywood Bowl, the Super Bowl. Oh, greatest country! I love thee and thine thick pine forests and thundering trout streams. I love yine valleys wet with dew and sunshine, yine golden meadows glowing in light. Oh, Americans! What hath we if not heaven right here? 'Tis ours, this emerald isle, this blessed plot, this earth, this realm, this America! I care not for vainglorious arrows that sling at me, nor do I care wenst they came. I am impervious to all mettlesome darts and such. I am an American. My name is Ron Burgundy and that, my good friends, is an American name.

WHAT'S WRONG
WITH AMERICA?

Okay, so you know my feelings for this country I call home.
It is the second-finest country in all of the Americas. However,
just because I love this land with more fierce love than my
love for Veronica Corningstone, my wife, it does not mean I
cannot be critical. For example, I'm in love with myself but it
doesn't stop me from occasionally staring into my thirty-foot
floor-to-ceiling mirror and saying to myself, "Ron, you could
lose a few pounds." Criticism is a form of self-love the way I see
it. We live in troubling times when criticism is seen as unpatriotic. There are a lot of red-faced blockheaded anchormen out
there calling themselves newsmen who wrap themselves in

patriot colors to hide the fact that they cannot handle reasonable adult criticism. This is an alarming trend the way I see it. The job of an anchorman is not to lecture the viewers on patriotism but to read the teleprompter as soberly as possible and let them decide what is right or wrong. To be honest you can really stretch the limits of sobriety and still achieve this goal. I've always had a nip or two before I go on. I usually have a few during the broadcast. My whole team enjoys drinking throughout the day. When I was at Channel 4, Ed Harken, the station manager, would have loud screaming meetings about being "over budget." People would pound their fists and raise their voices and stand on chairs and throw typewriters. It was a real sight but no one could ever figure out where the money went. Was it suits? Was it hair and makeup? Massage chairs? Fireworks? Archery equipment? Then one day some bold intern from Stanford University yells out, "It's the booze." Sure enough, over half our monthly budget was going to alcohol! That intern was fired immediately and I hope never works in news again. My point being, it doesn't take much to get the job right. Anyway, I will venture some well-thought-out criticism of this country and hope to God you idiots don't accuse me of being unpatriotic.

Our babies have gotten uglier. I don't know why this is but you can't deny it's happening. Is it inbreeding? Is it high levels of newfangled foodstuffs like yogurt and lettuce? Who knows? There is just no answer out there, but look around, babies are not cute anymore. Women seem to not notice it as well because often they become emotionally attached to their babies. It can ruin my whole day—some proud and delusional woman will shove her terrifyingly ugly thing right in my face and I am made to scream. It's just about at epidemic proportions. If it keeps going at this rate none of us will want to go outside by the year 2015 for fear of seeing a disgusting-looking infant. If women are going to keep having these gross little meatballs I think we need to start thinking about social engineering of some kind. Calm down. Not Nazi-type stuff here but just simple common sense. We could set up a tribunal of judges and decide which babies need to be shipped off to England, where there have never been good-looking babies. We could have this whole country looking beautiful and fresh in no time. I would say Thai babies can get a pass. I've never seen an ugly Thai baby. Never. We should as a nation be encouraged to breed with people from Thailand. It could solve everything.

I'm sick and tired of people driving too slow in the left lane. It just has got to stop, plain and simple. A few years back I was racing to a strawberry festival outside of San Diego up in the Laguna Mountains when I encountered a tan Honda Civic rolling along in the left lane. The driver had effectively set up a roadblock for those of us wanting to pass. I calmly waited for an opportunity but after about thirty to forty seconds of this bullshit I came down on my horn. I stayed on that horn for easily ten minutes and this guy just wasn't budging. All I could do was laugh. You gotta take these things in stride and live and let live. I relaxed and settled into the speed this guy apparently decided we all should drive. I bided my time like a Zen Buddhist until he slowly got in the other lane and slid off the highway. Well, I wasn't going to let this guy off that easy. I followed him down the ramp, turned the corner with him and drove on through several small towns around the outskirts of San Diego. When he stopped for cigarettes at a 7-Eleven I parked a half a block away and carefully waited for this joker to get back into his car. We rode on through the rest of the day, me following him ever so craftily. Finally he pulled up to a typical dumb shit suburban house with a little picket fence and some kids' bikes on the lawn. Oh boy, now was my chance! I waited a few hours until the sun went down and took out my gallon can of paint thinner. I scurried up to his car in the moonlight and drenched the car from the hood to the trunk with the paint thinner, then I lit it on fire. I left this note on the grass for him. It read: "Dear asshole, I want to thank you for making me miss the strawberry festival with your selfish and asinine driving. You are the worst person I have ever encountered and know that I am watching you. If you ever sit in the left lane again for any reason other than passing I will burn your house down and hopefully you in it! Ron Bu." I started to sign it but then I thought differently. Years later I found out I was suffering from something called "road rage" and it's a real medical thing! I'm still mad at the guy to this day but my actions were way inappropriate and I know that now. There have been so many advancements in human psychology.

College! This country has gone college crazy! Everyone and their dog has to go to college. If you make it through high school and you don't go to college, then you are an outcast. Well, this is ridiculous! I think we should go back to the good old days when nobody went to college except for homely women and pasty rich white guys from Boston. What's wrong with making birdhouses for a living? You don't need college to lay tar on a roof. Is there a better job than laying tar on a roof? You play around with hot tar, you're outside with your buddies cracking dirty jokes and then you head to the bar for some icy cold beers. Is college gonna get you that? Nope. Here's what college will get you: a sad, lonely, competitive longing for unattainable goals and a deep anxiety about impending failure and finally death. Studies show you will also get herpes.

People need to treat me with more respect. It should be a foregone conclusion that I am treated with the utmost respect, but there are people out there in my own country who don't respect me and that's just un-American. I know I said I wouldn't wrap myself in the flag like every other ham-headed idiot on TV today but frankly speaking, if you don't respect me then you are a terrorist. It's pretty simple. The government can stop the spying on its own people. All they need to do is make up a list of people who don't respect me and put them in Guantánamo Bay until they can make them respect me. I'm not completely serious of course, but really I am.

Let me tell you what else we got wrong in this country, and that's the whole gun situation. There are too many guns out there and not enough people. The gun-to-people ratio is like five guns to every person on the earth. That ratio is all wrong. At the very least there should be ten thousand people for every gun. By my calculations that means we need at least one hundred billion people. Let's start making more people to catch up with the gun population. Making people is easy.

You put your penis in a vagina and wiggle it around. Done. I've made a lot of people that way. A lot. Wait, no I haven't. You wouldn't be able to prove it anyway.

Another complaint I have is the way we treat the gays. Well, I don't like it! As you know, for the most part I'm a heterosexual man who likes to put my parts into ladies' holes. (There may have been a classier way to say that.) I think maybe I was born this way and apart from the few times when the situation got the best of me, like the aforementioned Bruce Lee incident, I have not desired romantic and sexual encounters with other men. In the seventies I ended up in a lot of hot tubs with all kinds of hands and feet groping around underneath the water. You can't keep track of all those hands and feet. You just can't. Did some guys go for my wiener? I have no idea and I don't care. It was good clean fun. (Just a little side note on the "clean" part: In '78 I donated my own hot tub to the prestigious Boston College of Medicine, where it still remains today as a source for the world's largest collection of streptococcus.) Apart from some drunken and good-time fun with a few guys, I would say I'm pretty sure of my sexual orientation. Now, on the other hand there are some guys who are made different than me. They are gay guys, or if you are in the science community you might call them homosexuals. They were made that way—just the way I was made to use my penis for entering vaginas and such. (NOTE: Think up a more scientific way to say this for final draft of book.) Honestly a gay man living his gay life in a gay way out in the world as a gay is a more courageous man than most of the straight men I know. That goes for gay ladies as well. The good news is this country has become more and more accepting of gays over the last thirty years and I've come along with it. I'll admit it, it wasn't easy for me to find out Paul Lynde was gay. That was a shocker. Then I got hit with George Takei and I was like, "George Takei? Is everyone gay?!" But then I started to think to myself, "Ron, what do you care if Lynde or Takei is gay?" Were they happy hiding it? Did I feel better living in a world where people had to hide who they were because of fear? Is our country that afraid? I hope not. Sure, there are some tobacco-faced old meatheads who take to the airwaves or dried-up old prunes or rabid young conservatives who are afraid of change, but why should they ruin it for the rest of us? I hate change too. I wish baseball was still a sport. I would like to see a return to bigger phones. I miss Burt Lancaster pictures. Whatever happened to MTV?

Let me tell you a story about a four-year-old boy playing with his new slingshot in his backyard in Iowa. The boy got pretty good at it. He could hit cans fifty feet away. He could hit tree branches and street signs. Well one day he took aim at a bird seventy-five feet away and he hit it. The bird fluttered and fell from the tree. The boy was elated. He killed a bird with his slingshot! He was a great shot. He ran over to it and there it was on the ground. It didn't move and wasn't going to move ever again. It had no future. It was that easy; the boy had stopped it from being a bird. He thinks about that mockingbird every day. I'm as conservative as the next guy when it comes to suits and cocktails, but not letting a gay guy be who he is is sort of like killing a mockingbird. That's my opinion on the gays.

Other than those few things I would say our country is perfect. Sure, you could complain about Wall Street hoodlums stealing our pensions and inflating our real estate, which I do in a later chapter; you could whine about oil prices going through the roof and athletes hopped up on steroids. If you wanted to you could complain about the toxic amount of food we eat and the decline of the public school system. The cost of higher education is going through the roof. Children are spending too much time on gadgets. That's gotta have some sort of effect on something and it makes for good complaining. I like to complain about the fact that there are not enough horse pictures at the movie houses anymore. The three-piece suit is nearly extinct and no one seems to care! These days bartenders often forget a drink on the house. There's been a dangerous backlash against polyester. There needs to be more shows like *Night Court* on television. If I see any more tattoos I'm going to go berserk. You could wake up every morning and start complaining, but then you would just sound like the "News Anchors" on cable news today. No, we live in the third-greatest country in the world and we should be pretty proud of it. I know I am. I wouldn't mind it if there were a few less old people.

WHAT KIND OF BREATH TURNS A WOMAN ON?

Hot breath on a woman's neck and face is an aphrodisiac. That's a scientific fact that researchers have proven—not that I needed some Murgatroyd with a lab coat to tell me that a hot, humid whisper delivered inches from a woman you've just met in an elevator or on a buffet line can often seal the deal without the usual handwork. The secret, however, is not in the force of the exhale or the distance; no, the secret is in the breath itself. What kind of breath turns a woman on? I've made a bit of a study of this over the years and here are my top seven food combinations for effective hot breath. There's just no way these won't work. Let's say you're a hairy little man, like an Armenian or a Greek, and on top of that you have one of those dog faces common among Slavic people and Corsicans. To further complicate matters you're sweaty and your penis looks like a burnt marshmallow in a bird's nest. You, my friend, are a big zero, but fear not; this hot breath stuff will work! Not every time. Sometimes it will have the opposite effect of what you're going for. Here's my list of recipes for effective sensual breath.

RECIPE 1: "THE DRIED-UP RIVERBANK"

Thick, musty, lonesome and dangerous, that's the smell and feeling of a dried-up riverbank. Women are terrified and turned on by it. How to capture it all in a breathy whisper? Simple. Shrimp dipped in stale beer and hot mayonnaise. Let it sit in your mouth for no less than five minutes; work it into your teeth. This one works from a long way out. Try it in a room full of women and see if any react—more than likely those who do won't be classy but they'll be moved by a memory long since buried that only the rancid smell of dried mud can recover. If that memory is a pleasant one—and often it is not—you are in business, my friend.

RECIPE 2: "THE FOREIGN ELEMENT"

If you've ever been to Europe, which I have, five times for pleasure, then you know the smell of a European café. It's absinthe and rich tobacco with a hint of an old-world standing urinal. It's a delicious smell that when delivered the right way can turn a frozen ice queen into a nonstop volcanic eruption of hot love fluids. But who's kidding who? Absinthe is expensive. Here's a way to get that same scent in your mouth on a budget. Take an onion. Let it sit in an open can of motor oil overnight. Put it in a blender with stale cigarettes and coffee grounds and drink. Voilà! European bar. If you can whisper a few words of French, like *mise en scène*, or gently sing an Edith Piaf song a few inches from her nose, that adds an extra element of continental spice. Some women find this irresistible. Others resist it, but stay with it; they give in eventually.

RECIPE 3: "THE EARTHY GARDENER"

Cabbage, broccoli, beans and raw bacon. This one is about timing. Once this hits your gut you have about fifteen minutes to go to work before the farts set in. I would describe the smell as "stomachy dirt," like blowing a fan through compost. I've had some luck with loose women with the Earthy Gardener, but then they were pretty loose, so it's hard to say if it really works. Give it a try! Treat every day like a prison break!

RECIPE 4: "SEVEN-CHEESE SAMURAI"

Just as it says. You eat seven different cheeses. Any kind will do but make sure you're eating at least a pound total. This one poses its own challenges. Women smell it coming from a mile away, making it harder to get in tight for real close breathing unless you employ the tactics of the samurai warrior. You need to keep your breathing to a minimum. Bring your heart rate down to a legally dead state. It helps to be hiding in a dark corner or under a desk or behind a filing cabinet. You must not move at all until the woman is absolutely within close range. Then the sleeper awakens and blows . . .

seven cheeses right at her face! It's a winner. Believe me. It has an effect.

RECIPE 5: "THE ROADKILL"

Find some roadkill and eat it. I haven't even tried this one but I know it would work. I just know it. Let me know if you do try it. It's gotta work.

RECIPE 6: "THE ANIMAL LOVER"

Who hasn't seen a beautiful woman come to her knees at the sight of a cute puppy? Oh how I've envied that puppy from time to time. Sometimes the envy gets to the point of really pissing me off. I remember a cute little basset hound puppy in particular who stole the attention of a woman I was interested in pursuing. I was as steamed as I ever get. I waited for the lady to get out of earshot and I laid into that puppy with every curse word my mouth could make. I hate curse words in general but that little dog got two earfuls that day! I had to lift the little guy's ears just to scream my anger right into his little dog head. Somewhere out there in the world there is a basset hound walking around with some very real psychological issues. I hope he eventually got some therapy. I'm really a friend to dogs, just not when they get between me and my own animal desires. Anyway . . . what is it about dogs that gets the ladies? Can't be their looks, because most dogs look like a pork roast with eyeballs. (Please, Baxter, do not read this!) Anyway I realized women love dogs because of their breath. "Eat a bowl of dog food, Burgundy," I said to myself one night, and so I did, and sure enough it was like cheating. Women go nuts for dog breath. (As an aside I should mention women in their late twenties really go for baby's breath. That's just a biological fact. I tried to find this breath—I ate jars and jars of baby food, cans of sweetened baby milk, even asked a woman to pump some breast milk for me, but no luck! You just can't get baby's breath unless you literally get a stomach transplant from a baby! Who would allow you to do that? I've befriended some very suspect "doctors" in my day but I doubt a one of them would feel comfortable replacing my stomach with a baby's stomach! Oh well, lucky babies! Sex appeal is wasted on the young!) When it comes to dog food I go right for the hard nuggets right out of a forty-pound bag. A handful will do you for the night. Word to the wise: If you're stealing the food from your own dog, be sneaky. Baxter put it together over several weeks that I had been taking his food and he confronted me directly. It was not pretty. We argued. Then he waited until I went to sleep and he bit my foot. He later told me he was so mad he would have bitten my face if it weren't for the fact that my face feeds us both. What a dog!

RECIPE 7: "THE EXECUTIVE"

Well, here it is, my favorite and a sure winner. I don't leave the house without the Executive because it's just a no-nonsense heavy breath that when gently whispered into any woman's face will drive her nuts. Sardines and an old cigar. Yep, it's that simple. I keep a tin of sardines and half a stale cigar in my inside vest pocket at all times. The cigar provides the weight and the sardines provide the spice. It's like a gentle breeze blowing over a garbage truck, just enough to say, "I'm here and you are in for a heck of a night . . . a heck of a night!"

MY NEIGHBOR: NEW DEVELOPMENTS

Just an update on the whole war I'm having with my neighbor Richard Wellspar. He borrowed my leaf blower and didn't return it. Baxter and I snuck into his backyard and I did indeed empty out my two garbage cans into his pool. The whole operation went off without a hitch. Baxter is a true professional. The next morning, who do you think is standing at my front door? Yep, Richard Wellspar, idiot! So he very calmly asks me if I know anything about the garbage in his pool. Well, I'm nothing if I'm not fast on my feet. I've spent a whole lifetime in the news game, where you have to be on top of it at every minute. I looked him square in the face and said, "It's not mine and I didn't do it." He looked confused. He showed me a wet Publishers Clearing House letter addressed to me. I was caught off guard for a second. Of course, all of the junk mail had my address on it! Ooooh boy, that was not smart. Baxter should have said something! Anyway, I came back at him with this: "Richard, here's the deal. This is something you should know about this neighborhood. You've only been here a few years, so how could you be expected to know this? Also you are a pool salesman or something and this kind of stuff is outside of your area of expertise. I'm a newsman, so I know just about everything. There are feral cats around here and they will take garbage cans and throw them in pools. Pretty standard stuff, really." He just said, "Okay, Ron. By the way, I am a money manager. I'm not a pool salesman." Then he walked away. Once again, nothing about the leaf blower! Incredible! I am beside myself.

THE BIG TIME, OR WHEN I KNEW I HAD MADE IT

My face is buried in a wine-soaked pillow. Slowly my left eyelid lifts to reveal a dark corner of the room. There's a naked body there slumped over itself, sleeping, maybe dead. Stale wine fills my nostrils. I take it in and it feels safe. I know that smell and I like it. I like what it says about my current predicament. I'm too brain-soaked to move fast. I say to myself, "Take it in, Ron. Enjoy the mystery." Something weighs on my leg. It's hefty, like the stale wine smell in the room. . . . Hold up . . . wine smell? Is this a distillery? Did I pass out in a distillery? I've passed out in distilleries before. It doesn't look like a distillery, although I've been in some inventive distilleries. People make distilleries out of anything—toilets, gas pumps, refrigerators, showers, swimming pools. My dear old friend Gus Cranshaw operated a distillery out of a converted mail truck. He painted it up to look like the current mail trucks you see today and me and him would drive around Dallas picking up mail and reading it while stoned on "Cranshaw's Crazy Juice." That was Dallas in the late fifties. You could get away with stuff like that then. It was a lawless town.

Cranshaw was an aeronautical engineer with a Ph.D. from Stanford but by the time I met him he had lost 90 percent of his thinking capacity—still a hoot, just had no ability to reason. It didn't matter because almost all of the mailmen in Dallas in the fifties were slower people and alcoholics. Reports of mail theft were common. I went back to Dallas in '71 to do a puff piece on Roger Staubach. Cranshaw was alive and well but he only had about fifty words left to his vocabulary. As the newly elected postmaster general for the greater Dallas–Fort Worth area he was asked to speak frequently and he confided in me that it was no easy task. Somehow he had retained the word *thermal*, either from his days at Stanford or maybe from his work on his distillery, and with only fifty words to work with the word *thermal* came up often, as in "I smell a thermal coming," "Look at that thermal," "We got us a thermal," "Us thermal look good, thermal." He was later elected six times to the state legislature with the slogan "We gonna go thermal!" . . . Back to my current predicament. Maybe there's a body decomposing? Is it fermenting flesh?

I know that smell, mold mixed with infection and dead skin. Am I in the Tarantula's Lair again? Is this Venezuela? A moment of fear surges through my usually calm disposition. For one second I am paralyzed with heart-stopping terror. Horrendous memories strike at me like coiled snakes jumping at my face, but just as quick I fight them off. No, Ron, those days are over. Look around the room. There are no guns, no cameras, no demonic symbols painted on the wall. You play it safe now. Cool down and take it easy. . . . Maybe I'm in some kind of whorehouse. It's too small for a whorehouse. Stop guessing! Slow it down, Ron. Slow it down. Let the mystery unfold. Back to the weight on my leg. I can feel the smooth skin on my haunches. It's sensual. Hello, Mr. Hammersmith (one of the many names I give my penis). He has awakened, bloated with wine and memory and possibility. "Now is not the time for you," I say out loud. It may be the place but it is not the time. I will admit, Mr. Hammersmith has no real sense of time or space. He's his own agent, bound to no rules made by man. Nature is Mr. Hammersmith's lawgiver and even she grants him free rein within her strict code. For I have witnessed Mr. Hammersmith defy nature many times, taunting her with his insolence like Odysseus yelling back at Cyclops, full of hubris. Mr. Hammersmith has thus taunted nature with many unnatural acts and yet Mother Nature loves her impish man-child. I envy Mr. Hammersmith. He's not bound to reason. I'm talking about my penis, Mr. Hammersmith. No, he's an epicurean all the way. His morning bloat is pure joyful defiance! He's a rascal and I love him for it!

Unfortunately I have a head—a head filled with brain cells—and I am intrigued by the mystery that surrounds me. What is that weight on my leg? Do I have the muscle control to lift my head and look or should I continue to sleuth it out like the newsman that I am? It's a female leg. I'm fairly certain of that, although there are men who shave their legs. World-class swimmer and nine-time Olympic gold medalist Mark Spitz shaves his legs to lose the aquadynamic drag that body hair might cause in the water. I asked him one time in a candid on-air interview if he felt more like a woman without the hair. He didn't know how to respond to the question so I rephrased it like this: "Does shaving your legs make you feel sexy, more feminine?" Again, he laughed but did not understand what I was getting at. Here is a transcript of my interview with Mark Spitz from that point on.

Ron
Come on, man.

Mark Spitz
Are you serious?

Ron
I'm an anchorman with sterling credentials.

Mark Spitz
You want to know if shaving my legs for my sport makes me feel more like a woman?

Ron
Does it?

Mark Spitz

You're an idiot.

Ron

I would think it would go a long way to putting you in touch with your feminine side. Do you wear dresses ever? Maybe a wig?

[Long stare-down]

Ron

Are you not comfortable with wanting to be a woman?

[Something begins to agitate Mr. Spitz]

Ron

I've seen men up in San Francisco in heels and dresses that I swear to God you would think are women. I did. I thought they were women.

[Mr. Spitz nods his head]

Ron

I don't know if that's something you're interested in but I should warn you—you can shave your legs and put on heels and the prettiest dress in the world but you'll never even come close to what these men look like. They basically are women.

[Spitz looks off camera, confused]

Ron

Hey! Over here. This isn't Howard Cosell lobbing soft-

balls at you, kid. This is San Diego and I am Ron Burgundy. Answer the question! Does shaving your legs make you feel like a woman? America wants to know!

[Spitz walks off set]

It was one of the few times I lost my cool on camera but gosh darn it, from time to time I let my insatiable need to know get in the way of decorum. I respect the NEWS just too much not to give a damn, and frankly he was hiding something. After the broadcast I ran after him. He took off like he was afraid of somebody or something but I gave good chase. I was fast on his heels all the way to the Coronado Bridge but then—again, maybe because something scared him—he dove into the harbor and at that point I threw up my hands in comic defeat. I laughed so all of San Diego could hear me. I certainly was not going to catch nine-time gold medalist Mark Spitz in the water! It made for a good story.

At any rate it couldn't have been Mark Spitz's leg draped over my own, that's for sure. This was before his time. More likely a beautiful woman. That would make all the sense in the world. Really quite simple: a night of drinks, maybe an after-hours gentlemen's club, a dip in someone's pool if we could find one driving around, a stroll through the natural history museum, a private party and then to bed, where Mr. Hammersmith could go to work in all his glory. How many nights have gone like this—every one of them special in its own way? How many times did I awake to this same sweet scene played out like a jazz flute solo with infinite variations on the same chords? I could almost describe the room before my eyes fully opened. There would be women, more than one, lying naked, and empty bottles and clothes hither and thither thrown about in passion's full fury. There might also be a half-eaten steak sandwich and some deviled ham. There could even be a fan of mine—a total stranger who had won a contest or something, "A Night on the Town with Ron Burgundy." The tales he or she would tell for the rest of his or her life! It was one of the ways I gave back and also it was one of the ways to get the station to pay for my nights on the town. In those days, '65, '66, a night on the town could run you three to four dollars, which was a good chunk of your paycheck. Newsmen were expected to party. Not like socialites and movie stars but like oilmen and footballers. There was a code amongst the real newsmen. You couldn't report the news till you paid your dues, and by *paying dues* I mean you had to out-drink and out-screw everyone else in the game. The code was a lifestyle and no one could outdo me. I was simply the best. I once went to have cocktails with Lana Cantrell and Bubba Smith. We agreed to meet in the Marina for a few afternoon drinks. I remember ordering something silly like a Naughty Squirrel. I was feeling zesty. I can remember the first sip. The next thing I felt was a boot to my rib cage. I woke up. I was in downtown Laramie with no pants, holding on to a bag of hundred-dollar bills. Another victory for sure. I know today people might look back and say, "Ron, you were an alcoholic."

Where was I? Oh yes, so I had regained consciousness in a strange small room with a naked or dead person in the corner and a female leg straddling my own leg. It was time to put on my thinking cap. First off, and this is something I do every morning to this day, I asked myself, are there any open wounds or bruises? I always like to assess the damage if there is any. Nope. I was feeling pretty good, maybe a bite mark on my arm but that hardly constitutes a problem. I noticed something gooey on my hand—a gooey substance. I knew I would have to sniff it but that could wait. I also noticed a sound. It was snoring, loud, contented snoring from a man. Aha! Besides the girl and the person in the corner there was someone else in the room with me. I tried to remember the evening. Was there another man with me, perhaps from the news team? We news people tend to celebrate in groups. If you get a bunch of us together, say at a conference, or maybe a big story brings the network affiliates into town, it's Katie, bar the door! Heck, Dan Rather and I aren't even allowed in the Flamingo hotel in Vegas anymore. That was a case where things got out of hand—unpaid bills, property damage, assault charges, etc. If it weren't for Rather's connection to the mob I don't think we would have left Vegas alive that night.

Rather is one of the best in the business. That is a fact I'm not afraid to report. With that smooth Texas drawl and that sexy I-will-mess-up-your-face-if-you-so-much-as-lay-a-hand-on-me smile, he is one classy operator. I've always said if I get caught in a Moroccan back alley and I'm looking at an all-or-nothing knife fight, Dan Rather or Charles Kuralt would be my pick for wingman. Both of these guys are as comfortable with a blade in their hand as a monkey is with his penis. Kuralt is legendary for quick-handed jabs and slashes, whereas Rather is the natural-born descendant of Gentleman Jim Bowie. He could toss a knife into a charging bear at fifty feet. I saw him do it one time back when bearbaiting was still very close to being legal. A man's bear got loose from his chains and headed into the crowd. Rather happened to be there on a story about Ross Barnett, the governor of Mississippi. Barnett was a big bearbaiting fan and an old-school racist. He had the Freedom Riders thrown in Parchman Farm, where they were strip-searched and humiliated. He said this about Bobby Kennedy:

"I say to you that Bobby Kennedy is a very sick and dangerous American. We have lots of sick Americans in this country but most of them have a long beard. Bobby Kennedy is a hypocritical, left-wing beatnik without a beard who carelessly and recklessly distorts the facts."

The bear headed straight for Governor Barnett and Rather dropped him like a sack of old beef. I asked Dan about it a couple of years later. I knew him to be a lefty from way back when we both were members of the Commie Party for a couple of weeks. He said, "I didn't want that bear to make a martyr out of that sack of shit." Rather could swear up a storm but I'll save that for later (see chapter 8).

Well, it was coming to me. The whole setup started to make sense. There had been a big story in San Diego that week.

The minor-league San Diego Padres became a Major League Baseball team and it was a huge, huge story! All the big network affiliates were in town. Every newsman—Mudd, Reynolds, Cronkite, Reasoner, Wallace, Huntley, Brinkley— they were all in San Diego to cover the story. So here's what must have happened. We got our stories in and then, because San Diego is my town, I hosted the evening. I took the whole gang out to my favorite watering holes. I'm sure one thing led to another and here I was in a small room with a contest winner, a naked woman or two and another man. All that was left was for me to sit up and survey the room to see who'd survived the night. I did just that. I sat up. My head hit something and I immediately saw that I was in the cabin of a small schooner. Sure enough Walter Cronkite, America's most trusted news source, was snoring away in a hammock three feet from me. His beard was maybe four or five days old. The person in the corner was Korean, a sixty- or seventy-year-old woman (still breathing thankfully), and the woman lying across me, sans undergarments, was none other than a young Barbara Walters. A slow smile formed.

Here I was, the boy from Haggleworth, Iowa, in a boat, drifting aimlessly at sea with two of the greatest newsmen who ever lived. (There's always been some confusion over whether to call a woman in the news business a "newswoman" or the more proper "female newsman." If she's risen to the level of a Barbara Walters, then she damn well deserves to be called a "newsman." The end.) I took in the greatness of this important scene. How did I get here? Not the nuts and bolts of how I got on the boat—Cronkite stole the boat off the harbor pier, yelling, "I'm the greatest sailor that ever lived! I'm better than Sir Francis Drake! And that's the way it is!" And off we went. We were four hundred miles off the coast when I woke up. Weeks later we ended up in the Solomon Islands on a remote outcropping, shipwrecked, because Cronkite is NOT the greatest sailor that ever lived. Two months on that island with those three people fighting off monitor lizards is a whole other story. What I'm really getting at is clearly I had reached the pinnacle of success. I was number one in San Diego. Soon I had just put together the news team that would come to dominate that town for nearly a decade and I had just spent a night or maybe a week of lovemaking with Barbara Walters . . . and most likely Walter Cronkite and the old Korean woman, but let's focus on Walters. I can hardly think of a more prestigious honor than a night of wine-soaked sex with two respected newsmen like Cronkite and Walters. That morning, with nude bodies spread out in the cabin and the smell of body fluids everywhere, was the moment I realized I had made the big time.

It's no big deal but I'm taller than the guys on the team. I look shorter because I'm kneeling down. If you look, you can tell that my knees are bent. Clearly I'm not standing straight.

ABOVE: I'll be honest, Jackie O gave me the creeps. She looks like Jeanne Tripplehorn though. I'm wishing she was Jeanne Tripplehorn in this picture. No that's stupid. Tripplehorn was three years old when this photo was taken. BELOW: Norman Mailer was a real puss and I enjoyed beating him at everything.

Mark Eaton, Utah Jazz.

My great friend who I never shut up about, Lance Bullwright.

Ancient dinosaurs like the Tyrannosaurus rex terrorized the first Mexican peoples.

ABOVE LEFT: Having a whale of a time! (I put that in here for laughs because of the word "whale" and there's a real whale in the picture. I've always liked jokes.) ABOVE RIGHT: My favorite bird of prey, Lady Samantha Hutchinson. BELOW: God's majesty knows no bounds.

ABOVE: Pointing at something. BELOW: Caught in the bubble! I go to jail for an $80 billion real estate mix-up. I've done longer stretches for public urination. Only in America!

ABOVE: Baxter refuses to get a job but I still love him. BELOW: My wife. My lover and a damn fine woman anchorman.

MY TWELVE RULES FOR LIVING THROUGH A PRISON RIOT

Prison riots are boisterous affairs. You really want to try to avoid them if you can, but at one time or another you can just bet you'll be in the middle of one. I've been in eight of them. Three in this country and another five in various countries around the world. I've even started them! Here are my twelve rules for living through it.

RULE NUMBER 1: Use it now. If you're not an idiot, then you've spent your time in jail wisely, making weapons. You should have at the very least a zip gun, a carved wooden shiv, a broken-glass-covered soap ball, a garrote wire and a chair leg with some rusty nails in it. A lot of guys will have more than this but if you have these few simple tools you'll be okay. The key here is to recognize this is the moment to use these things. It's a not a collection to take pride in and show the other guys. Prison is not a craft fair. You made these things to hurt other people, so get to it!

RULE NUMBER 2: Look for weakness. There's always fear in the air. You might as well accept it and embrace it. Some men can't handle it. They buckle under the fear. These are the ones you need to attack. Hit them fast and hard and often and if they get back up, then you didn't do something right. Hitting a weaker man will gain you confidence when you have to go after the really big cats.

RULE NUMBER 3: Use a verbal assault. Different theories abound here. Do you come across as more fearful without talking? Are a few choice words all you need? The scariest man I ever came across inside or outside of prison was a man who could squish a human head in a fight and all he ever said was, "I'm going bananas!" He didn't open his mouth for any other reason but to say those words, and if he was saying those words, it was too late, my friend! So sometimes a man of few words can indeed be a terrifying thing. However, I like to yell out a torrent of threats while running right at my victim. You should practice these in your cell at night. Practicing lines with your cell mate is fun and helps pass the time. "Here comes the face eater" is a good one. I've also said this:

"I will rip your balls off and sauté them in garlic butter with basil and ground pepper. I will then add a garnish of shaved orange peels and a side of fresh-cut sliced beets misted with lemon juice. I will beautifully plate it and enjoy a glass of white wine with it while dressed in a tuxedo. It will be a Michelin three-star meal and you will not be invited to join me! Do you understand?"

RULE NUMBER 4: Go naked. Take your clothes off as soon as possible. It adds to the insanity of the whole scene. When watching scratchy security tapes of the riot later it's always a moment of pride and levity when someone yells out, "Who's that crazy naked mofo?"

RULE NUMBER 5: Paint your face. This is a must-do. When you walk out into the yard with a painted face you already have an edge. I like a simple "one side black, the other side white" look, but have fun! I've seen skulls, clowns, Jackson Pollock paintings, Egyptian symbols, brown paint that may or may not have been feces (see rule 8) and many more. If you can't do it yourself most prisons have a face-painting station for a cigarette or two.

RULE NUMBER 6: Play dead. It's not the strategy to use right out of the gate, mind you, but about midway through the riot there's no shame in curling up on the ground like you're dead. You might need to stab yourself to make it convincing but it's worth it. You get to watch all the pounding and kicking and sticking with sharp objects from a nice safe place. Again, afterward there's nothing funnier than one of the guys in the infirmary saying, "Ah shit, Burgundy, you wasn't dead!" and then having a good hearty laugh over it.

RULE NUMBER 7: Stay with your group! A prison is a population of men organized around different social groups. There are men who are uncomfortable around black people and other races. There are men who belong to various urban societies and motorbiking clubs. Each one of these groups can be very protective, so join! Be a joiner! I'm a loner, which is not the way to go in a riot, so I try to side with the homosexuals. These crafty she-hes know how to survive and thrive in a bloody riot. They are some devious tricky bastards and if you turn on them, out come the claws and the metal shivs and other stuff they hide up their butts.

RULE NUMBER 8: Have poop ready. Save up bags of your own poop and be prepared to throw it everywhere. No one likes to be hit with poop. Make sure you have lots of it too. The closer it can be to diarrhea but still be held in your hands, the better off you are. It's just basic human nature, going back to when we were monkeys. All animals, except dogs, try to avoid getting hit by poop. Aim for the face. It's magical stuff in a riot.

RULE NUMBER 9: Try reasoning. If you're cornered by a few thugs who want to stomp you to death, now's the time to try to reason with them. Every man carries within him a sense of fair play. We all have it, be it from our fathers, our ball-playing days or just spending time out in the world with other men in daily combat. You can count on this one basic truth. All men will see the logic in your argument and give way to a more peaceful, alternative solution. I am clearly messing with your head. (Something you learn to do in prison.) Prison riots are the very definition of unreasoned mayhem. You need to be on your toes at all times and trust no one.

RULE NUMBER 10: Be prepared for a life sentence. It doesn't matter if you've killed a man or if you're only doing a ninety-day stretch for forgery; you have to go into the riot believing you will never leave jail and like it. If you're dreaming of the day you leave, your opponent might smell hope on you. *Hope* is just another word for fear. Destroy all hope and turn yourself into a killing machine.

RULE NUMBER 11: Masturbate. Never tried this one but I saw it once in a Colombian prison, and let me tell you, everyone just left the guy alone. It's a bold move—not my style, but effective.

RULE NUMBER 12: Have fun. This might be the most important rule but so many people seem to forget it. It's a prison riot; have fun! Make a game of it. Sing to yourself. I sing songs from the musical *Hair*. Get punched and punch other people and smile. Don't forget to smile.

MY NEIGHBOR RICHARD WELLSPAR

Last night around dinnertime I took a bag of dog crap that Baxter and I had conspired to save and set it on Richard Wellspar's front doorstep. I lit it on fire, rang his doorbell and ran away. Sweet revenge! I hurried back in the house and got to the window just in time to see Wellspar stomping out the fire on his stoop! What an idiot! It worked perfectly. Baxter was ecstatic! I said very loudly to Baxter, "That'll teach him to borrow something of mine and not return it." So about five minutes later, Richard comes to my door with the charred bag of poop.

"What is the meaning of this, Burgundy?" He's obviously very angry.

"I don't know what you're talking about, Richard. Is something the matter? I've been working on this airplane model for the last two hours." He didn't expect that, I'm sure. That was my strategic mind at work! I had gone to the hobby shop that morning and purchased a Grumman Bearcat World War II fighter plane model and put about half of it together. It actually was starting to look pretty good with the two wing pieces attached but I left it half-done and when I appeared at the front door holding the half-finished model it looked like I was in the middle of something that demanded great concentration and time. How could I have been involved in the flaming bag of poop? I was busy making my model.

"I heard you yell out your own name!" he barked. (It's true; I do sometimes yell my own name when I'm running and when I'm overly excited.) "Half the neighborhood saw you running from my house. What is wrong with you?"

"I'm a respected News Anchor," I said to buy some time while I thought of a better response. "Here's the situation, Richard, I am afraid of fire . . . so when I saw the burning bag of poop on your doorstep I rang your doorbell to warn you and then ran away in fear. You see, my daughter . . . Richardessa"—I came up with that fast!—"whose name is sort of like yours when you think about it—you two would have really hit it off—she died in a terrible awful fire about a week ago."

"Stop it, Burgundy. I don't like what you are doing and I want you to stop it. It's not funny."

"I wish I knew what you were talking about, Richard. We are neighbors and good friends. We say hello in the morning and borrow stuff from each other and return stuff. We're neighbors."

"You're not being a good neighbor, Burgundy. Just stop it." And he walked away. The leaf blower? Didn't even come up. So now I have determined that he means to steal my leaf blower. I am furious. It's time to put this little feud that he started into overdrive.

FROM HUNTING TO PROTECTING: BURGUNDY AND THE ANIMAL KINGDOM AND THE DAWN OF THE JACKALOPES

I went jackalope hunting with Peter Lawford and Bobby Kennedy. I was in beautiful Las Vegas, where the women are loose and the slots are tighter than a librarian's vagina. Pardon my French! Anyway, I had an opportunity to meet both gentlemen when they took a fancy to the lady I was escorting. I was invited up to Lawford's private penthouse suite, where the three of us traded stories and sang show tunes all night long. Bobby was an excellent piano player before we lost him that blackest of days in California. I shall miss him dearly! He was a good man, ethical to the core—not like some of these politicians you see today. All of the Kennedys were made of the highest blue-blooded moral fiber and Bobby was no exception. Anyway we passed around three or four women between us, rotating and changing our styles, and then decided it was time for breakfast. They have the most sumptuous and amazing breakfast buffets in Vegas. If you've never been to one you are simply an idiot, an idiot to your friends and family and an idiot in the eyes of God. If there was a higher form of idiot, like a circus idiot's illegitimate child with an idiot donkey, then that would be you. Here's why: They have meat like you've never seen before! Three or four different types of bacon. They have Canadian bacon. They have regular or hickory bacon and thick-cut bacon. They have ham. They have steak. They have pork. Don't get me going on the merits of a Vegas buffet. Seriously! Get this, there's usually an omelet station and you can choose your own ingredients, be it ham or bacon or beans or cheese or all of it. The breaded material is limitless. Crescent rolls from France, sweet breads and doughnuts. Oh, and pancakes! Big fluffy, buttery pancakes like you've never tasted before. There are some fruit cups, for women I guess, but not really necessary. Two kinds of sausage, flat patties and wiener shaped. Holy Moses, I forgot the best part. When you are done scarfing all this down you simply hand the waiter your dirty plate and go back and get another clean plate for another round, free of charge! You heard me. It's all-you-can-eat! I would not lie about this. I know what you're saying: "Ron, some of the stories you tell in this novel are unbelievable." This buffet story is absolutely true. It's not the main gist of the whole story. It's really a story about hunting jackalopes with Bobby Kennedy and Peter Lawford, but I wasn't going to tell the story without the buffet part.

So there we were eating breakfast from the buffet when Kennedy starts talking about the legendary and elusive jackalope. A jackalope is a stronger and faster jackrabbit with antelope horns. They are believed to exist only in folktales and postcard shops throughout the Southwest. Anyway, Kennedy is going on and on about jackalopes when—wait one second, I forgot something about the buffet. The pancakes, I did them a real disservice. Yes they are fluffy and buttery, but they've also got different flavored fruit syrups you can pour over them, strawberry, blueberry, peach, whatever! AND— and this is big—whipped cream. So these pancakes are more like dessert than breakfast food. Just thought I should mention that. Also free refills on the coffee!

So Kennedy is going on about the jackalope when Lawford shouts out, "Let's go jackalope hunting!" Next thing I know I'm in a convertible Mercury Monterey rolling outside of Vegas in the high desert with Peter Lawford and Bobby Kennedy. Each one of us holds a service revolver handed to us by Kennedy's security team. Lawford swears that the only way to hunt jackalope is with handguns. I know what you're thinking: Ron Burgundy is a friend to animals; he wouldn't want to hunt them. Very true, I am, indeed, a great friend to all the Animal Kingdom, but I wasn't always. In fact there was a time when I just loved to hunt. You heard it here! Ron Burgundy, nature lover, hunted and killed animals for sport. Crossbows, rifles, knives, snares, traps, throwing stars, slingshots, dynamite, my bare hands and of course guns—I used them all. My lust for the blood sport was only outpaced by my lust for lovemaking.

Some weekends the whole news team would pack up the camping equipment and head up into the mountains for a few days of relaxing and hunting. I would bring the chow. Brian Fantana would bring various scents he said were useful for attracting "prey." It was usually just an assortment of his various colognes but they were also highly effective in attracting animals. I would say many of his colognes were better at attracting animals than women! Bears especially liked Night Stalker.

Funny story: One night we were all out on the town having a few drinks, seeing what we could stir up, when Fantana walks in drenched in Night Stalker. It's a heavy scent. Not all women go for it. It smells like cat box and old meat. This is downtown San Diego, mind you. Anyway Brian hits the dance floor, where he can show his moves to the ladies. Suddenly everyone is screaming and running for the doors. It's a bear, not a grizzly but a pretty big black bear. It probably traveled a hundred or two hundred miles to get to what it was smelling, Night Stalker. Poor guy quickly became disoriented and angry in the dance club. Bears are not cool with disco lights and Donna Summer. That's a bear fact not everyone knows. Suffice it to say it was a real mess! After that, San Diego made it illegal to have Night Stalker within the city limits.

Anyway, back to our hunting trips. Brick Tamland would usually pack a lunch box full of yarn or secret notes, and

Champ Kind, who to this day enjoys shooting and killing animals of any sort, would bring about forty to fifty guns of all sizes and makes. Too many guns really. (We once got pulled over by a state trooper in Nevada because Brian was driving 130 miles an hour through downtown Reno. The trooper asked to search the camper and was surprised by—and I think maybe a little scared of—what he found. None of the hundred or so guns we had in the camper or the trailer were registered. More than a few of them had been used in violent crimes and were sought after by prosecutors throughout the Southwest. There were even some grenades back in the trailer and a Russian-made rocket launcher. Luckily it was Nevada. We got out of there with a slap on the wrist and a twenty-dollar fine. That particular trip turned out to be a huge disaster, which is an entirely different story! Let's just say there's a big difference between hunting and insurrection.)

Mainly our little hunting excursions didn't amount to much more than four drunk guys in the woods shooting off guns and eating cans of soup! I don't even remember bagging many animals when the news team got together to hunt. It wasn't about that. It was more about friends yelling and not shaving. However I do recall one time when we probably killed a mountain lion, or maybe more than one. I say that because we spent a night in Montana fighting off mountain lions. Once again Brian had one of his colognes with him, I think it was something he called Erotic Dawn. Whatever it was, it sure attracted mountain lions. I don't care what naturalists say, mountain lions are not solitary creatures. They can organize and work in groups if the need arises. They can even work with other animals, like raccoons and hawks, if they want something bad enough. They wanted Erotic Dawn real bad. We spent that night completely sober shooting semiautomatic weapons out into the dark, just praying we were hitting the lions. Scary stuff. Fond memories. I can now look back on those days and laugh! I'm a different man today and soon enough you'll see why. My transformation happened almost all at once at a point in my life I still call "the Dawn of the Jackalope."

So back to the jackalope tale. Me, Kennedy and Lawford are driving in the desert. There's plenty of booze in the car—this was back in the days when you could legally drive drunk. Most men in the late sixties who were responsible and held down respectable nine-to-five jobs drove home drunk every night. No one said anything then! I don't know. Times change. Frankly it would not have mattered if we were swerving all over the highway, because we were definitely off the main roads in the middle of nowhere. At one point I remember asking Lawford if he knew where we were going and he said, "To hell!" Kennedy just laughed and shot his pistol into the air. After about five or six hours of driving through the desert we came to a spot where we parked the car. Lawford got very quiet. He whispered, "We are in the land of the jackalope. Keep all of your senses alive." We got out to walk. We carried whatever bottles of beer and bourbon we could find in the car along with some flares and boxes of ammo, then headed out on foot. We walked for hours, only stopping to drink the bourbon. The heat was punishing. The sole force pushing us on under the brutal sun and over uneven desert terrain was the chance encounter with the vicious and fast-attacking jackalope.

I'll tell you this. If you want to get to know a man, I mean really get to know him, go jackalope hunting with him. We three got very close out there as we slowly started to die from heatstroke and dehydration. Bobby confided in me that he was responsible for Marilyn Monroe's death. He had been in love with her long before his brother John but if he couldn't have her, then no one could. He forced pills on her and left her to die. Peter told me he once had a three-way with Frank Sinatra and his daughter Nancy.

There's a chance none of this was true of course. Men say strange things before they are about to die of heatstroke. Our brains were like hot cream of barley soup. I confessed to both of them that I stole dinosaur bones from the Museum of Natural History in New York City. (That actually was true. I did steal those bones, but I needed them.) We wandered aimlessly for days. When the beer and bourbon ran out we experienced a new kind of torture. Bobby Kennedy would not shut up. He was a bit of a Boy Scout and a know-it-all. He was arrogant, like every Kennedy. The kind of arrogance you admire and appreciate and look up to until you have to listen to it all day. Lawford and I quickly grew to hate him and his endlessly blathering mouth. Unfortunately we also knew he was our best chance at survival. He found us water underneath the sand and sustenance in lizards, snakes and cacti. He was an excellent marksman with a revolver as well. Crossing him might have cost us our lives, so we toed the line and nodded our heads when he talked. The sun came up maybe six or seven times on us while we were out there. Buzzards began circling on day five. Meanwhile we hadn't seen one jackalope. Lawford was beginning to scare me with his Captain Ahab–like declarations. "Gentlemen, there's jackalopes afoot." Or "I smell jackalope." I was beginning to think maybe the jackalope was some sort of hoax made up for tourists!

Without upsetting Peter Lawford I walked Kennedy out into the desert where we could talk alone. We sat on a rock under the moonlight while Lawford painted his own blood on his face. I quietly spoke to Bobby of my doubts. He confessed to me he hated politics and that he really wanted to be a maintenance man in a luxury hotel but that his father, Joseph, was a real asshole. I tried to stay on point with my concern about the existence of jackalopes and whether we needed to be out in the desert at all. He confided in me that Jackie O was a better lay than Marilyn and that the woman had a mouth on her that could suck the chrome off a trailer hitch. I wanted to listen to his concerns and confidences but I really felt we needed to form a majority opinion so we could talk Lawford into heading back toward civilization. He understood, I think, but wanted me to know that his brother Ted was gay and couldn't handle it and so he drank. I took this in—that was a big one—but I straight-up asked him if he thought jackalopes were real! He didn't answer for a long time. I could hear coyotes howling off in the distance. They would be getting close soon. Somewhere a desert owl announced his loneliness with a mournful hoot. The desert is a cold mistress. Finally, Bobby sat up and said these words to me from the poet Aeschylus: "Wisdom comes alone through suffering." He then walked out into the darkness. I didn't see him again. Like everyone I was shocked and saddened by his death. I had the solemn duty of having to report it on the evening news. I ended the night's broadcast with another Aeschylus quotation that maybe Bobby would have appreciated: "Call no man happy until he is dead." When I awoke the next morning Peter Lawford was standing over me holding a pistol to my face. "Where's Kennedy?" he yelled. I told him that he'd walked off into the night but he was having none of it. He was sure I had eaten him. Lawford had smeared a clown's smile on his face and three lines across his forehead. He also had blisters all over his head from the sun. He was nude. I tried to reason with him. I told him how much I liked Bobby and that I would never eat him. Peter was not convinced. He told me he was going to have to kill me to see if he could get his friend Bobby out of my belly. This was nonsense, I thought, but he cocked the gun aimed at my face. Now, here's where the story gets kind of unbelievable, but it's absolutely true, as is every word of this novel. As I was about to get shot by Peter Lawford, a voice so smooth and soothing came from the wind and spoke these words: "Kill not this man!" Lawford and I were stunned. Who spoke? Peter started spinning and shooting into the air. It was no use. There was no one there. Both of us were trembling in fear . . . but then we saw it: a jackalope! And then another, and soon we were surrounded. Thousands of jackalopes, squealing and thumping. It was unbearable. Then after several minutes the squealing and thumping stopped. The biggest jackalope of all approached us and spoke. "My name is Sekannawan, son of Kokatah, cousin to the wind, king of the jackalopes. This violence you wish on each other cannot happen on our sacred ground. You, the one called Ron Burgundy"—he looked at me—"why does this man wish to bring you into eternal darkness?"

"This man," I said to the jackalope, "believes I have eaten Senator Bobby Kennedy. He believes Mr. Kennedy is alive and in my belly."

"Is this true, Peter Lawford?" asked Sekannawan.

"Yes, proud mythical beast. I believe the senator has been eaten by this man."

"Not so," said the jackalope king. "Bobby Kennedy was given permission to walk free from here and with our aid he made it back to civilization. He is enjoying the breakfast buffet at the Desert Inn even as I speak."

Well, you can imagine how this really burned my britches. Suddenly I didn't care a lick about this talking jackalope king and I let him know it. "Now, you listen to me! My name is Ron Burgundy and I'm not going to sit here listening to any half rabbit, half antelope blabber on while Bobby Kennedy is enjoying a delicious breakfast buffet. I WILL NOT STAND FOR IT!"

"Then you have no choice but to enter the Ring of Lost Horns and fight me unto the death!" said Sekannawan the jackalope king.

"Then I shall fight you!" I cried.

"Be careful, Burgundy." Peter was back on my side. "He will tear your limbs off and eat your liver while you are still alive. He will feed your eyes to his children while you can still feel the pain. The raw sound of gnashing baby jackalope teeth on your eyes will drive you to insanity before you die!" It was truly the most emotive I had seen Peter Lawford since his turn as Theodore Laurence in *Little Women*. I told him as much and he was grateful for the notice.

We were paraded some miles to a circular patch in the desert. The ground was littered with the horns of dead jackalopes. It was a gruesome sight to be sure but my mind was focused on that buffet. I couldn't stop thinking about maybe one day possibly wrapping two pancakes around a western omelet in the shape of a huge spongy burrito. I would call it "the Breakfast Burgito" and it would be enjoyed the world over. In my reverie I hardly heard the sounding of the jackalope yell signaling the beginning of the fight. Sekannawan came at me fast. His little jackrabbit feet exploded his muscular body off the ground. His antlers pointed right at my face as he flew through the air. It was like a grenade had gone off and the shrapnel was coming at me. I had time for one move and one move only. My two hands went instinctively to guard my face. The antlers hit my hands with surprisingly little force. He was a lightweight. I grabbed ahold of both antlers and tore him in half. The fight was over. A thousand jackalopes stood in mute silence, stunned by the death of their king. But soon the silence grew to a murmur and then a growl. "Kill him!" they yelled! And just like that they were on us, Lawford and me. Ripping and gnashing and tearing, they tried their best, but we were killing jackalopes faster than you can say *omelet fixins*.

"ENOUGH!" came the cry of a female jackalope. Suddenly they all stopped attacking. When she spoke I knew that she was their queen. "My name is Kokenta, queen of the jack-alopes. I say free this man! He has honored the law of the Ring of Lost Horns. He is worthy of our respect and admiration and shall hereafter be known as Ron Burgundy, king of the jackalopes." I think she was trying to save face, because clearly Lawford and I were going to rip up their entire population in about ten minutes.

"Great queen," I said, "I do not wish to be worshipped as your king but only to return to the Desert Inn for their breakfast buffet."

"You can return, Ron Burgundy, under one condition," she spoke.

"Name your price, wise jackalope queen."

"From this day forth you shall harm not beasts of the wild for any reason other than survival of thyself."

I was slow to answer but when the words finally came I felt a great relief, like a magical feeling of being one with the universe had overtaken me and I was suddenly free. I answered her demand thusly: "I will indeed honor your condition and from this day forth, this dawn of the jackalopes, I, Ron Burgundy, son of Claude Burgundy, will harm not any beasts of the wild unless my own life is challenged."

"Go in peace, Ron Burgundy," my new friend Kokenta said. "Your name will forever be sung in our epic songs. Your deeds will not be forgotten by the jackalopes! Make haste. The breakfast buffet ends at eleven thirty." And off the thousand jackalopes went, racing into the desert. I have not seen one since. But, yes, they have seen me.

My experience with the jackalopes was deep and life alter-ing. I began a journey of new understanding in relation to the Animal Kingdom as a whole. Baxter, my very best friend and dog, was my constant companion and guide through this new consciousness. I am a sensitive man unafraid to express my feelings. I have been known to cry from time to time. I've never made it through the movie *One on One* with Robby Ben-son because I get too choked up. It's so very emotional. If you haven't seen it, do so, it's a real treat. A young college basketball player with great one-on-one skills is forced to play in a system of offense and defense that severely constricts his style. It's torturous to watch. The overbearing coach, played by G. D. Spradlin, simply won't let the kid create on the court. Whatever you do, don't tell me how it ends. I have never seen the ending and I doubt I ever will. The waterworks start flowing as soon as I hear the Seals and Crofts song "My Fair Share" and because of my loud sobbing, almost screaming re-ally, I am always asked to leave the theater. Annette O'Toole plays a bitchy but softhearted tutor—Oh boy . . . I'm having a hard time getting through this right now! Forget I brought up the movie *One on One*. It's just too damn emotional for me to even write about it.

My point here is simple. I am a sensitive man. I'm not afraid to pick a flower or delight in a butterfly or go for a skip. I care about the world around me and all of its creatures. Now when I see a manatee or a dingo or a hyena or a toucan or a giraffe or a leopard or a tortoise or a cow or a baboon or a

Gila monster, I have no desire to kill it. Take the wild baboon for an example. If you run at a baboon with your arms waving, yelling with your shirt off, which I have done, the animal will see it as an act of aggression and run full speed right at you. His only thought will be how to get at your face and tear it off so he can eat your head meat. I don't speak baboon. I confess I don't speak any animal language. However, Baxter can communicate with almost all of God's creatures and I can converse with him. On that particular safari when I ran out to a baboon to play a joke on him I was nearly torn to shreds. He was feet away from chewing off my whole face when Baxter barked out, "No, proud race of ape! He is your brother!" To which the baboon responded, "This thing is no ape!"

Baxter would have none of it and he said to the baboon, "He is an upright ape, no more dignified than you, great baboon, but simply one that can drive a car and uses small sharp knives to cut the hair on his face."

"Why is he running at me?"

"The human man is not smart. He does not understand basic body language."

"He could have gotten killed," the baboon warned. (All of this conversation was related to me later by Baxter on the plane ride home.)

"I have had to save him many times from all sorts of animals in the Animal Kingdom," said Baxter.

"I don't understand, what's in it for you?"

"He puts dry dog food in a bowl for me."

"A devil's bargain!"

"He is my friend. I sleep with him when he has not 'scored.' I sleep with him often."

"What is your name?"

"My name is Baxter and his name is Ron Burgundy."

"Well, Baxter, you tell your friend Ron Burgundy not to run at baboons the way he did. It's weird."

"I shall relate that to him. You are a gentle soul."

"And you are a wise dog. Go now. I am hungry and I will want to eat either you or the Ron Burgundy."

"We will take our leave. Can I smell your red butt?"

"Of course."

An animal that understands that you respect him, from the fearsome white shark to the impulsive and grumpy bear, will be more willing to treat you with respect.

Over time I have come to understand the Animal Kingdom as one great hierarchy. The noble eagle sits at the top. He is God's greatest creation, soaring through the skies with magnificent splendor and grace! His watchful eye looks over us all. I am in awe of the eagle and I believe one day when the skies fall and great chasms of doom open up to swallow mankind, it will be the eagle that rescues and guides those of us worthy (that would be me and my news team for sure) into the next land. I have several wood carvings of eagles in my home for this reason. One of them has a removable head and a hollowed-out body where you can hide some keys or half pencils like the kind you get at a golf course. If the noble eagle is at the top of the Animal Kingdom, then surely the lowly sea otter is at the bottom. They are the dumbest, most stupid animals out there. I can't even imagine what kind of hell we would be in for if the sea otter ever took control of the world. Simply put, they would ruin it. I don't hate them but I sure wouldn't trust them with maintaining order. Baxter confided in me once that talking to sea otters was like talking to aerobics instructors. I don't doubt it. They are self-centered and boring and all they want to talk about is fish. Meanwhile Baxter tells me that most eagles think like ancient Greeks with minds sharper than Socrates'. Baxter has also told me on several occasions that eagles intimidate him. His small dog brain is no match for the cerebral majesty of the eagle.

As a kind of sidebar I would like to say wild eagles do not make great pets. I was offered a wild eagle by a Russian I had come to know through the world of high-stakes archery. We both had an interest in falconry. (I have owned several world-class falcons over the years.) This man—I will call him "Glavtec" because he would definitely not want me to reveal his true identity—had six bald eagles in the trunk of his car that he was trying to unload. He was in to me for a lot of archery money. I REALLY wanted one of those eagles but I knew it was illegal to own a bald eagle in this country. I decided if I kept the eagle inside my house no one would be the wiser and I could have my cake and eat it too. I threw the eagle in a pillowcase and took him home. Well, day one the eagle tore up everything in my house. Day two he scratched up Baxter and me pretty badly. Day three he got caught in a fan and while trying to rescue him I got scratched up worse than before. Day four he sat on the couch almost lifeless, watching TV and possibly contemplating suicide. Day five he began working on a strategy for escape. Day six he was polite and even ate dinner with us at the table. Day seven he allowed me to place a small Uncle Sam hat on his head and posed for a picture with me and Baxter in our red, white and blue swimsuits. Day eight I taught him to drive a miniature fire truck in a comical way and he looked like he was enjoying himself. On the ninth day Baxter and I decided to take our new best friend for a walk on the beach. The minute I opened the door he flew away. He had been planning it all along! He was just playing with me to get free. Ingenious! He still, to this day, attacks me when he sees me. I'm forever watching the skies. He truly is a magnificent bird.

Where does man fit in this great chain of being? I'll tell you. Right between the narwhal and the puma, and that's pretty close to the top, my friend. I would say humans are positioned maybe a hundred or so animals from the top. Pretty good considering there are more than a thousand animals. Things like cheetahs, hermit crabs and salmon are definitely higher than us, but then donkeys, parrots and daddy longlegs are below us. It really puts things in perspective when you come to understand the science of the Animal Kingdom and where we as humans stand within it, or Human Positionology, as it is known in science circles. I try not to lord it over the dumber lower animals, like horses and woodpeckers, because I always know there are more intelligent animals, like the squirrel and fruit bats, that can look down on me! Through my experiences with the jackalopes and my understanding of the great chain of being I have become a friend to all nature. I no longer hunt for pleasure. I don't condemn those who do.

CHART OF HUMAN POSITIONOLOGY

Champ Kind, my friend and an award-winning sports journalist, kills, on average, around five to six hundred animals a year. He loves to hunt. He would hunt caged chickens if it were legal. Maybe he does anyway! I know every year he goes off on his annual hunting trip to some secret island with a group of men known only as the Dark Watch. I don't know what they hunt. I don't want to know. I say live and let live, which might not be what they say at all. Funny situations.

Finally, I want to say a word about cats. They are wonderful!

ABOUT WOMEN

Over the years I've had an ever-evolving understanding of the female sex. I credit Veronica Corningstone, my wife, my lover and my sex partner, as the lady who changed my views on women. Before I met Veronica I had some antiquated ideas of how women should conduct themselves in the world. For the longest time I didn't like seeing a woman in the workplace unless she was getting me coffee or bending over or both. Often I would put a cup of coffee on the floor and ask a woman to get it for me. I know it sounds crazy but I wasn't sure women could read. When I saw them typing I just assumed they were copying shapes or making noise for no reason. I didn't know if women knew how to count money. I thought women had underdeveloped brains like the brains of softheaded people. Then there was the whole idea of men-struation. It made no sense to me and science didn't seem to have any answers. How could a person dying of blood loss be allowed to work in a man's office? Frankly I'm still hav-ing problems with this one. The science just isn't there yet. We need greater study in this area but I'm willing to concede women should be allowed in the workplace alongside men. I can laugh at some of the naive things I used to think, but much of it you could write off because of the times. The times were different. Before 1970 women were here on this earth to cook food and give men boners. You certainly couldn't as-sociate them with delivering the news. There was the whole credibility problem. I wasn't alone in believing that women could not be trusted. I once bet Edward R. Murrow that a dog would anchor the news before a woman, and I believed it. Women were considered nothing more than sex objects. They were valued more for their legs, their butts and their tits than for anything else. Times sure have changed! Heck, now in television news and I guess just about everywhere else women are respected for their brains. Appearance means very little! Go figure! When I see a woman walking down the street in high heels and a short skirt I no longer drool like a hungry zombie. I think to myself, "Hmmmm, I wonder what kind of brain that foxy mama has?" Veronica did that to me. She's got brains, all right, and I married her for that reason. Of course Veronica also just happens to have a grade-A dumper and some first-class tits.

For many years I was asked to attend sensitivity training. I got hit with sexual misconduct suits left and right, at least twenty a year for a while. My hands were always leaving me and going places. I stood too close to women. I used words like *boobies* and *knockers* and *jugs* and *jigglers* and *melons* to compliment my coworkers. At one point I was told by my lawyer that it was safer if I never talked to women. But of course that is ridiculous. My old-fashioned transgressions aside, I do know a lot about the ladies. Without being modest, I've found that women cannot keep their hands off me. It's true. I've slept with more women than six Wilt Chamberlains. I've made love to women in the same room—heck, in the same bed—with Wilt. Wilt and I have—oh no I won't; that's a story for a different kind of book. Besides, the young women we were with that night, Tracy Karns and Debra Sanlinger, may not want me to tell that story. It's pretty dirty.

Suffice it to say I've learned quite a lot about the fairer sex over the years just through experience alone. If you add to that my extensive reading in scientific journals and my interviews with great lovemakers like myself and Geraldo Rivera, you could say that I'm probably the world's greatest authority on the subject of women. I could write a whole book just about women. Someday I will, believe me. It would have a bunch of pictures—not just nude women either. They would be on horseback or in cocktail outfits or wearing cheerleading dresses. I would show them in natural settings like offices and beaches, or maybe even on the farm. Each woman in the book would talk about her favorite things, like what turns her on and what her measurements are, stuff like that. Then I would have pictures of these women in their underwear, probably just so you could see a little bit more. After a few photos of the women in their clothes I would then have nude photos of them. Maybe one part of this book I'm thinking about could have a special unfolding-page section in the middle that gives you a big picture of one of the women completely naked. I don't know! The book is not fully formed in my mind just yet. Perhaps if I had chapters about stereo equipment and new suit styles it would be helpful for men too. I bet a guy could put a book like this out every couple of months! I would sure read it. My point is I know an awful lot about women.

Women on the whole tend to be more emotional than men. I may be the rare exception. I'm more better at emotional stuff than women. I'm actually more better than women at a lot of stuff. I can balance a basketball on my finger for more than twenty seconds. I bet I can run faster than most women. Cheetahs are the fastest mammals on earth. I know how to spell *Mississippi* backward—what am I doing? This isn't a contest. Anyway, women turn on the waterworks for just about any reason but mostly for manipulation. No one likes to see a woman cry and women know it. They use the crying thing all the time to get what they want. It starts when they are babies and doesn't stop until the dirt is shoveled over them. For whatever reason men stop using tears at around seven years old and start using their brains instead to control their surroundings. In scientific terms women's cranial development is said to be retarded but their powers of manipulation are far in advance of most men's by the time they are five years old. This is basic developmental stuff, by the way, and you could read it in any journal of human development. There's a special "manipulation gene" in women that has been discovered or will be discovered. This gene, which surely exists, controls the crying and lying sections of the frontal cortex lobular section of the brain. It allows women to trick men into all kinds of situations.

A woman's sneaky and underhanded manipulation can take many forms and can be quite cunning and subtle. Here's a standard conversation I might have with my wife and glorious sexual partner, Veronica.

Ron

I was thinking about going out with the boys tonight, maybe having a few drinks?

Veronica

Sounds fun.

Ron

Just me and the boys.

Veronica

You need to get out. You've been working very hard.

Well, you can see how infuriating this kind of subtle manipulation can be! Every word is so well chosen to cause pain. It's like they control your mind! I once wore a motorcycle helmet with a dark shield on a date with a woman I thought was trying to control my mind. I was too afraid to take it off for fear she might try to change my plans using manipulative word combinations and crying. I literally could not hear or see her the whole date. In the end it worked out. We made sweet and long-lasting love but I stayed inside the helmet so as not to let her connect to me and my mind.

Of course, for most of the women in my life I didn't need a helmet to protect me from their controlling ways. I have an automatic shutoff switch inside my brain that lets me listen to a woman speak without hearing a word. For about a ten-year period, up until I was smitten with Veronica, I used the time that women spoke to me as a chance to think up songs or poems or make up new games. It was a valuable use of my time. A woman would come up to me and maybe start a sentence like "Ron, I need to speak to you. . . ." If she was serious I would nod and look concerned and say "Okay" and "Right away" every so often, but inside I was off thinking about something else, something fun. I made up the game Piddly-Woop while some woman was talking to me. It's a complicated but fun game for the whole family.

I'm not going to lie, I heard this a lot from women throughout the sixties: "Are you listening to me?" A lot. So to be honest I'm not sure I perfected my "shutoff switch" method. I know that my colleague Champ Kind has never listened to a woman talk for more than eight seconds. He shuts off and just smiles and waits for them to stop moving their mouths. If you asked him I don't think he could remember two sentences a woman has said to him. It's remarkable really. For him it's like they don't even exist as speaking animals.

Looking back on it, I think plenty of women thought maybe I was rude. It didn't really matter though. In those days there were so many women who wanted to make it with a number one News Anchor that it was just the law of averages. The way I figured it, if I batted one for twenty, that would make for a batting average of fifty. Those are Hall of Fame numbers, my friend, Hall of Fame.

As a Hall of Fame ladies' man (an institution I am lobbying to create, by the way), I don't think anyone in the world would mind if I gave up some of my secrets for how to meet, bed and marry the woman of your dreams.

HOW TO MEET,
BED AND MARRY
THE WOMAN OF
YOUR DREAMS

Courtship is as old as the earliest days of fire. Men have forever pursued females in poetry and song and with feats of daring. Little has changed from those early days of courtship. We gentlemen still recite poems and sing and try to outdo other men for the hearts of women. I often dream of the medieval days, when men wearing robes made of thick woven carpet lifted heavy goblets of wine and sang to their paramours. Even though the great banquets and royal feasts of olden days are long gone, I feel like I would have been right at home in their giant halls. I've often imagined myself atop the turret of some noble castle on the Rhine with my falcon, Leander, perched on my arm. I think in a past life I was maybe a baron or possibly an earl and that I had many lands and great wealth and an eye patch. I was known throughout the region as a generous landowner but ruthless when I had to be. I could be quite swift with justice but I was never accused of being unfair. If you've seen my dining room in my house, then you know it's a passion of mine to imagine such things. I've commissioned murals on the walls of my dining room with scenes of me throughout history. A local artist by the name of Vincent St. Vincent-Pierre was paid handsomely, perhaps too handsomely, to illustrate me in heroic situations throughout time. While dining at the Burgundy house, guests enjoy rich oil paintings of me as an explorer on a clipper ship sailing for the New World. They can turn their heads and I'm represented as a proud slave in the Roman Colosseum, having just vanquished a lion! St. Vincent-Pierre also portrayed me as a noble savage who first lays eyes on Lewis and Clark from a bluff high above the wide Missouri. Guests often comment on the painting entitled *Justice for All*, where I am standing with my arm around my good friend Nat Turner in a field of bloodied and hacked white slave owners. It's really quite a room! On the ceiling, above the table, St. Vincent-Pierre painted his masterpiece, Veronica and me making love in the nude as a panoply of exotic animals look on in wonder. It's the room I'm most proud of in my house. I suspect the room will be carefully dismantled when I pass and donated to the San Diego fine arts museum. Look at me! I was supposed to be talking about courtship. There I go again. The problem

I'm discovering while writing this chronicle is that I'm just too darn interesting!

I don't have the facts in front of me but I'm pretty sure the ratio of women to men in this country is approximately one and one-quarter women to every eight males. It's a problem and we should really import more women into this country— not from England, Jesus Christ, NOT FROM ENGLAND. Some countries, like France I believe, have thirty women for every man, which accounts for why Frenchmen always have beautiful girlfriends and wives. If you put a Frenchman in a country where he had to fight it out with real men for the love of a woman, he would fail miserably and be left with only the dogs.

With such a low ratio of women in this country it makes it hard to meet and then court them. Hanging out at the ball game or the Elks Lodge is not going to do it. You could go where they go—the hair parlor, for instance, but you end up looking pretty stupid in a hair parlor. I've sat in women's hair parlors before. It's only a matter of time before you are asked to leave. The best places to meet women are places where both sexes mingle—churches, parks, department stores and supermarkets. There's a strategy for each location.

For instance, let's talk about supermarkets. Women like a man who is confident, and nothing says confidence more than beef. When I'm in a supermarket, whether it be to pick up a gallon of milk or to get some coffee, I take my cart straight for the meat department and pile it full of steaks. Make sure the cart is overflowing with steaks. Don't worry, you don't have to buy them. It's only for show—you can ditch the cart later in the bread aisle, but while you're in the supermarket, for two to three hours, you need to push around a cart weighted down with cuts of red meat . . . and NO CHICKEN. Maybe some pork, but make sure you have lots of sirloin and ribs. Women go nuts! They see all that beef and it triggers within them something from the cavemen days. They just start thinking of procreating. I promise you if you push around a shopping cart with two hundred pounds of meat cuts in a supermarket you will get respect from women. I like to throw in a few cans of beans and twenty or so packages of bacon to add some variety. A box of condoms is too suggestive and shows a real lack of class. No, the best course is to simply walk around the supermarket, humming along with the piped-in music, pushing your cart of meat in front of you like you don't have a care in the world. You can sometimes "accidentally" bump into a woman and then say something like "Sorry, it looks like my meat got away from me!" If the woman smiles, then follow her—by all means follow her. Some won't smile. The crabby ones will look at you like you're some kind of homeless man and recoil. They are not worth the effort. They're not real women anyway. They might even be lesbians. More than likely women who do not fall for the ole meat cart routine are lesbians.

In a department store you can't walk around with a cart full of meat. It's stupid, and frankly you look crazy because most department stores don't sell meat. The thing to do in a department store is to carry around eight or nine suits. Go straight to the suit department and get eight or nine suits and then start walking around the whole store. Purchasing power alone is a real turn-on for all women, but when they see suits they react like they've seen a shopping cart full of meat. You have the money to buy eight suits. You have the class to wear a suit. You are desirable. It's simple. Some guys will head over to the women's wear section, maybe grab a bra to hold, and start crying and talking about the "breakup." It's a good ruse. There are women who fall for it but ultimately you need to look secure, and bawling on the floor with underwear in your hand is not very secure looking. If you need to shout out, "I'm buying eight suits today," that's okay. Imagine being a woman (not putting on the clothes and walking around in front of a mirror; I mean just imagine it with your brain); now imagine you're in a store and you see some handsome man with a new toaster in his hand and you are intrigued, but then out of nowhere you hear a loud voice proclaim, "I'm buying eight suits!" And around a corner comes a man holding eight suits. I rest my case.

PTA meetings are real winners. It doesn't matter if you have a kid in the school. Walk in, sit down and wait. When people start popping up and talking, stand up and talk, maybe cry, but whatever you do make it passionate. I usually try something like "We need to address the issue of safe zones. I know it's controversial but I am for it!" I blabber on for a bit about keeping children safe and then I might wrap up my speech with something like ". . . and one more thing: I drive a Chrysler LeBaron." Women love that you care about children but it's even better when they hear you drive something like a LeBaron or a Stratus; they get wet down below. It also helps to have a step stool. You really want to tower over everyone else in the room. If some nosey body gets in your face and asks you what grade your child is in at the school, you need to run away. No harm no foul, just keep running until you are safely out of the neighborhood. If you're jumping fences, look out for the bigger dogs.

Fortunately for me meeting women has never been a real issue. I am a very big deal. I have been for some time. When you are the number one News Anchor in San Diego you are basically a rock star. When you make it to the network you are a god. Women just want what I have. They want to be close to it. They want to be a part of the magic. Brian Fantana, who does a lot of reporting from the street, literally has to fight the women off with a stick. He once confided in me he's never masturbated—not once—because it has always been easier for him to just go ahead and have sex with a woman. In fact he sometimes fantasizes about masturbation while having sex with women. That's what being in the news game is like. Just ask Brian Williams. That guy uses Velcro to keep his pants shut. He doesn't have time to keep buttoning and unbuttoning them with all the classy tail he gets. Being a News Anchor is so close to being a god on so many levels that you start to think like one. You start to believe it's your right to descend on women and impregnate them with demigod babies. Those were simpler times, of course, when gods could just come down and have sex with any mortal they wanted. I would give my right nut to live in those days with the gods, but no such luck; I got stuck in this age of horseshit. Anyway, I digress. Once you've got the woman interested it's time to think about stage two: How am I going to get this woman in the sack?

Here again it helps to be a number one News Anchor. Women just want to jump in bed with me. I can't help it; it's just something I live with. Every once in a while a woman comes along who does not want to sleep with me. It's weird but it happens. My first reaction is always the same: Do I look like the man who killed her dog? If it's not that, then I know she's just a psychologically damaged frigid woman who needs a little Burgundy thaw. I start by asking her out on a date. Now is not the time to be cheap. Take her to an Olive Garden or a Red Lobster. If you have a skill, like playing the flute, or you can juggle, now is the time to spring it on her. The mystery you have inside you unfolds. She's probably thinking, if you can juggle, what else can you do? She's going to be intrigued. I sometimes will hit a woman with my amazing knowledge of dinosaurs. I might tell her that birds are considered a subgroup of dinosaurs by many paleontologists or that the word *dinosaur* means "terrible lizard." Women can't believe what they are hearing. They see how smart you are and then you tell them it's just the tip of the iceberg! This is also a great time to blow hot air her way. Women respond well to humid, pungent hot air (see chapter on effective breath).

Get them talking. Women love to talk. You don't have to listen, as mentioned before, but you do have to let them talk, and believe me, they will yammer on like howler monkeys. Pretend you are interested if you can. It's not a deal breaker if you can't, mind you, but it helps. Most women understand that you are not interested. Scientists have proven that by the time a woman is in her late teens she knows that men will not pay any attention to the noises coming out of her mouth.

That's not to say women have nothing to say. Please, don't misinterpret me. The last thing I need is a bunch of angry feminists picketing my house and throwing pies at me. I know what that feels like and I don't like it. You would think I would like it! Pies are delicious, but pies can also be hurtful. There have been some great women talkers over the years. I could list so many! Smart women have made their mark on history and I know the names of many if not all of them. (NOTE: Find list of smart women for later draft.) Anyway women love to talk and if you can manage some fake interest it's a great way to get them comfortable.

Once she is comfortable it's time to be direct. Nothing works quite like leaving a lady in a room for a few minutes and then returning wearing only your best Nordstrom or Crabtree and Evelyn bathrobe. Talk about a winning strategy! Women will react in different ways but believe me, you will always get a reaction! Leave the bathrobe open for a hint of what awaits within. A glimpse or suggestion of chest hair, maybe a little belly, can send a girl to the moon, wild with anticipation—not all women, mind you, but a select few. Keep in mind these time-tested strategies are all from before I married my best friend and sexually adventurous wife, Veronica. The bathrobe ploy, as I called it, was used many times to great success in the home or outside just walking around. I sometimes wore the open bathrobe through the supermarket or at work. I think now there are laws that prohibit open bathrobe wearing in places of business. I don't know, it's hard to keep up with all the laws people make. Sometimes I think people who can't build stuff or report the news or do anything useful spend their time making up laws. The world would be a better place if men and women could walk around in open bathrobes.

Once you are in the sack there's very little I need to tell you that you can't find out on your own. I was lucky to have Jenny Haggleworth, sixeen years my senior, for my first go-round. She knew what she was doing all right! For most young men learning to make love I recommend cruising retirement villages to see if they can scrounge up some old tail. Women in their seventies and eighties make great guides through the complicated world of the sensual arts. A young man of twenty can really benefit from a few days in the sack with an old prune or a French whore. Of course, where are you going to find a French whore in times of peace, huh? Anyway after a night d'amour you can usually sneak away unharmed. Unless you have fallen in love. If that's the case you might have to start thinking about marriage.

The Holy Bible teaches us that marriage was invented by Helen of Troy to keep men from ruling over Canaan. It's in Deuteronomy somewhere, I believe. The exact quote is, "So sayeth Helen of Troy that unto her Joseph shall be husband to the woman soeth he hath not manly poweres hence forth and the woman shall have dominion over the domain." Something like that. I'm paraphrasing I think, or I made it up. It doesn't matter. Most historians believe the King James Bible was written by Shakespeare anyway, and we all know what kind of ladies' man he was. The real point I'm making here is you need to go into marriage lightly, my friend. The two sexes were never meant to live together and that's just a fact.

I don't have the numbers in front of me but I believe that all marriages in this country end in divorce. I can't for the life of me think of a marriage that hasn't ended in divorce. There must be one. It would be interesting to find that couple and ask them what went wrong. Why did they stay together when they obviously needed to get away from each other? Are they lying? Are they secretly divorced but they just wanted to be on the news? How could they look each other in the face for so long? This is all hypothetical of course. We don't even know if such a couple exists. Go ahead, get married, I don't care. Get married over and over again. It's very American and for that reason I am for it.

MY NEIGHBOR: THE PLOT THICKENS

My neighbor, the one who borrowed my leaf blower and didn't return it, is dating an old broad that I slept with thirty years ago. Cynthia Spaller is her name and honestly she's still got it. I want to shake the hands of the plastic surgeon who kept those two boulders up in the air. Frankly she's too good for him. Anyway he's throwing a block party and he didn't invite me. How do you not invite Ron Burgundy? I'm a living legend. Okay, Wellspar, let's see where this goes.

MY HISTORY OF MEXICO

I decided to do it. I'm going to write a history of Mexico. Someone's gotta do it! I figure it's my gift to the Mexican peoples. I'm passionate about history and I'm not sure we want to leave it up to Mexicans. I brought it up in an earlier chapter and I just couldn't let the idea go. This is just the first chapter and the book is in no way designed like I would like it. As I said before it will definitely be bound in rich Corinthian leather, about two feet by three feet in size and about eight inches thick. It will have many fine illustrations and smell like a new pair of cowboy boots. So without further ado . . . here is the first chapter of my long-awaited history of Mexico.

THE
Fabulous Fables
&
Rich Tales
OF
Olden Mexico
AND ITS
Regal Peoples

In the beginning there was only the land. A great land that stretched on and on as far as the eye could see. Savage dinosaurs roamed the earth unaware they were even in Mexico, for it did not exist as a country then. Thunderous fights occurred between mighty sauropods and crafty spinosaurs. It was a wild land full of passion and brute lust. Two hunters, Kah and Miko, cautiously walked through the forest in search of sustenance for their families. They were dressed only in small loincloths. Miko was nervous, for he had seen a herd of hadrosaurs not far from where they made camp the night before. Neither hunter, although they were skilled in hand-to-hand combat, was a match for a hadrosaur. The two hunters were tired. It had been a long day and they had come up empty. Soon the rainy season would be upon them and it would be time for the great migration. Kah was the stronger of the two. He reached out his arm and rested it on Miko's shoulder. It was a reassuring touch for Miko. He had been worried that they would find no food. Kah wanted Miko to not worry. He suggested they make camp and went about finding kindling for a fire. The two men did their tasks with well-rehearsed precision and soon they had a suitable camp. They had hunted in these pre-Mexican woods often. As the blazing hot sun sank into the blue mountains outside of current-day Mexico City, Kah once again put his hand out to reassure Miko that everything would be all right. He rested it on Miko's bare shoulder. Miko could feel the big man's hand on his shoulder and felt comforted by it. Kah then slid his hand along Miko's muscular back, stopping right before his firm buns. Miko instinctively stepped away but Kah held him and pulled him in. Within seconds the stronger man was pressing his hungry lips onto his friend. Miko struggled to get free but Kah was strong. He held Miko in a tight hug and now both his hands firmly held the smaller man's round buttocks. Miko was terrified and strangely aroused at the same time. He had often stayed awake dreaming about what the big man would feel like and now it was actually happening! As Kah pulled Miko into his broad muscular chest Miko could feel his willpower draining. He would give over to his desire once and for all—but suddenly there was a great crashing in the forest. A *Tyrannosaurus rex* burst through the trees and wrapped his mighty and awesome jaws around Kah and snapped his body in half. These were dangerous times. They were the best of times if you could avoid the dinosaurs but the worst of times if you could not. Miko never could erase the image of his friend mercilessly slung back and forth like a rag doll in the mouth of that *Tyrannosaurus*. He hiked back to his village and became known as Mikothelan, lord emperor of the Incas.

The Incas were the first inhabitants of Mexico. Where they originally came from remains a mystery. Many historians believe aliens brought the Incas here from a planet outside of our solar system, so if you were thinking Mars or even Pluto, think again; you're way off. I'm not buying it! Aliens did not bring the Incas to this planet. The Incas were just too dumb. More than likely, as more and more research demonstrates, the Incas probably just grew up in Mexico naturally and built some cities and lived good lives, occasionally eaten by dinosaurs. There really isn't much we can learn from these people. They weren't cavemen but they weren't rocket scientists either. They enjoyed about a million years of peace and tranquility and then the Mayans came, and that's when the shit hit the fan.

The Mayans probably were brought here by aliens. They were too smart to be born in Mexico. They invented a calendar. A calendar? Really? That's not something you invent every day if you're born in Mexico. They "built" pyramids. Right! Earthlings living in mud huts built pyramids. Sorry, not buying it. The Mayans were definitely aliens. They were much more civilized than the Incas. They wore suits and went to work and made up games like football played in giant stadiums. I once had the opportunity to visit one of their stadiums. Not really that great but considering it was built by people whose average height was two and a half feet, you can't help but tip your hat to the Mayan people. They slaughtered the Incas in no time flat. They took them from their houses and whacked their heads off and used the whacked-off heads in their football games. (Don't worry, they get what's coming to them later. What goes around comes around.) They built great cities and established trade routes. They grew as a race and were said to be numbered in the millions. Their king, Esteban, was considered to be a god. Scholars now believe that he had contact with the aliens and so he had more knowledge than everyone else, but this is only reasonable speculation. What we do know is that he was a boastful and proud man who ruled with an iron fist. He had been a great footballer in his day and a star athlete in the school system. If my reading of the Florentine Codex is correct, then he studied law and went on to marry a woman with great wealth. (Not too bad on the eyes either!) With her wealth and his natural good looks and grace they quickly climbed the ladder of success in the backstabbing, drama-filled world of the Mayan court. They were natural-born politicians, so when election time came rolling around they had run such a smooth campaign that they easily had the votes to be declared the new king and queen. They would stay atop the throne for many a year until a politician so smooth and fun to be around, the kind of guy you would drink a beer with, entered the city and won the hearts of everybody.

Montezuma grew up in the farming community outside of Tijuana. He wasn't a Mayan but an Aztec. He had wanted to be a town planner and to some degree that's what he was—maybe the greatest town planner in history. He built Mexico in a few weeks. He was no Thomas Jefferson, mind you, but he was pretty good. Jefferson was our greatest thinker when it came to cultivating the land. He understood the delicate balance between the growth of civilization and croppery. I consider myself a gentleman farmer in the Jeffersonian sense. Before I was asked to leave San Luis Obispo I had a nice half acre of land with about a hundred head of donkey. They were a stubborn lot of animals and a half acre inside the town limits is not enough land for them to really stretch out on. They needed way more land and way more food than I supplied. A day didn't go by without a donkey in my kitchen. They ate me out of house and home until Baxter talked them into making a break for it. They stampeded through San Luis Obispo and headed up into the Sierra Nevada mountains. Technically, by California law, I still own them, but I'm happy enough to let them roam free.

Montezuma had bigger fish to fry than donkeys! He marched into the town where the Mayans were and quickly set up shop as the new guy in town. He was a cool customer from what we historians know. He had the ladies dripping wet with his handsome looks and self-confident attitude. In no time at all he was the most popular guy in the region. Archaeologists claim he loved the ladies. He had many wives of all shapes and sizes, although legend has it that he enjoyed huge knockers. If you go to certain areas in Mexico today women with really big jugs are said to have "Montezuma's Bazumas." I think there's a limit to how big a set of breasts should be. Some of the women in Mexico have tits way out to here—floppy big'ns that make them so top-heavy it looks like they are going to fall over. No thank you, Mr. Montezuma, you can keep your size 50 E-cups for yourself; I like mine big, but not THAT big. If I'm going to have a pair of boobs jangling in my face I don't want them to threaten me with suffocation! I like to get my hands on 'em and enjoy the ride.

Under Montezuma, Mexico and the new Aztec empire grew to magnificent splendor and opulence. Gold adorned every woman who walked the golden streets. Elaborate parties were given every night, with giant ice sculptures and fountains of hot gold. The excess saw no boundaries, for these were the "go-go" years, when everyone overextended themselves and cheap credit was the name of the game. On the top of this all-too-fragile wealth and lavish lifestyle sat Montezuma without a care in the world.

Meanwhile, a million miles away in Spain, at the court of Fernando Valenzuela, a young, handsome adventurer by the name of Hernán Cortés was dreaming big and shooting for the stars. Valenzuela had just granted the stout explorer a legion of ships and casks of red wine to set sail for Mexico in search of gold. Cortés was a hard man. His chiseled features and rugged good looks suggested a soldier of fortune, which he was, but he turned out to be much more than that. He was a conqueror of lands and a loyal subject to the queen of Spain. He was also a ruthless bully who tamed a people and forged a destiny for Mexico that would last even to this day. He set sail on Tuesday, July 5, 1776, unaware that a far greater country than his own had just declared its independence. The ships were stocked with casks of red wine and goblets for drinking. For drinking fine red wine was the sailor's life in olden times. Also each man had his own broadsword made from the finest iron ore mined in deepest, blackest Africa. These swords were so great they often were named. Names like La Legion, Excelsior, Magnifico, El Cartagena, Beatrice, Fontanello and Esmeralda ring out among broadsword collectors far and wide. At the Sword and Shield, a high-end-replica sword shop specializing in rapiers and broadswords, a group of us meet once a month to discuss these ancient weapons. We often make up our own wondrous deeds done by these legendary swords. I have several replicas and I've created histories for them that I enjoy telling to people if they're over at the house. Cortés sailed with many fine broadswords and horses and leather and casks of red wine. The wine poured down the Spaniards' bearded faces under the hot sun but they had not a care in the world, for soon they would be in Mexico with all the gold they desired.

Montezuma, the dumb Aztec, never knew what hit him. Cortés was a man who knew what he wanted and he just reached out and grabbed it. He had a lust for life and he showed it. Using his broadsword, Gabriella, he cut a hole through Mexico, hacking and chopping off faces and limbs and enjoying his red wine with a hearty laugh. The smell of sweaty leather and dried wine hung in the air like the smell of sex in a whorehouse. Soon all of Mexico would smell of the Spaniards, and they would like it. Pungent were the days of Cortés! His men were ripe with lusty doings and bold adventure. They had hearty laughs and enjoyed roasted mutton chops dripping with olive oil. They would just toss the uneaten parts of the mutton in the street like they didn't care. They were a band of brothers known only as "the Conquistadors" and they were the true Mexicans. Their more handsome European looks were an instant draw for all of the Aztecs and the Mayans, who were not a great-looking race, but they had one problem. Although not much scientific record exists concerning penis size, we can judge by ancient Aztec drawings and paintings that the Aztec people had huge penises. Some of them appeared to be two feet long! With that kind of size, how could any man compete for a woman's affection? The Conquistadors quickly realized they would have to cut off every penis bigger than their own in the land. If we can believe oral history, this period was called the Time of the Great Castrata! Soon the Aztec women forgot their desire for giant penises and settled into comfortable lives with the much smaller Spaniards. But could a memory be extinguished so easily? Hardly. It explains why even to this day Mexican women secretly lust after that which they lost, a truly giant penis.

But who was their leader? Who was Hernán Cortés? And how did Maximilian get into this picture? Read on, dear reader, for more glory and excellence follows in chapter 2 of *The Fabulous Fables and Rich Tales of Olden Mexico and Its Regal Peoples*.

END OF CHAPTER ONE

My Favorite Doodles

Doodles are a unique form of expression for me. A way to release stress and clear my mind . . . and if I don't say so myself, some of these are pretty darn good.

"Alien"

One of the friendly aliens who brought the Mayans to Mexico. Possibly named Glabbo.

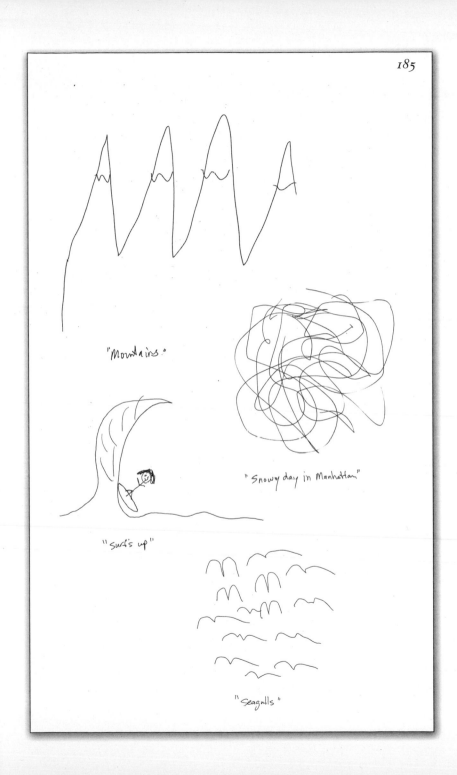

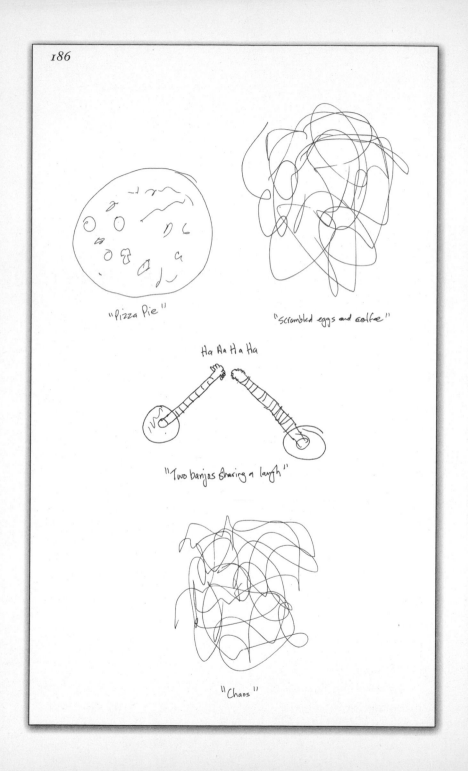

"Pizza Pie"

"Scrambled eggs and coffee"

Ha Ha Ha Ha

"Two banjos sharing a laugh"

"Chaos"

I DISH THE DIRT!

I've enjoyed a great life with many friends and wonderful acquaintances. My time in local news and cable TV gave me great access to personalities from every walk of life. Far be it from me to turn this noble chronicle of my life into a smut-filled smear campaign against those who confided in me over the years, but I will not stand by and allow these same people to drag my name through the mud without putting up a fight. Even if they haven't tried to bring me down, I know that's what they're thinking and I'm a firm believer in the preemptive strike. If it's good for American foreign policy, which clearly it has proven to be, then it's good for Ron Burgundy.

For starters, just to put to rest a rumor floating around, I did make love to Katie Couric. It was wonderfully slow and filled with passion. This was about two months ago. Veronica and I had rented a secluded cabin up in the Finger Lakes district in upstate New York. Nights were alive with the sounds of crickets and cicadas and the trees bending in the breeze. You could hear the gentle lapping of the water on the hulls of the boats across the lake. It was like we'd stepped into a more genteel time. It was the kind of peace we both desperately needed. I spent my days relaxing by the lake and my nights on the porch with my pipe and brandy and my best girl. On the third day we were awakened by a thunderous sound exploding across the lake. I took out my binoculars, and by the teat of Arachne, what did I see? It was Katie Couric in a cigarette boat called the *Blazin' Bitch* bouncing over the water. I knew that she was a bit of a tramp, but this was a ridiculous breach of decorum! I got in my golf cart (everyone up at the lake has a golf cart, okay?) and I drove around the lake to the dock. Sure enough, Katie roars in, paying no attention to the "no wake" signs, and as she's coming into her mooring she sees me and starts waving. "Ron! Ronny! Ronny! It's meeeeee, Katie."

Knock me down with a feather! I come all the way over ready to chew her a new one and gosh darn it if she isn't the cutest little bug there is. She just radiates health and beauty. I can't help it. Every time I see Katie Couric my insides just go to mush. I don't know what to say. . . . I manage a "Hi, Katie, it's me, Ron Burgundy." She laughs and then yells back, "Get over here, you dog. I have some Natty Lights in the cooler down below." So next thing you know I'm making my way across the deck of the *Blazin' Bitch* and heading for the cabin. Katie's about ten steps ahead of me. When I get down into the cabin she's got a marijuana cigarette and a bottle of Captain Morgan spiced rum in her hand. The whole cabin is upholstered in Ed Hardy–tooled leather. John Mayer is piped in over a built-in Bose sound system. "Money. Makes it all happen, right, Ronny?" she says to me.

"So I've been coming up to the lake for a while now and I haven't seen you before," I venture.

"Shit, Burgs, I just go where the *Blazin' Bitch* takes me."

"Where's your new fiancé?" I ask.

"We all gotta break away, right, Ron?" And then she puts her foot on my crotch. And that's as far as I'm going to take this tale. There's still a little friction over this incident in the Burgundy household. Besides, I've never been one to kiss and tell—but since there was no time for kissing, suffice it to say Katie Couric is a real wildcat with an insatiable desire to be loved, and I loved her. Enough said.

What else . . .

George Stephanopoulos wears women's underwear when he delivers the news. There is absolutely nothing intriguing or interesting about him at all except for this strange anomaly. Is it sexual? Is it wrapped up in some kind of identity crisis? Is he a thrill seeker? Nope to all three. He just confided in me that wearing women's panties while delivering the news lets him stay in touch with his feminine side. He also said women's underwear is made from softer materials and it feels better on his ball sack.

Or here's one . . .

If you remember the Captain from Captain and Tennille, he's always claimed he wasn't a real captain, but hold the boat! He *was* a captain. I was on board the *Angelica Nora* when he quite drunkenly guided it into some rocks off the coast of South America. The rusty old ship was overladen with stolen Chinese art and an assortment of international spies. I had agreed to work in the engine room in return for passage home to San Diego. How I got to China is a whole other book. Anyway, we spent the nights on deck drinking rum until we passed out. The Captain—his real name is Daryl Dragon but he went by Scardworth in those days—left the navigation of the ship to his pet seal. I know it sounds ridiculous, like I'm making the whole thing up, but seals make great navigators. This seal, Stinky was his name, just happened to be unfamiliar with the Southern Hemisphere and he got confused. When the Captain woke up he thought we were coming into San Francisco when in fact we were off the coast of Peru. Those are some of the toughest waters to navigate for seal or man and, well, Scardworth wasn't up to it. We hit rock and tore up the hull good. Only the Captain and I survived the sinking. In the lifeboat he tried to eat me but I grew to like him anyway. I told him his secret was safe with me but I warned him never to become a captain again. I guess the pull was just too great.

Maybe I shouldn't but what the heck. . . .

Vice President Walter Mondale and I ran a cockfighting ring for six years. I was just starting out in the news and he was the attorney general for the state of Minnesota. He used state funds to buy an old twin-engine mail plane, which he flew down to El Paso, where we had our ring. We ran twenty fights every Friday and Saturday night. He bred his own gamecocks, cut off the comb and wattle himself to prepare them for the fights and raked in a small fortune. He named his best cock "Sir Humphrey," after his good friend Hubert Humphrey. Sir Humphrey still holds the record for consecutive kills at 947. He was almost more eagle than rooster. He remains a legend in cockfighting lore to this day. There's an old Mexican-style *corrido* that goes,

Sir Humphrey, Sir Humphrey
Has entered the ring
No one can beat him
For he is the king
His beak is a razor
His feet are like knives
He's come from the devil
To take God from our lives.

It was used for many years to scare Mexican children into eating their vegetables. Anyway Walter Mondale loved Sir Humphrey. We both cried the day we ate him.

Now you got me going, so why not spill the beans about this. . . .

There was a time when Warren Beatty, the movie actor, was quite promiscuous. It's the truth. I know what you're thinking—not Warren Beatty! No way! From what I have heard from very reliable sources he would use his good looks and Hollywood power to attract women into the bedroom. Yes, that Warren Beatty. Get over it. He would meet them at parties or while shooting his movies and take it from there.

Believe me, I was as shocked as anybody when I first heard this, but apparently it's true. I guess you can't judge a book by its cover! I've known some promiscuous men in my time— Brian Fantana, World B. Free and of course myself come to mind—but Warren Beatty? Who would have guessed it?

The stupid old urban legend about Elton John collapsing after a concert and having a gallon of semen pumped from his stomach never seems to die, but I can say with complete certainty that this never happened. I have made an in-depth study of this ridiculous semen-swallowing legend and those falsely accused of it, and I can tell you there are only eleven people who have swallowed more than twelve ounces of semen and had their stomachs pumped because of it. They are: Rod Stewart, David Bowie, Duane Allman, Jeff Beck, Jon Bon Jovi, Andy Warhol, Britney Spears, Tonya Harding, Dick Cheney, Andy Roddick and Anita Bryant. Let the rumors about others stop! This is the complete list as it stands today. We need to set the record straight on this story. It's important news and we have to get it right.

Here's some investigative reporting. . . . After Barbra Streisand ended her relationship with Elliott Gould she carried on a yearlong, torrid affair with a young news reporter then anchoring KNBC-TV in Los Angeles by the name of Tom Brokaw. You heard it here! Fantana and I got the scoop from Ted Koppel, who was jealous of Brokaw's success at the time. News Anchors can be pretty catty and we knew it. To corroborate, because after all I am an investigative journalist, I broke into Streisand's room at the Beverly Hilton and snuck under the bed with a tape recorder and a typewriter. I waited patiently for six or seven hours but then got hungry and left. Meanwhile Fantana spotted the two lovers in the Sportsmen's Lodge over in the San Fernando Valley. We then decided to disguise ourselves as an out-of-town married couple on our second honeymoon. We checked into the Sportsmen's Lodge, with Fantana as my wife, and set about looking like a normal older married couple. We sat by the pool, went to the breakfast nook and spent our evenings at the bar. Bob Hope was there every night with a different lady, of course, but that was hardly news. No, we were onto something big. The Vietnam War was still happening and the military was in the middle of the Tet Offensive, but what we had on our hands was the kind of news you dream about as a young reporter but know will never happen. Ed Harken was furious with Fantana and me. He was yelling at us to get back to San Diego and report on the war—but of course he didn't know the dynamite we were sitting on. So one night after about two weeks of surveillance, we see them. We're posing as this innocent couple from Decatur, Illinois, and Fantana, dressed as my wife, runs up to Barbra and asks her for her autograph. While he's making small talk about recipes I slip into their room and place a tape recorder under the bed. The whole thing went off without a hitch. The first half of the tape is just a lot of mumbling and squeaking bedsprings, but then there was this:

Barbra
Tom, I can't do this anymore.

Tom
Why? Why not?

Barbra

I won't be a home wrecker. You love your wife. This is nuts!

Tom

I've explained it over and over again. I've got too much passion in me for one woman. Don't you see I need you and Joey? [He was having an affair with Joey Heatherton at the same time.]

Barbra

I need more. I need a man who will be there for me.

Tom

I'm here. I'm right here, baby.

Barbra

Tuesdays and Sundays! It's not enough, Tom. I want love. Love like you read about in the dime-store books.

Tom

I'll leave my wife. I'll go on the road with you. I'll learn to sing or dance. I could be in the chorus.

Barbra

It would never work. You would only resent me.

Tom

Oh, Barbra!

Barbra

I need you to know something else.

Tom

You're cheating on me?

Barbra

No, of course not. You need to know I'm pregnant with our child.

Tom

Nuh-uh! No way! Couldn't be mine—you're pretty loose, you know—I'm guessing there's been a lot of guys—could have been Donald Sutherland. There's just a lot of guys. NO WAY! I'm not responsible for nothing! Not a chance. Don't put this shit on me, Barbra.

Barbra

Don't worry, Tom. It's okay. No one will ever know. I want to have the baby. I'll put her up for adoption and the two of us can watch over her. We can see to it that she gets breaks in this world, breaks she might not even deserve, but we'll look after her. She will be a living testament to our secret love.

Tom

That is beautiful. Barbra, I will always love you. One more time for old times' sake.

Then the bed starts squeaking again for about another two hours. We had it. The biggest scoop in decades. We were sure to get the Pulitzer. We drove back to San Diego with the evidence but somewhere along the freeway Fantana and I made a big decision that has affected the news business ever since.

We decided that this was a private matter between Brokaw and Streisand and it really wasn't news. It was a huge shift in the way we, and ultimately America, thought about news. Our decision and subsequent focus on hard news rippled across the country until Americans simply lost their taste for salacious gossip and celebrity news. One more thing about this story. The love child? Her name is Jennifer Aniston and she is America's sweetheart.

MY NEIGHBOR: BREAKING NEWS

I spent the night in jail. As you know, I've been at war with my neighbor Richard Wellspar over my leaf blower. He borrowed it and then never returned it. It's been three weeks. Enough said. Anyway I crashed his little block party yesterday. I brought some very interesting pictures of his girlfriend, Cynthia Spaller. I had some old photos of her I took on a boat nearly thirty years ago. Bob Guccione would have paid me American money for them, if you know what I mean. So I start passing the photos out to everyone there, moms, dads, children, etc., and Wellspar flips his lid!

"Burgundy, this is the last straw!" he yells. "This woman is my wife!" (That I did not know, but I'll admit it: Sometimes I can be pretty unobservant.)

"Well, this woman and I did stuff on a boat that everyone needs to know about!" I yelled back.

"I'm calling the police!"

"Not before I make it plain to everyone at this party that

your wife, Cynthia Spaller, and I did stuff in every position imaginable with absolutely no regard for safety for hours and hours. We did not make love! We did it like zoo monkeys with no compassion and no end in sight but multiple dumb orgasms. It was debasing and humiliating and we enjoyed it! That is all. My name is Ron Burgundy."

I stormed out of there, only slowing down to key his car. I did spend the night in jail but I think he got the point. He won't be borrowing anything of mine anytime soon!

THE REST OF THE STORY:
THE NINETIES

Of course in writing a novel about my life I realize that much of my story has already been told. I've starred in two factual documentaries about myself. The first one I titled *Anchorman: The Legend of Ron Burgundy*. It covered a period in the news business of great change. It was the battle of the sexes, and you know what? . . . We all won! It's a better world with female anchormen. It also was a delightful retelling of my courtship with the lovely Veronica Corningstone, who then later became my wife and the woman I do it with. The documentary was a great success enjoyed by billions of people across the world and it quickly spawned a sequel, which reveals an even more adventurous time for me. I've titled this one *Anchorman 2: The Legend Continues.* This documentary also covers a game-changing moment in the history of televised news reporting, namely the epoch of twenty-four-hour cable news. As both these documentaries do an excellent job of chronicling my life in those tumultuous eras, I see no reason to waste the reader's time with descriptions of what they can see in color for a few bucks extra. I highly recommend *Anchorman 2: The Legend Continues.* It's very accurate. We stuck to the facts with no bullshit. I tip my hat to the filmmakers and my own acting ability. I'm no film critic writing for one of these vitally important Internet blogs, but I will say it may just be the finest film ever made. It bears a second and third screening to be sure, for there are many nuances that are only enriched by multiple viewings. These two documentaries combined with the facts I've presented in this book form an accurate picture of my life up to a certain point. I shall not embellish on the years covered in the documentaries other than to say documentaries are not a complete life! During that whole period I ate cereal, I blew my nose, I shit my pants, I costarred in a movie with Sylvester Stallone called *Over the Top* and I went to the grocery store. So much of life is not worth spinning into tales that we forget that tales themselves are little more than omissions of choice. For instance, during the period chronicled in *Anchorman: The Legend of Ron Burgundy,* Brian Fantana and I ran a very successful car-detailing shop in San Diego. This was in the original thousand-page script, along with a very funny story about the day I bought a comb that then broke. Well, some of this delightful storytelling just had to be omitted in the interest of time. The comb story was a real doozy and if I ever get a chance to do a documentary about that alone I will take that opportunity, but you know what they say about letting go of things you love in a script: "When in Rome."

Sadly even here in this sweeping tale of my many adventures and wonderful deeds I am forced to omit details in the interest of space. What needs to be told and what needs to be left out? People still want to know where I was the night of the O. J. Simpson conspiracy. I have some details that would shed new light on the whole mix-up. Is it worth throwing in here? Did I barter a peace between Bears quarterback Jim McMahon and Commissioner Pete Rozelle? Was I best man at the wedding of Sean Penn and Madonna? Did I squeak some bedsprings in the Ozarks with a governor's wife by the name of Hillary? I mean, what is a good story and what is just more stuff that happened? In point of fact there's a good story everywhere you look. During a short separation from my wife and sex friend, Veronica, I took a run at every Spice Girl. I'm not the kind of guy to kiss and tell but Scary Spice was the very best in the sack and aptly named. I was terrified and aroused the whole time. I invented the Wonderbra and the Super Soaker on the same day. I was minutes away from preventing the whole Chernobyl disaster while doing work for the State Department in Russia. Is that a story or is that just a guy doing his job? Anyway, you can see my problem here. What stands out?

One thing comes to mind I've never talked about. In fact I've never written a word about it for fear of reprisals. I did some government work in the early nineties for George Herbert Walker Bush. I'll admit that politically we didn't always align but I'm nothing if not patriotic, and when the president calls on you to do a job, well then you do it and you don't ask questions. You just do it. You blindly march into battle because he's the president. That's just what being an American is all about, my friends.

Because I was such good friends with Manuel Noriega, the leader of Panama, Bush 1 asked if I could broker a deal between Noriega and the U.S. This was before Operation Just Cause, which sent twenty-four thousand troops down into Panama to broker a different kind of deal. Before that deal, which wasn't really a deal at all but just a military invasion to take over a country, there was a much more complicated deal involving ███████████, Noriega, Saddam Hussein and Margaret Thatcher. I flew to Panama, where I had a summer house near the palace and where I enjoyed the bounty that came with being great buddies with the misunderstood Noriega. While in his company I was to offer him ████████████████████████, among other things, including a Land Rover with custom Kenneth Cole leather seats. To help navigate the complexities of the deal I was accompanied by Secretary of Defense Richard Bruce "Dick" Cheney. I did not like him. From the very beginning we fought. There was something so cold and calculating about the man that I immediately sized him up as a world-class idiot who was surely going to blow the whole thing. His judgment in all matters of foreign policy was counterintuitive to natural reason. For instance, in a meeting with Saddam Hussein, Cheney suggested

██████████████ ████████████████████ loved
boiled eggs ████████████████████. Thatcher was
insufferable; she insisted that ███████████
███████████████████████ at an advance show-
ing of *The Bodyguard* with singer/songwriter Dolly Parton
and King Fahd. Also present were General Norman Schwarzkopf, VP Dan Quayle, rock guitarist and presidential adviser
Ted Nugent, ████████████ and myself. The meeting was a
lively one, with ███████████████████ as a
suggestion. Pat Robertson, who was also in attendance, indicated that he would ███████████████████
████████████████████ several other S & M followers
███████████ ████████████████████
Glenn Miller ███████████████████ having
███████████ wistful ████████████
███████████████████ forty kilos of Panama-
nian █████████████ ████████████
████████████████ because Thatcher loved the smell of it.
I was taken to a room in Kuwait with a hood over my head.
I knew that Soviet general secretary Mikhail Gorbachev was
going to play ball but I also knew that I had to act fast. I handed
over ███████████████████████! I
couldn't believe it! Dan Quayle, probably one of the hand-
somest politicians I've ever met and a great doubles tennis partner, was behind the clandestine handoff from the
beginning. He was carrying the briefcase with ██████████.
How Ted Nugent gained such access was not my concern,
but Thatcher said, "████████████ went ██████████ fifteen ████████████████████ hammerhead sharks

█████████████████████████████████ dead with one word. A chill went through the room. Only Dick Cheney was laughing. Noriega looked sweaty and I felt sorry for him. I gave over my package to ████████████. We got on a plane, James Baker and I, and flew to Saudi Arabia, where Afghan freedom fighter and American ally Osama bin Laden were waiting with ████████████. We went out to dinner. James Baker ordered the ████████████. I must say I've never been one for Mexican food in foreign countries. If you're going to have Mexican food it's best in America. The conversation centered on ████████ in ████████. Bush had agreed to ████████████ without reservation. ████████ any ████████████ before ████████ ████████ Runnin' Rebels Greg Anthony and Stacey Augmon. Fahd, of course, was a huge booster for UNLV basketball and a personal friend of Jerry Tarkanian. This was all going nowhere fast and I had had enough. I called Dick Cheney from ████████████. He was not happy and he let me know it. "If you can't ████████ patriot ████████ water-board ████████████ American way of life ████████████ my legacy ████████████ to buy Liz a toaster oven. Son of a bitch, Burgundy, I thought we had a deal." And then he hung up. It was the loneliest I've ever felt. To be stranded in Kuwait holding all that ████████. I went to Noriega and warned him. Thatcher would ████████████ Harrier Jump Jets ████████ nuts ████████ Armen Gilliam as well. I knew if the press got ahold of this they would have a field day. It put me in quite a bind as a committed journalist. I had the entire three-hundred-page brief in my hotel room. I was asked to ██████████ not because but ██████████ Parton's song ████████████████████████ nudity included. The ██████████ glass ████████████. "Holy balls!" I shouted. "Is this where ██████████?" ██████████ but Schwarzkopf tried to take a swing at him and I stepped in. The outcome was ██████████ mission ██████████ not in the Bush library. ████████████████████████ paper-shredding machine on the eighth floor running nonstop for days. CIA operative ██████████ stepped in to ██████████ gloves ██████████ disposed of the ██████████ like lumpy soup ██████████ field of un-marked graves. That's where it turned. Suddenly I was in real danger. It's a feeling I cultivate. Like sexual pleasure, danger sets off certain life-affirming emotions in me. I quickly sprang into action. The drugs were in my suitcase. The money was in the hands of ██████████. ████████████████████ ████████████████████ wet ██████████ *New York Times* ██████████████████████ firing at me and Jerry Tarkanian. The plane was one hundred yards away. Dolly Parton and ██████████ heels and red leather ██████████. I hadn't even flown before but there I was in the plane with ██████████, Cheney, Thatcher and ██████████. Back in the States I locked the documents in a private vault I had hidden under an auto junkyard outside of Gary, Indiana. I believe in transparency. I believe we the peo-ple should know what our leaders are up to when it comes to vitally important foreign policy. Now the story can be told, and let the consequences fall where they may. If ████████████ ████████████ grapes in the ole basket!

Throughout the rest of the nineties I turned more and more toward investigative news. I hosted an hour of television on PBS called *The Burgundy Journal*. The whole news team stayed together as we tackled big subjects well beyond our ken. We were out of our league over there on PBS. There were guys in the mailroom who knew more about the state of the world than any of us. So we told the news the only way we knew how: directly, forcefully and without substance. It was, as always, a hit. The highest-rated show in the history of PBS. Unfortunately the pay was ridiculous. Champ had more restaurant ambitions. Brick wanted to run around on grass and I was beginning to feel like an old man in a young man's game. After about a half a year of *The Burgundy Journal* I retired from the news business and walked away on top—a champion and a winner, the number one guy of all time.

A couple of years later I received the highest honor any News Anchor can be awarded—the Golden Anchor. It was usually reserved for network anchormen, but it was only fitting that after a career unmatched by anyone's I should receive this prestigious award. They all came: Cronkite, Jennings, Curtis, Brokaw, Rather, Sawyer, Mantooth, Couric, Lehrer. The room was filled with news greats. A lot of scores that had gone unsettled got settled that night. I wasn't able to even get to my thank-you speech before a fight broke out between Rather and Koppel that then grew to a regular old-fashioned donnybrook. Tables flew, chairs broke, bottles were smashed, machetes were drawn, shots were fired—it was the most fun I'd had in years. It seemed fitting that the night should progress into a good old-fashioned news fight. It seemed more fitting that in the end only four men were standing over the broken bodies piled up in the room. I looked around to survey the wreckage and a smile came to my bloodied face. There beside me was my old news team, triumphant again, standing tall and victorious over the battlefield.

HOW TO RELATE
TO CHILDREN

As a father I've experienced many ups and downs raising
a child. Parenting can give us so much joy. To see the wonder
in a child's eyes is as close to heaven as I've ever come. (I'm
speaking metaphorically of course. Physically I've come very
close to heaven, as I was on the summit of Mount Kilimanjaro
with game show host Gene Rayburn and Beatle Ringo Starr.)
There can also be great dissatisfaction when it comes to children. I've had interactions with them that have left me feeling
sad and alienated and hollow inside, to the point of wanting
to kill myself. If you're not careful a child can spin you into a
suicidal drain from which only pills and sex and circus rides

can save you. Their brains are mysterious puzzles that con-
found all human reasoning. I've been very frustrated talking
to children and I'll admit it, I'm always a little terrified of
them. If you get in a room alone with one you can't help but
start thinking about how irrational they are. It's only a matter
of time before you begin to wonder if they are going to attack
you or start flying around the room or speak backward. I was
locked in a room with a small girl one time who started to
speak backward. I nearly fainted but summoned the courage
to try and kill her. I was moving toward her with that intent
when the child's mother entered the room and stopped me.
She explained that they were from Poland and the child was
trying to talk to me in Polish. I guess they speak backward in
Poland. My point here is that children say and do stuff that
makes no sense. It can be very unsettling. I keep a candy bar
in every room in my house just in case I'm left alone with a
child. So how do you relate to a creature that lives by no rules?

Every summer for one week I run something called Camp
Ronny. I get a bunch of poor kids from broken homes and bad
neighborhoods and take them out into the woods for some
hot dogs and sing-alongs. It's my way of giving back. There's
only one rule at Camp Ronny, and that rule is, have fun!
Many of the kids come from environments where they hardly
ever just have fun. The first day I teach them some basic Boy
Scout/American Indian stuff like making smoke signals and
tying knots. Boys and girls just love this kind of outdoor fun.
On the third day they are on their own. They have to make
their own shelters, forage for food, make tools and fire. The
little ones, in the eight-to-nine-year range, always have prob-

lems with this, but eventually they get it. When they see I'm not going to help them they get it. Over the years we've had some close calls with some of the children and animals. Some nosey child welfare do-gooders have shared their opinions with me about Camp Ronny, but I'll tell you what, many of these kids go on to become prominent wrestlers, stockbrokers, Realtors and bouncers. Do these children become part of our great social fabric that ties us all together? No, but that wasn't going to happen anyway. What I've done is instilled in them a ruthless instinct for survival at all costs. Kids who come out of Camp Ronny are some of the scariest and worst citizens in the country. Famous alumni include Kenneth Lay, Sean Hannity, Junkyard Dog, King Kong Bundy, Paul Wolfowitz and Laura Ingraham. They may be hated and feared by regular Americans but they are survivors, and that's what's important.

If you can instill a little confidence in a child, then you've gone a long way to being a great parent. A ten-year-old will feel on top of the world if you can teach them to drive on a freeway. From what I understand the Chinese allow their children to operate heavy machinery making garments and fabricating car parts at a very young age. This must do gangbusters for their confidence!

Apart from that there's not much more I can say about relating to children. Scientifically speaking the medulla oblongata of children is smaller than that of adults, and so that's something I'm sure.

MY NEIGHBOR: MY BAD

Weird development in the whole Richard Wellspar affair. I found my Craftsman leaf blower in my garage sitting on the workbench with a plate of cookies and a very nice handwritten note dated a month ago. Can you believe it? He must have returned it the day I lent it to him! What a goof. My bad. Sometimes life gets silly. Only in San Diego, folks, only in San Diego.

WHERE I'M AT TODAY

Don't you worry, life's pretty good for Ron Burgundy these days. It was touch-and-go there for a little while but counting my chips, I see I came out the big winner. When all is said and done I will walk away from the poker table of life richer than when I came in—except I will be dead, which in many ways is not richer than when I came in. Someone once said one day we all end up at the banquet of our own consequences. For many men that banquet is an unsettling and fitting end to a life of poor choices. For me I'm at the banquet of my consequences and there's roast beef and mutton chops and red wine and cheeses and pancakes and a stack of Heath bars and creamed corn and succulent other foods like shrimp cocktail, hot dogs with sauerkraut, ravioli and three-bean salad, to name a few more—ice cream too—anyway it's quite a banquet, really, and it's all consequences of a life well lived. But it didn't feel that way a few years back and I'll tell you why.

In 2004 I was basically retired. My day consisted of a round of golf with Merlin Olsen, a five-dollar lunch at China Buffet, some checkers with Captain Willoby Faloon, a few personal appearances and then home for dinner. If I was lucky, and frankly I'm always lucky, I got some you-know-what from Mrs. Burgundy. She's still got it. Even at our advanced age we can still do stuff that would make a Nevada prostitute sit up and take notice. Anyway, that's how a typical day went before the fall of 2004. Somehow through one of my many personal appearances I got involved with a gentleman by the name of Fast Eddy Keel. People in and around San Diego know the name and face of Fast Eddy as it appeared on many bus stop seats advertising home loans. He approached me early in 2004 with an opportunity too good for me to pass up. I've never been one to try and profit from my name unless there's money in it, but here was a case that spoke to a particular passion of mine—namely building a high-end gated housing community. The Burgundy Estates, as they later were so named, was to be an ambitious housing development of fine homes heavily guarded and protected from the disintegrating social contract threatening our way of life. Each home would have fifteen rooms, including a screening room and a great room; a granite-topped kitchen; huge stainless appliances; a four-car garage; two swimming pools; a guesthouse; an indoor rock-climbing wall; an old-timey "make your own sundae" ice-cream parlor; his-and-her walk-in closets; koi ponds in every room—in short, only the best! Not to mention all the gadgets and gizmos the world had to offer at that time. Land clearing and building started in the spring of 2005. Each house was presold at about $2.5 million. With thirty houses to be built Fast Eddy and I were looking at a nice tidy profit. I supervised some of the building myself. I designed the houses on cocktail napkins and scraps of paper. It was kind of an indulgence but I walked around the construction site with a hard hat on and really got to know the gang working on the houses. There was Jose, with his infectious laugh, and Hernandez the happy whistler, Manuel the prankster and Jesus and Raul and Pepe—just a buncha construction guys whose names I made up every day. Here I was, retired, in my golden years, and I should have been enjoying an easy chair and Turner Classic Movies, but instead I was hanging with the guys, pouring footings and slingin' drywall mud. I really loved it.

One day Fast Eddy comes to me and says we should do our own financing. Now, I don't have millions of dollars sitting around so the idea seemed too risky to me, but Eddy is one of those guys who has all the angles and he tells me how we could start financing the whole development with different types of loans and deferred payments. Before you know it Eddy Keel and I have a new business—Eagle-Eye Mortgage. Now, on paper Eagle-Eye had no assets whatsoever. There was only debt in the form of some questionable loans, but in 2005 debt of any kind meant one thing and one thing only—future money. In the very first year Eagle-Eye Mortgage had holdings worth two hundred million dollars. We quickly started buying up other loan operations all over San Diego and then jumped on Liberty-Cougar, the biggest home lender in the area. The new company was renamed Eagle Eye Liberty and we now had holdings valued at nearly a billion dollars. Heck, I was happy to walk around the development site with the fellas and grab a cold one after a hard day of roofing, but things began moving very fast. Eddy Keel was quite the salesman. He used to walk into laundromats in San Diego and get guys with absolutely no income to sign home loans for half a million dollars. Was it ethical? Was it the right thing to do? Anyway, Eagle Eye Liberty became Red White and Blue Lenders and then just as quickly became the American Fund, which we leveraged to buy SoCal Homestead, which later became Yankee Doodle Mortgage, which merged with Betsy Ross Financial, which had just taken over Hearth and Home Securities and became Stars and Stripes Money Tree. By early 2007 we had the biggest home mortgage company in the Southwest, servicing Southern California and Arizona. We named the company the Loan Barn. You probably remember the TV ads we did with the jingle "Need a home but you ain't got the dough? Down at the barn we never say no! The Loan Barn." We paid Donald Fagen a boatload of money to come up with that jingle! Anyway in the spring of 2008 the Loan Barn was valued at eighty billion dollars. I still didn't quite get it. I mean, I would often sit in my booth down at the Alibis with the work crew drinking my cans of Coors and think to myself, "Ron, all the money they keep saying you have is money that's in the future. Does it make sense that people are spending future money in the present? Shouldn't we wait till we get to the future to get the money and then spend it on futuristic stuff like dino-bots and hover-cycles and phones with cameras?" I don't know, call me old-fashioned but I like to see my money. I always had the news station pay me in stacks of twenties. I always bought my cars with stacks of one-dollar bills. When someone tells me I have eighty billion dollars, I say show me the stacks. Show me the stacks! Well, I don't need to tell you what happened in the fall of 2008. All our future money was deemed un-moneyable. (That's a word. No need to look it up.) We had nothing, and what was worse, the Loan Barn was being investigated for securities fraud, for overstating assets, for going around lending laws, blah blah blah blah, the list of infractions went on and on. When all those loan payments came due we had to come up with eighty billion dollars. That's a lot of money. Fast Eddy Keel stayed true to his name and beat it fast. I believe he now operates something he calls a "party barge," which is a boat full of deviants he takes out of Argentina into international waters for so many nefarious reasons it would sicken the reader to list them, but one of them involves cat glands and human scat. He called me one day—he spoke fast and maybe sounded a little paranoid— and asked if I wanted in on "the wave!" He kept saying "the wave." And by "the wave" he meant did I want a party barge of my own. I said no and asked him where he was and told him that federal investigators had taken all my possessions and were looking for him. He said he had to go and then I heard some gunshots on his end and I haven't seen him since.

Fortunately Veronica had squirreled away some money for us to live on and I played a hunch that put me on top once again. After all the politicians and egghead editorialists had spun their wheels about what went wrong in 2008 I was in a heck of a lot of trouble. I found some slow-moving lawyers and set about "defending" myself but mainly stalling for time. The Loan Barn was indefensible—*predatory lending* and *fraudulent underwriting practices* were words being thrown around at the time—but I knew something all the Washington idiots didn't know. I knew that places like California and Florida got so excited by future money that they would not be willing to give it up. They were, and are, so addicted to future money that they can't give it up. Like any drug addiction, it would take a concentrated twelve-step program to cure Californians—heck, the whole country—of their addiction to future money. But in 2009 the country was at an all-time low. Every day a new commentator would come on TV with new gloom-and-doom scenarios. A lot of finger waving at consumers and Wall Street bankers and brokers. The home lenders took the brunt of the blame, and frankly we deserved it. Fast Eddy and I once loaned a five-year-old girl a million dollars just because we could! That money was on the books at 20 percent interest. Future money! If you listened to the facts, we wrecked Iceland, we wrecked Italy and we wrecked Greece. We almost took down Europe. It was worse than the Depression. And just like a repentant drunk, we felt really bad . . . for about a day. Then we got thirsty. Out of the shadows like stubborn little jackasses, a breed of News Anchor—I'll call them "News Enablers"—started to whisper, "Hey, the economy isn't so bad." These guys, who called themselves reporters, began suggesting that the losses were overstated and that everyone panicked and that future money was good and real and we could start spending it again. Well, as a student of human nature I saw this coming. We are essentially a country of ham-headed idiots. We love to forget about debt and go water-skiing. I think we all can agree it's better to live in the beautiful fable of future money than live in a boring world like adults where we pay our debts. We are not adults. We are children, and it's just more fun! About three years ago Californians started to buy houses again with money they didn't have—the Loan Barn held on to so many bad loans and toxic assets that it seemed like nothing short of killing everyone involved would clean it up. But that didn't happen. Instead I was able to unload the Loan Barn to a refi company called United American Yankee Liberty First National Mortgage and Security for the tidy sum of forty billion. Now they have all those risky loans on the books and they are valued at ninety billion dollars. The country of Greece has invested its entire pension plan in the company and just can't believe their good fortune!

In the end I didn't need forty billion dollars. I gave most of it away. Some of it went to my favorite charities, Candy Canes for the World and Dolphins for Children. I gave about twenty billion to Iceland because I did feel in a way that I ruined their economy, and gosh darn it if that country just doesn't intrigue the hell out of me. It's a whole land of ice, where ice people live in ice houses. I've never met anyone from Iceland but I would imagine them to be about eight feet tall with long pointy noses and blue skin. I would visit, but no way. I hate the cold.

Today I'm as comfortable as a man of my advanced age

can be. I enjoy cooking and lying out by the pool in the nude. I enjoy that my neighbor Warren Moon and his friends can clearly see me out by the pool in the raw and there's really nothing he can do about it. Occasionally the old gang gets back together to reminisce, sing show tunes and take in a bum fight. Every Christmas I drive by Wes Mantooth's house and throw a brick though his window. He returns the favor every Easter . . . with the same brick! Most mornings Veronica and I can be seen bouncing up and down the coast on our Jet Skis. Most nights we can be seen bouncing up and down by the pool. I still breed labradoodles for anyone who wants them. I'm good friends with Reba McEntire. My long-standing feud with Oscar Mayer meats is over. They were right and I was wrong. My steak knife collection is very famous. I have many honorary degrees but wouldn't say no to a few more. There's nothing so bad on God's green earth that can't be made good by a tall glass of scotch.

MY FINAL THOUGHTS

Well, that's the end. I know I did a lot of bragging in the beginning about the greatness of this book. Those are just the
kinds of straight-faced lies we authors tell you people to get
you to read a pile of garbage. Frankly I really thought I had a
huge pile of garbage on my hands but I've just read it over and
I have to admit something to myself: I'm a great book writer.
Will I get the Nobel Prize for this baby? Probably not—maybe
an outside chance if a couple of guys die, but probably not.
Is it worthy of a Pulitzer? You bet. It really turned out to be
a great book that I'm sure will be required reading in colleges for years to come. Oh sure, somewhere down the road
it will lose favor with intellectuals and go through a period
of neglect, but then some smart professor will find it again

and resurrect its greatness and there it will sit on the highest throne with the greatest books of all time. I can accept that fate for this little book.

Before I end it though I thought I'd share a final thought. There's a lot of anger out there. I feel it in the streets. I see it every day on the roadways and in the air. I guess we're a pretty angry bunch of idiots all around. Why is that? Why does mankind hate his brother? Is it as simple as some people have got stuff that other people want? I don't know, but I've got a lot of stuff—Jet Skis and trampolines and football-shaped phones—and sometimes my anger still gets the best of me. I don't think it's just about the stuff. I think, if you really get down to it, we are angry because we are scared. Scared of what? Well, I'm scared of children and elephants. I'm also scared of losing and, heck, I'll say it, I'm scared of dying. When you think about lying in that mud hole and someone shoveling dirt on you, it makes you angry. You start to think, "I don't have as much as I want! I'm not doing what I want to do! I'm not being who I want to be!" Well, it takes courage to do what you want and be who you want to be, and it takes courage to admit you're afraid. I'm afraid all the time. It's hard to say it but I'm afraid right now, afraid an elephant is going to come crashing into my den and crush me. It's a very real fear. The way I deal with it is by staying classy. That's the best medicine of all. If you're busy going about doing what you want to do and being who you want to be, unafraid of what everyone else thinks, you'll be classy too. Sure, the other guy has a flying car and a camera in his watch, but you can have something better. You can have class. Stay classy, America. You know I will.

Ron Burgundy

One other thing: The last time I wore a swimsuit while swimming was June 8, 1976. Had that in my notes and it didn't fit anywhere in the book, so I just added it on. Stay classy.

PHOTOGRAPHY CREDITS

(In order of appearance)

INSERT 1

© Library of Congress
© Lisa-Blue/iStockphoto
© Library of Congress
© Mammuth/iStockphoto
© PF-(bygone1)/Alamy; BrianAJackson/iStockphoto
© AP Images
© AP Images/Suzanne Vlamis
© Ammit/iStockphoto
© Mihail Dechev/iStockphoto

INSERT 2

© 2013 by Paramount Pictures Corp. All rights reserved.
© AP Images/Bill Chaplis
© AP Images
© Tim DeFrisco/Hulton Archive/Getty Images
© Mediaphotos/iStockphoto
© Corey Ford/StocktrekImages/Getty Images
© Lowell Georgia/Corbis
© 2013 by Paramount Pictures Corp. All rights reserved; PaulShlykov/
    iStockphoto (falcon)
© Moodboard/Alamy
© SharpPhotoPro/iStockphoto
© Belinda Images/SuperStock
© 2013 by Paramount Pictures Corp. All rights reserved (both
    photos).